Journal of John Charles Philip von Krafft ... 1776-1784

You are holding a reproduction of an original work that is in the public domain in the United States of America, and possibly other countries. You may freely copy and distribute this work as no entity (individual or corporate) has a copyright on the body of the work. This book may contain prior copyright references, and library stamps (as most of these works were scanned from library copies). These have been scanned and retained as part of the historical artifact.

This book may have occasional imperfections such as missing or blurred pages, poor pictures, errant marks, etc. that were either part of the original artifact, or were introduced by the scanning process. We believe this work is culturally important, and despite the imperfections, have elected to bring it back into print as part of our continuing commitment to the preservation of printed works worldwide. We appreciate your understanding of the imperfections in the preservation process, and hope you enjoy this valuable book.

BIOGRAPHICAL SKETCH OF LIEUTENANT VON KRAFFT, WITH A PREFATORY NOTE, BY THOMAS H. EDSALL, ESQ.

[PREFATORY NOTE —About three years ago, through the courtesy of a descendant of its writer, there came into my hands seven detached sheets of tabulated German manuscript Each sheet was about six inches long by eight wide, and bore the heading "Dienst Tabella" (Table of Service), followed by the journalist's name, rank, regiment, and company, the names of the commanding officers, and the year of service (the several sheets covering the years 1778–83). It was ruled underneath into numerous columns, which were respectively entitled with the special duty, service, or command, which he had performed or held Horizontal lines divided the page into twelve spaces, for the respective months of the year, which were named in the left margin Opposite to the name of each month in its proper column, was entered the date of each service or command, sometimes with brief comment, or "N B,' referring to fuller comment elsewhere. In the right-hand column, entitled "Annotationes," was noted the station or location of his regiment or command in each month.

The dates of the month were invariably accompanied by the signs used at that time to denote the days of the week—*i.e.*, ☉ Sunday, ☽ Monday, ♂ Tuesday, ☿ Wednesday, ♃ Thursday, ♀ Friday, and ♄ Saturday.

The reverse side of each tabulated sheet was entitled "Anmerkungen" (Notes by the Way), followed by memoranda under separate dates, beginning on January 1st in each year Sometimes a part of this page was devoted to his Pay Account ("Tractements Liste") or Provision Account.

The handwriting was exceedingly minute; so much so in places that it could hardly be made out with a magnifying-glass It seems incredible that it could only have been written with the goose or crow-quill of that day

The language was High German, but somewhat antiquated in its grammatical construction. The meaning of some obsolete words had to be conjectured. A few could not be deciphered.

The "Notes by the Way" on each sheet ended early in each

year It was apparent after their translation that they were incomplete in themselves. This induced further research, which brought to light some seventy additional pages, of the same dimensions and equally minute chirography, containing the writer's Journal for the remainder of the years 1778–1783, inclusive The seven original sheets had been only its commencement for those years respectively

The following pages contain a translation of this Journal, with the interpolation of the facts noted in the "Dienst Tabellen" The translation is almost literal, in order to present the quaint style of the writer The elongated sentences in the original have not been divided, except where their extreme length and involved construction would have obscured the meaning in English

My acknowledgments are due to Mr. William Freeman Goldbeck, of New York City, for his invaluable assistance in deciphering and translating the manuscript

Since the translation of the Journal, its owner has kindly placed in my hands several maps and sketches made by his ancestor, which are reproduced herewith. Their historical interest is only equalled by their exquisite delineation.

From his Journal and other memoranda, and from family tradition, the following sketch of the life of the journalist has been prepared]

John Charles Philip von Krafft was born in Dresden, Saxony, on Thursday, August 21, 1752 [1]

He is said to have been of a baronial family, whose seat was at "Delitzsch-on-the-Hill," near Leipsig, in Saxony, and to have borne the title of "Baron" A drawing of his coat armor, made by himself, has inscribed on its reverse, in his handwriting, "Related to the Princes of Hohenlohe" He was also related to other families of rank, in Prussia and Saxony, and was descended from ancestors who had been officers in the military service of Prussia for generations

On the 4th of July, 1773, he was commissioned Ensign in Major-General von Luck's regiment of fusiliers, in the Prussian army, under Frederick the Great, and on the 29th of December in the same year, Second Lieutenant in the same regiment. In the beginning of 1776 he was Lieutenant of the second company of Grenadiers, Captain Westphal, in the fusilier regiment of von Luck. The regiment was then stationed at Braunsberg, a garrison town of Eastern Prussia.[2]

[1] "Den 21st August 1752 nachmittags 3-4 4 bin ich gebohren, in Dresden" —From the leaf of a German almanac of 1750, in von Krafft's handwriting

[2] Braunsberg is the capital of a circle in the government of Konigsberg, on the Passarge, between three and four miles from its mouth, in the Frische Haff, an estuary of the Gulf of Danzig, Baltic Sea.

During the early part of 1776, becoming wearied of the life of a garrison town, with its dinners at the General's, jolly sleigh rides to Heiligenbeil, flirtations "outside the upper gate," duels with his fellow-officers, etc., he determined to resign his commission and seek advancement elsewhere. The King refused his application for some time, but finally granted it on the 10th of May. The following morning he reported for the last time to the General and his staff, and they wished him much success in his proposed undertaking. The last of May he went to Russia, visiting St. Petersburg.

An abstract of the Journal prior to January 1, 1778, gives an account of his wanderings until that date, when he appears as a volunteer on board of an American privateer, bound from France to Philadelphia.

Full details of his life from this time to the close of 1783 will be found in the Journal. His commission as Free Corporal in von Donop's regiment is dated September 5, 1781, and as Second Lieutenant in von Bose's regiment, December 15, 1782.

In 1783 Lieutenant von Krafft was secretly married, in New York, to Miss Cornelia de la Metre, the daughter of a widow residing "past the 5th Mile Stone, King's Bridge Road, on New York Island." This course was adopted, no doubt, to keep the knowledge of his marriage from his proud widowed mother in Saxony, until he could present himself in person and secure her consent. It seems to have been his intention to visit his mother for this purpose, when he sailed for England with his regiment, in 1783. Before reaching England, however, he had already resolved to resign and return to America. Whether he was led to this by dread of meeting with his mother, or controlled by yearnings to rejoin his young wife in New York, does not appear. After a stay in England until the middle of February, 1784, he boarded the ship Vigilant, in the Thames, on the 18th, sailed in her on the 11th of March, arrived off Sandy Hook on the 22d of April, and was anchored off Fly Market Wharf the next afternoon.

On the 16th of May, 1784, he was publicly married in the First German Church, New York City, by the Calvinist minister, the Reverend Daniel Gross, and on the same day his eldest son, born April 30th, 1784, was baptized "Cornelius Frederick," the sponsors being Dr Appel and his wife.

For several years thereafter Mr. de Krafft, that being the surname which he adopted, and afterward bore, supported himself and his family by teaching in New York City. Then he became employed as surveyor and draughtsman to the Treasury Department. When the seat of Government was removed to Washington he went thither with his department, and continued in its service until his deccase.

A few months before his death Baron von Humboldt, who had known him and his family in Germany, spent several days on a visit to Mr. de Krafft, at his home in Georgetown Humboldt informed him of the death of his mother, with whom he had ceased to correspond for many years, and advised him to return to Germany and lay claim to his estate, which was in the possession of a venerable maiden relative He had made his preparations to do so, when he was seized with an attack of congestion of the lungs, which terminated his life, July 24, 1804

Mr. de Krafft was a man of commanding presence and of courtly and fascinating manners. He had a quick temper, and was sensitive to affronts During his military service—1770 to 1784—he was the principal in some twenty duels, and was several times severely wounded

His descendants have held responsible positions and high rank in the civil and naval service of the United States

THOS HY. EDSALL

GLENWOOD SPRINGS, COL ,
February 22, 1887

VON KRAFFT'S JOURNAL.

1776.

Commencing May 23, 1776, Thursday. Out of service.

Von Krafft left Braunsberg by post-road and arrived next day in Danzig, putting up at a house where he had lived two years before. June 7, Friday, he left by the schooner "Jacob Wolffram" for St. Petersburg, where he arrived, Tuesday, June 25, (distance from Danzig 280 miles). He was offered a position as *Cornett* in the Russian army, but seeing that he would have to serve as a volunteer for two or three years before being entered on the pay-list, because there were about 700 other applicants ahead of him, he decided to join the Hessians in America.

He took passage on the schooner Werkhooven, bound for Amsterdam, which left St. Petersburg on Thursday, Aug. 8. A Major von Bose was one of the passengers.

Von Krafft says that his journal, from July 18 to October 7, 1776, is written from memory, the original having been confiscated by the English

Off the island of Bornholm they saw a water-spout. They stopped one day at Helsingor, near Copenhagen. Sept. 6, Friday, they arrived at Amsterdam and landed, (distance from St. Petersburg about 300 miles). Von Krafft visited the beautiful Hague with von Bose.

A merchant by the name of *Chabanell* gave him letters to several "grandees of the Congress" in Philadelphia—he had forgotten all the names excepting *rob*, which the English call *Manasches* (molasses) and which tasted very good. There were not more than forty people on the whole island and these made a living by catching great quantities of cod fish "

When provisions ran low they had to send to the little French island of St Peters, 60 miles distant, where a French captain held the position of Governor, with 30 soldiers. It took the boat two months to make the trip there and back.

De Prijce offered Von Krafft one of his suits to wear, but the latter declined—" because De Prijce was very tall and I would have been obliged to get some one to carry my train for me "

April 19, just before the ship was to leave, Von Krafft gathered a lot of *Indian Tea* and *maiden hair* that grew on the island, also a number of mussels, which the English called *Coks et Hens*.

April 20, they set sail.
    " 21, Monday, they passed St. Paul and Cape Breton.
    " 25, they passed *Anticosty*.

When within about 9 *leges* of Quebec they saw houses along the shore and the Captain sent out a boat to investigate. It returned with the information that Englishmen, Scotchmen and Canadians lived there; furthermore that two American ships with two of the greatest American generals had, a short time before, been captured there, in consequence whereof peace was soon expected. The joy of the Englishmen on board was so great that they hurrahed and fired off several guns to express their delight at this good news.

On the 5th of May, Monday, they arrived at Quebec where General Carleton was Governor. Von Krafft immediately set to work to better his condition. A merchant by the name of Cramer gave him some necessary information about the neighborhood and he met with a certain von Tonnerfeldt, one of Gen Carleton's adjutants This man tried to assist him to a position with the Hessians; the latter, however, being stationed near Boston, it took some time for letters to go to and fro. and Von Krafft, who had but one ducat left, determined to set out on foot to the Braunschweigers, who were stationed at Trois Rivieres, some 16 German miles from Quebec, under Gen. von Riedesel. He started with many misgivings on May 11.

After going some distance he was ferried over a small stream, in a birch bark *canuth*, for "two *habbene*", and later on met with a French woman and her daughter, going the same way. They treated him very kindly, insisting upon his partaking of their food and showing him all kinds of attentions, though they were unable to exchange a single word of conversation, because he was entirely ignorant of the French language.

On the 16th after having stopped at the house of a man to whom he had a letter of recommendation from the Quebec merchant, Cramer, and who lent him 3 piasters, Von Krafft arrived at Trois Rivieres. But Gen. von Riedesel refused to give him an engagement in his regiment, it being contrary to the wish of the Duke to have strangers enlisted without his express order.

Greatly discouraged Von Krafft started out to return to Quebec. On the night of May 18th he met with Capt. von Schlagenteufel, who at first suspected him of being a deserter, but afterwards treated him with the greatest kindness and generosity.

On the 26th he got on a boat at *Cap Sante* and proceeded to Quebec by way of the St. Lawrence river. He arrived there at 10 P. M. on the 27th of May.

At first he was undecided whether to try to get back to England, and thence to Germany, or to go on and join the Hessians. He finally decided to do the latter, but met with great difficulty in procuring a pass thither.

For several days he was compelled to rely on Cramer for support. Cramer raised a subscription for him among some German merchants. Then the Lieut Governor gave him 16 piasters, but still refused a pass until Gen. Carleton had returned from Montreal.

On Friday, June 13, he met with a Hessian, Lieut. von Meyer, who had just arrived with a number of Hessian recruits from Portsmouth, on their way to join the Hessians Meyer showed much interest in Von Krafft, and persuaded him to sail with them in their ship *Methiadeur*, which he consented to do, and started off with them.

On the 17th von Meyer got into a dispute with another officer, while the ship lay at Trois Rivieres. Though entirely innocent of the trouble that ensued, Von Krafft was held under arrest on board the ship. On the 27th they arrived at Montreal and landed. Here he was treated politely by the English, but compelled to return by ship to Quebec and try to justify himself before Gen. Carleton. They arrived there on July 3

On July 4th Von Krafft was put in prison with the worst class of evil-doers without being able to get a trial.

He was kept there for a long period, in great distress of mind, " tired of life," " but still with a something of hope left." " Live and suffer till you see it is impossible to hope and live any longer, then—die !"

On July 12th he heard the news of Burgoyne's having taken Ticonderoga, but with a loss of 800 men.

Gen. Carleton, on being interviewed by Capt. Tonnerfeldt in Von Krafft's behalf, decided to send him back to England as soon as a ship left.

The days passed without any relief coming to Von Krafft. He grew desperate and longed for death

On the 19th of July he was finally released, but found little relief in his liberty, as he was without money. His friend Cramer assisted him a little and he managed to exist till July 23rd, when he received an order from Gen. Carleton, through von Tonnerfeldt, to return to England by the three-master Nottingham, which had been appointed to carry the news of the fall of Ticonderoga to England. He got 3 piasters and an order for three months' rations, which were dealt out to him on the ship On applying to von Tonnerfeldt for letters to England, he was told that he must expect no further aid ; this drove him almost to despair and he contemplated self-destruction, deciding to wait, however, and see how things turned out in England.

At this critical juncture he made the acquaintance of a young French girl, named " Mademoiselle Lisette Amiott," whose charming manner and sweet disposition had a most potent and salutary effect upon his sinking spirits. He rapidly fell in love with her and felt that this was his first experience of sincere devotion. She lived in a house, adjoining the inn where he was lodging, and thus their accidental meetings were naturally frequent. On the 26th he was suddenly called to his ship, which was every moment expecting the order to sail. The departure, however, was delayed for some reason and Von Krafft hastened back to his adored Lisette, though the Captain warned him that the ship might leave any minute. But love made him reckless He struck a bargain with two Frenchmen to row him to the ship in case he should be left. This mishap actually occurred. The ship sailed without him, at the very moment he was escorting Lisette to church. The two Frenchmen came running up to him with the startling information. He tears himself away with bleeding heart and is only able to catch up with the ship in consequence of the Herculean efforts of his two boatmen, whom he rewards with half a crown a piece. Scrambling up on the deck he stands there in a dazed condition, his eyes cleaving to the receding scene of his passionate love—nor does he retire to the cabin till distance obliterates the last lingering landmark of his past misery and joy.

After an uneventful journey they arrived off Ireland

on Aug. 23 The ship dropped anchor at *Cove of Cork* and for several days Von Krafft wandered about Cork waiting for a chance to get to Holland. At last he met with a German ship-captain, who was about to sail for Bordeaux, France, and this man offered him free passage thither.

Thinking it would be easier for him to get to Holland from Bordeaux than from Cork, Von Krafft accepted the offer and set sail on the 3rd of September. The ship was the Maria Catharina, the captain, Gottfried Samuel Parlow. They arrived at Bordeaux, Sept. 14th.

Among the ships in the harbor were a number of American privateers and giving up all hope of doing anything better, Von Krafft resolved to join one of these, not from preference, but deeming it his last resort. After many unsuccessful attempts he finally made a bargain with an American captain named *Lyle* to take passage with him to Philadelphia, for which Von Krafft was to get a *douceur* of £10, and a share of any prize that might be taken. On the other hand he was expected to fight and defend the ship, if the occasion demanded it.

He spent several days viewing the city with chance acquaintances, "but if I were to describe my anxiety during this time, more blood would have to flow here than ink!" A few days before the departure Von Krafft ran across a German tailor, who wished to get a place on board the American privateer. The tailor had several dollars in his pocket, so they both made friends and started out together to spend the money in amusement. They went to the comedy every evening and spent the days walking about the town and drinking wine. At last the tailor's money was all used up and they had to deny themselves the comedy and get their meals on the ship. A profitable disposal of a couple of silk neck-cloths, however, enabled them properly to celebrate the day of departure with a bottle of wine

The ship sailed November 13th. She had 16 guns and had been newly repaired and painted. After passing the French guard-ship they got along smoothly until they sighted a strange ship in the distance They prepared for a fight, but the ship, which turned out to be an English merchantman, taking a load of wine, salt and all kinds of delicacies from Lisbon to England, surrendered without any resistance.

On the 19th the crew of the captured vessel was taken on board the privateer and one Lundcranz put in command with orders to follow to Philadelphia.

The same day another brig hove in sight, "but immediately recognizing our character they tried their best to escape us. This, however, was impossible, as our brig sailed astonishingly fast. We spread all sails, fired a gun at them, whereupon they hoisted the English flag and, lowering their sails, surrendered. The ship was named *In Thebe*, hailed from Newfoundland and had on a load of fish and salt. The crew was again transferred to our ship and chief lieutenant *Tomson* took command of the prize which he was ordered to sail to Martinique and sell there."

They encountered several terrible storms but met with no accidents. The prisoners on board were handcuffed every night and on the approach of any suspicious looking craft.

On December 18th they emerged from a dense fog that had enveloped them for some time and beheld "a part of New York" lying at their right. This sudden and unexpected approach alarmed them considerably and they feared being discovered by English men-of-war; but they passed unnoticed. Renewed storms of the most malignant nature seemed to Von Krafft a fitting close of this year of misery and despair.

1778

1 Jan. Thursd   There was a calm till towards evening when a good but light wind blew up, and it became bright weather.

2 Jan. Friday. Early at daybreak all was excitement on board our ship, because a *"Scunert"* was again quite near us (the watch having been asleep) and asked us where we came from and what we wanted here. It had six guns, and as we could not yet see distinctly nor understand our position, there was much confusion among us. But we prepared ourselves as quickly as possible. In the meantime our captain spoke through a speaking-trumpet to the other one, but neither seemed to wish to let the other know who he was. Finally the other moved off a little, apparently to wait for the break of day to observe us more closely. When that time came he was just behind us and had run up his flag which we however could not recognize We ran up ours, whereupon the other fired three guns and steered directly for us. We fired one shot, turned about and awaited him. When he had come nearer we saw that he was a *"Bostonier,"* and he soon informed us that General Burgoyne had been defeated with 10,000 men by the Americans, but that Philadelphia had gone over to the English. These last tidings embarrassed us exceedingly, as we now had to change our course. Towards evening I lost a tooth.

3 Jan. Sat. There was a light fair wind. The captain directed his course toward the province of Maryland, aiming for a dangerous inlet there near *Synntebox*.

4 Jan. Sund'y. About noon we caught sight of a schooner and a sloop on our right—they were running away from us, and, taking no notice of them, we soon lost sight of them. We never dared to inter-

fere ourselves, always suspecting that they might be English.

5 Jan. Mon. At daybreak we beheld America, a little to the right, ahead of us. The wind was very light.

6 Jan. Tuesd'y. Towards evening we turned about and keeping the land to our left we cast anchor.

7 Jan. Wednes The weather was dark and the wind contrary, so we could not sail far, and seeing that we were being driven toward the land, we soon had to cast anchor.

8 Jan. Thursd. At eight in the morning we weighed anchor and arrived, in the afternoon, in the neighborhood of *Synnteboxent* where we saw a ship, 2 brigs, and 2 sloops lying at anchor. We saluted them with our sixteen guns. It was very dangerous, however, to run in there, since it was no regular port and full of sandbanks, on one of which, owing to the carelessness of our pilot, we ran aground and were almost wrecked; but after much trouble we finally got off again and cast anchor at 5 o'clock.

9 Jan. Frid'y. Visitors came on board in whose honor the guns were made to thunder and we were treated to fresh meat. I alone was overcome with depression , for though I was again rid of one misfortune, I saw great uncertainty before me and was far from what I had planned. Here I sold an old white Prussian cloth vest with silver buttons for $6 (Congress money) to a sailor.

10 Jan. Saturd. This morning they commenced to unload the ship's cargo which consisted chiefly of tea, and this was continued for several days. Several other volunteers being on board and wishing to leave I went to speak with the captain, in the afternoon, 16 Jan. Frid. and tell him that I wanted to go on shore. I asked him for the ten pounds he had promised, which he immediately agreed to give me , but, as it was already late, he promised it by the next morning.

17 Jan. Satur. At 8 o'clock this morning I got

$28. Congress paper money [and $1. computed at 7 shill. 6d.] from the captain, and our captured ships not being there I was put off for my prize-money [Note I was to receive my portion of the prize, when the ships had been sold. But afterwards when I was in Philadelphia and had entered the Hessian service I could not obtain anything. What the future will bring about I know not.]

A letter was given me to take on land to the military colonel so as to procure a pass from him. At 9 o'clock boarded a sloop with an old German, named *Lechleidner*, who had been a drummer with the *Palatinate Kurpfalzer Dragoons*, but was an arch-scamp as I found out afterwards—and together with several others and my few traps I started for shore. The tide being low we could not avoid running aground several times with our sloop and had to sail in different directions before we succeeded in gaining the shore Thence we had quite a long walk, so that we did not reach our destination until half past ten o'clock and exposed with our baggage to a severe rain storm. [Marginal note " From this time again dependent upon myself in America."] I got a pass from Col. *Parmy* to the headquarters of Washington, and started out immediately in spite of the pouring rain After walking for about an hour I stopped at a fine-looking house to my right which, I found out, belonged to a young widow. I requested admittance which, on account of the bad weather, was granted. The old Drummer was with me. I decided to remain there over night and we were treated very handsomely. I made them some trifling presents, (there were two pretty young sisters of the widow there besides herself), among other things my little coffee kettle which I had brought with me from Braunsberg. During the night I slept in a very good bed and

18 Jan. Sund in the morning at 10, after an excellent breakfast, the weather being good, I asked how much I owed them. With many compliments I paid

$1, and leaving the box there which I had brought with me from Quebec, I packed my shirts and a few other things in a cloth and continued my journey; but halted again as early as 2 o'clock at the last house in *Synnt;* being received very cordially by the English people there, we decided to stay over night.

19 Jan Mond After breakfast this morning the journey was continued, but the people would not take any payment. At 8 in the evening we arrived on a muddy road at a house belonging to poor people The man had overtaken us on the road. We had to content ourselves with poor accommodations.

20 Jan Tues. We left at 6 A. M. I noticed, when I gave the woman a dollar, that five dollars had been stolen out of my pocket-book. To all appearances no other was guilty of the theft but the Drummer. From that hour I endeavored to separate from this fellow. In the afternoon we passed through the little town called, in English, *Blackfort*, which is estimated to be about 30 English miles from *Synntebox*. Here I bought a pair of shoes at the inn, paid $4 and gave the tops of my Russian boots besides. At 6 P. M. we halted again at a house belonging to an old widow where we lodged quite comfortably.

21 Jan Wed. At 8 in the morning journey continued after I had paid $1. At noon we overtook a wagon that, as I learned by inquiry, was going in the direction of the camp So I put my things on it and walked leisurely behind. At 8.30 in the evening we put up at an inn where we had quite comfortable quarters.

22 Jan. Thurs. In the morning we left after I had paid $1. At 6 P. M. we stopped over again at an inn.

23 Jan. Frid. At 6 A. M. journey continued, after previously paying 12 shillings. At 7 30 drove through the town of *Doves Town*, but did not stop there. From *Blackfort* to here, 54 English miles. At 1 30 through the town of *Duck Crack*—to here it is 12 Engl. miles further. Here I dined at the hotel

called *Gl Montcummery* and, as there were several other wagons there, the Drummer had to join another one At 3 30 we rode through the little town of *Cross Roads*, half an English mile from the former place. In the evening at 6, as it grew very cold and dark and began to snow, the driver stopped at a blacksmith's in the woods, where I found very fair accommodations.

24 Jan Sat. This morning early, journey continued. I paid half a dollar. In the afternoon my driver showed me the huts where the English and Hessians had camped a short time before, when they were on the march to Philadelphia. At 7 in the evening we arrived at the little town of *Newark* in *Chester County* where I stopped at the inn called *St. Patric* I paid my driver $2, for from this place he went in another direction. In an inn not far from here I sold a silk handkerchief and a linen one for 1 guinea.

25 Jan. Sund. At 9 this morning after breakfasting and having to pay $2, I met another wagoner who was going from here along the road towards the camp I gave him my things to put on the wagon, for which I intended to compensate him. This old man was very agreeable, called himself *Thomas Anderson* and lived 6 miles beyond *New Arck* at the place called *New London Town Ship, Chester County, Pennsylvania Mode*. When we reached his house he pressed me so kindly that I at last went into the house with him. Here, judging from outward appearances I expected very little, but verily I was treated very well. This honest old man and his wife overwhelmed me with kindnesses, washed my soiled linen, and I was obliged to stay there till the

27 Jan. Tues At 3 30 in the afternoon I left in spite of their protests, bid farewell to this good old man and his wife and seven children. They would not, with all my urging, accept any compensation, but wished me all good luck and the old man accompanied

me over half a mile. Then I thanked him again and bid him, Good bye ; but I did not proceed more than half a mile and, as the sun was about to set, I stopped at an inn to sleep there.

28 Jan Wed   Early at 9 30 continued my journey, after having to pay 12 shillings   At 4 in the afternoon I stopped at an inn, which was kept by one of the American Militia, a major by the name of *Bell*. Here I drank some cider (Seiter)   A short time after, a man addressed me in German.   I spoke with him and he tried to induce me to go to his house and stay with him.   I at last yielded.   It was already night.   He took me on his horse and in that manner I rode with him about 1½ English miles to the left, when we arrived at his beautiful and elegant house.   Here I met with a large family.   He was a Quaker and had come over here from Germany when a child.   His name was *Muller* and he lived in a part of the country called *New Canada*.   I was entertained here superbly and had a room and bed to sleep in unsurpassed by any I had ever had before.

29 Jan. Thurs.   At 9 in the morning it was raining hard   I had first to take breakfast, for which I was only permitted to thank them, and then Muller accompanied me back to the inn.   Having remained a while with me he finally bade me good bye, and as it had stopped raining I went leisurely on my way.   It was frightfully muddy, however, and I consequently stopped at an inn again at one o'clock, remaining there the rest of the day.

30 Jan Frid.   In the morning journey continued. Paid 10 shillings 9 pence.   At 2 P. M. I had myself carried on a horse across the so-called *Brandywine*. In the evening I again put up at an inn, where I eventually got into conversation with a Lieutenant of the Americans, of the 10th Pennsylvania Musketeer Regiment.   He was a German of *Lanchester*, named *Backerstoss*.   He had been ordered to the camp with a supply of wagons and asked me to go with him.

31 Jan Sat. We started at 9 A. M. after I had paid 11 shillings. I again placed my things on a wagon and left them to proceed a little in advance, as it was raining hard. Soon, however, I followed. At 10 o'clock we passed through a very small place called *Downings Town* On the way we stopped several times, owing to the continuity of the rain, and thus only accomplished a distance of 8 English miles from the inn where we had spent the night. Finally we reached an inn called *The Weit Harst*, which, by the way, was the last stop before we got to the camp. We arrived at 3 P M and remained there the whole day and night on account of the rain.

1 Febr. Sund. It was fine weather, so we pursued our journey at 9 o'clock in the morning It was only 9 English miles from here to General Washington's camp, but, the road being so muddy, it took us until 3 P M. before we reached the camp. I immediately sought out the house of Colonel *George Nagel*, where *Backerstoss*' quarters were too, (the whole camp consisted of houses built of trees). I was very politely received, especially by Colonel *Nagel* who offered me a position as Second Lieutenant in the 10th Pennsylvania Reg. which he commanded, but I refused it. I was retained, however, as a volunteer and received double rations (provision) the same as the other officers.

2 Febr Mond At 2 o'clock this afternoon I went with *Backerstoss* to Genrl. Washington's headquarters, which were distant one mile and a half and situated in a place called *Valley Forge* near a stream called the *Schulkill*. I wanted to speak to Washington himself, but he had ridden out, so we returned to our house

3 Febr Tuesd This morning I went there alone, but before I had reached the house Washington was pointed out to me in the act of riding out. I accosted one of his adjutants, who very politely referred me to the Genrl. Regmt'l Quarterm^r whose

name was *Letterloh* and who was a German having the rank of Colonel. It was one mile and a half farther on, but I went there directly. The Col spoke with me and directed me to another Genrl Ad-. jutant, who was lodging at a place on my way back, but I did not find him at home. So I returned to my house again, and as it grew more and more unpleasant to me here every day the longer I stayed and the more I heard and saw, I decided to go to Genr'l Washington again and obtain a pass from him to enable me to leave the camp Col *Nagel* tried to dissuade me from this and said that I would not be able to procure the desired pass I replied that I was a stranger and that nobody was going to detain me, nor would I enter the service in any other capacity than as a Captain. I was going to see who would dare to keep me back, and therefore went off 4th Febr., Wednesday, a distance of 2 English miles, and stayed in a house, in which two Lieutenants were lying sick. They persuaded me to remain there over night, assuring me that I could not get thro' the picket without a pass. So I stayed there all night. Here a queer thing happened to me during the night: a fellow lying on a bed of straw was so drunk that, in his sleep, he disgustingly soiled me and another of the officers.

5 Febr. Thurs. At 10 A. M Col *Nagel* sent Lieut. *Backerstoss* to beg me to return. He said I would only incur trouble, if I should leave the camp without Washington's permission. I was prevailed upon and returned with them, lodging in my previous house. To-day Col. *Nagel* left the camp to go to a farmer's house, because he was sick and wished to be taken care of there.

6 Feb. Frid. I felt rather ill, but it was nothing serious; yet I stayed in-doors.

10 Febr. Tuesd. I saw by the General Order that some officers were wanted who had knowledge of field fortification. They were to apply to the Adjutant General in writing. I went to what was called

the German Battalion, found the Reg^{md} Quartermaster and had him make out a document in the proper form for me. From this man I heard that their Colonel's name was *Br. v. Arndt*, and had been in the Prussian service. After further inquiries I found out that this same person was the Lieut. *v. Arndt* whom I had met in Amsterdam in 1776. I did not tarry long, but returned to my house with the English letter.

11 Febr. Wed In the afternoon I went to the Adjutant General's and had the application given to him, whereupon he spoke very politely with me and asked whether I had already served. Then I showed him my commissions and some drawings upon which he complimented me highly and declared his intention of speaking with Gen'l Washington about me I then went back to my house and waited until

13 Febr. Frid. At 9 A. M. the already mentioned Lieutenant *Backerstoss*, who had again been taken sick, went on leave of absence to *Lanchester*. I accompanied him, since he had done me a great many favors, as far as the picket, a distance of 3 English miles. At 10 o'clock General *Green* and General *Ween*, 3 Colonels, 6 Lieut. Colonels, 16 Captains, 32 Subalterns, 32 Sergeants, 32 Corporals, 16 Drummers and Fifers, and 1200 men crossed the *Schwlkill*, but it was not known, in camp, where they were going In the afternoon I wrote a letter to Col. v. Arndt, who was not in the camp, but had gone, on account of his sickness, to a house a little way out in the country. I sent this letter by a Sergeant to the Quartermaster of his regiment, to have it sent to him. However, I did not care to wait long for an answer, because in the meantime I left and it was some distance from the camp to where he resided.

14 Feb. Satur This afternoon I went with a Lieutenant and the Regt Quartermaster a little way outside the camp to take a walk.

15 Feb. Sund. This afternoon I went with a Lieutenant to the German Battalion which lay at a

distance of one English mile from my house. I met an Adjutant of the regiment there, who had also served as a soldier with the Prussians. He entertained me very generously and an hour later I returned to my quarters. The same evening I got into a devilish quarrel with 2 Captains, who, however, finally gave in. The quarrel arose about the Hesse Casselers.

16 Febr. Mond. At 10 A. M. I again went to the Adjutant General's and after a while he went with me to Washington, who was again not at home. I spoke with his Adjutant Col. *Laurens* who asked me to leave my commissions and discharge there—he intimated that he would show them to Washington. I did so and went away again.

17 Febr. Tues. At 9 A. M I went to Headquarters again and on the way met the Adjutant General on horseback, who accosted me politely and said · that my papers were at his house and that I should go and ask for them there, and because they were in German, which General Washington did not understand, I was to go to the Regmt[1] Quartermaster Col. *Letterloh* and get him to accompany me to Washington. I went, got my papers and proceeded to *Letterloh*, finding him, however, a very envious man. He pretended to be indisposed and incapable of accompanying me. I met a man there who was called Captain, who told me that he had served with the Prussians in the last war among the Green Dragoons. He told me also, after some conversation, that Major *von Bose* had arrived here about 4 weeks before, but, not getting a position, was serving as a volunteer in Washington's Army. I went away feeling greatly distressed and spoke again with Col. *Laurens* telling him that I wanted to leave, and go to a seaport, to try and get back to Europe again. He promised me to speak to Gen'l Washington about it, when the latter returned home. He said he would have me called then. So I returned to my house again.

19 Febr. Thur. Nobody sending for me and not

wishing to wait any longer myself, I again went to Headquarters. I found Adjutant *Laurens* who told me that Washington offered me a position as First Lieutenant, with which I was, however, not satisfied. I then asked for a pass, which was finally given me in the direction back to *Synnebox*, besides another for free rations on the way and for a horse, if I should fail to get along on foot, besides $30, in paper money. I rendered thanks and went back towards my house. Towards evening I went walking again with an Adjutant and a Lieutenant. [Marginal note· "Henceforth again dependent upon myself."]

20 Feb Frid. At 10 A. M. I left the house, bade farewell to the officers staying there and went to the German Battalion, because I had caused them to believe that I was going to await the return of *v. Arndt;* for I did not intend to disclose my real plans to any one. In the meantime it began to rain hard I went off, but I noticed several times on looking around, that they were watching me. So I walked on until they could see me no longer and, turning, reached the Lanchester road by a circuitous route, arriving at the picket I was allowed to pass without delay on showing my pass. The snow was deep, owing to which I lost my way several times, but at last, by asking the way, I reached an inn called the *Weet Horst.* Some time before reaching this place I met a man on horseback who was a German After some talk and questioning, though my real intention was to go to Philadelphia, yet, having to avoid all American posts, I got the man to point me out another safe road. I took him with me to the inn where I got some dinner and a quart of whiskey for the man. He persuaded me to ride home with him, which I did after many protests. The man was so drunk that, being on the horse with him, I was in imminent danger, the man hardly being able to sit up. However, when it had become dark night, we at last arrived through deep snow and dense woods at his house. Here I perceived

that they were poor people who had to work for wages. They gave me a pretty good bed where I slept very well.

21 Feb. Satur. After I had breakfasted they would not hear of accepting any payment. Then I asked the man to show me the way back (2½ miles) for payment, which he willingly consented to do So we started at 8 A. M. passing the inn and straight on over the Lanchester highway to *Beicklandt.* We arrived at the inn there at 10 A. M. and knowing that my companion was fond of drink I told him to drink as much as he wished and I would pay for it. I stayed here so long that I didn't get away till late. However I found out, that I would have to cross the stream called the *Schulkill* at a place where there was a house owned by Adam Hallmann. So I left there at 4 P. M. and walked 5 English miles further. Here I remained over night at a widow's house On the whole way I have met hardly any but German people

22 Feb. Sund. At 8 A. M. I left there after paying $½. There was a heavy snow-fall and I lost my way several times. It snowed so hard that I could not keep my eyes open. At 12 o'clock I arrived at Hallmann's, but was somewhat startled when, upon entering the room, I unexpectedly found soldiers there and heard that, in the next room only, there was a Rebel Captain. But I did not let them notice anything and said I had a pass to go to Germantown to see some friends there. I ordered "*Tschille Wiske*" and gave the landlord and soldiers a treat and succeeded, after a while in making them all so cordial, that the landlord took the opportunity to order his boy to take me across the stream on horseback. I gave him a shilling and stopped there no longer, but hurried across, fearing all the time lest some one might ask to see the pass, or some one come from the camp who knew me (for it was hardly four English miles distant) Then I would have been placed in a very disagreeable situation. As soon as I had crossed the water I walked

off with long strides. But soon I lost my way again and wishing to take none but the road along which the most Germans were to be found, I was directed by three horsemen to go back a distance of some two miles to the so-called *Trap*. I pursued this way with energetic step through heavy snow and arrived at about 2 o'clock at a small house, which, however, looked very clean and was inhabited by poor people. I only wanted to warm myself a little, but when the people heard that I was a German and a stranger, they prepared something for me to eat, and the weather being so bad they offered to have me stay over night with them. I was very glad to accept. The woman had twins three weeks old, who occasionally furnished me with what I must confess was rather disagreeable music. However, I received a good bed and was treated very kindly

23 Febr. Mond. At 8. A. M. I left there after having breakfast. I actually had to force these good people to accept 8 shillings in payment. At 10.30 I arrived at a stream, across which I was carried on horseback for 14 pence. Here I came across an American soldier from whose talk I soon discovered that he was a deserter. For that reason I quickly separated from him and went my own way alone. At 2 o'clock I crossed the water again on horseback near a mill for 2 shills. 6 pence. As soon as I got across I went to an inn and had some chocolate made for me, and eventually remained there till

24 Feb. Tues. At 6.30 A.M. I left after paying 1 doll. 6 shill. 3 pence and arrived at 8 o'clock at a fine-looking and indeed elegant inn. There were several officers of Congress here, who wished to examine me thoroughly, but, they having no authority to do so, I dismissed their inquiries so energetically that they soon grew silent. I drank a cup of coffee and then proceeded to the next house, where, meeting with different roads, I asked a man to show me the right one to Germantown. The man spoke German

and showed me the way, asking me very artlessly whether I was one of the Hessian prisoners, for in that case I had better be very careful, as there were many traitors in that neighborhood. He told me also that I would have to pass several Rebel pickets. He told me, however, to go straight ahead and inquire for several people whose houses and names he had written down for me. I thanked him and continued my march. When I had proceeded about 2 Engl miles I met a German in a thicket of whom I inquired the way to Germantown, which he showed me, saying, moreover, that on that very morning the English, numbering about 200, had made a sally from Philadelphia putting all the American posts to flight. Hearing that I intended to go to Philadelphia he told me to keep on along the road, intimating that, owing to the general confusion that still prevailed, there was no doubt but what I would get through safely. So I went on. On reaching the next inn I found many of the American soldiers there, who were fleeing in dread before the English. I ate something here and then went on to see whether I could succeed in getting through. I went as far as an inn called *Weit Harst*, where the first Rebel picket of *Leidhorst* was stationed When I had come within about 300 paces of the place, I already saw some of the *Leidhorst* hurrying about. I spoke with a Negro or Indian, who accosted me, and learned from him that 20 *Leidhorst* were again on a sharp lookout. Reasoning with myself that it was impossible for me to proceed further, being so ignorant of the roads, I turned back again with the intention of going to the man whom I had spoken with before in the thicket and who had voluntarily invited me to come to his house, if I could not get through, to stay there until some better opportunity offered. I went back, but only as far as to the inn where I had last eaten something. I arrived there at 3 and, it being very muddy, I decided to stay. Though questioned by many Rebel officers, who came in, as to my destination, I always managed to give them a satisfactory answer.

25 Febr. Wed. At 9 A.M I left after breakfasting and paying 9 shills. 6 pence. I directed my course to the house of the above mentioned man, whose name was *Adam Bender*, a shoe maker, who, however, no longer practised his trade. The house stands just opposite the 19th milestone. He received me very kindly, but asked me not to disguise my real intentions and draw him into misfortune. When I had sufficiently reassured him, he promised to assist me as much as possible in getting to Philadelphia. Then I had to take a little walk with him and in the afternoon ride over on horse-back to a rich friend of his, whence we did not return till towards evening. I fell with my horse and owing to the heavy rain got very muddy. My foot too was hurt by a kick from the horse so that I suffered with pain and a swelling for over two weeks.

26 Febr. Thurs. In the forenoon I stayed at home —in the afternoon we rode out a little while.

27 Feb. Frid. Stayed in the house again.

28 Feb. Sat. *ditto*. but occupied with manifold meditations and inward counselings—as also on the

1 March Sund. until the

2 March. Mond. At 8 A M. a German came to the house who had butter and some chickens with him, in order to find a market for them in Philadelphia. I spoke with him, and agreed, when night had come, to accompany him. Accordingly at 9 P. M , after being permitted to reimburse my host with thanks only (I had, however, made him a present of a few things) I started off with the man. Bender himself went with us more than an English mile As we were approaching the first inn (we were walking in the fields alongside of the road) we hardly escaped being discovered Some dogs set up a terrible barking, but the matter passed off harmlessly. When we arrived in the neigh-

borhood of ———— where the first picket of Rebel Dragoons was stationed we took a roundabout course to the left about 100 paces and succeeded in passing safely though not without a mixture of some anxiety. Then we proceeded straight ahead along the highway, sometimes listening attentively. We got as far as *Baeren Huhel* Church, not far from the 12th milestone, without interference. But we were so near the Rebel picket stationed there, which consisted of about 300 men under the command of Col. *Nagel*, who has been mentioned before, that we could hear them gathering their firewood. My traveling companion, who was a very timid person, and had several times taken old trees in the distance for ferocious *Leidhorst*, had not courage to attempt passing the picket. So we knocked at the door of a house whose inmates he knew. It was already past 12 o'clock, but the people let us in and warned us not to go any further, as it was very improbable that we could succeed in getting past. So we remained there that night hoping for a better opportunity next day—our chief wish was, however, that the English might soon sally out of Philadelphia and rout the pickets.

3 March. Tues. I learned from my host who had made further inquiries, that it would be difficult for us to get through, as all passes were most carefully guarded by the Rebels to prevent outsiders from carrying fresh provisions to the English. So I had to make up my mind to stay there awhile especially as our kind host and hostess offered to keep us until a favorable opportunity was presented. The host was a young man, a cooper by trade, named *George Crossmann*, a German. He was also an ensign in the American militia, but an enemy of the so-called *Wiecks* (whigs). His wife was also still quite young and unusually handsome, with a mind constantly wide awake. They both tried to entertain me and so I remained there with my traveling companion, amidst conflictin rumors, till

5 March Thurs. half past three in the afternoon. Having no longer the slightest hope of getting through in face of the conflicting reports, my old traveling companion decided to return and therefore sold his butter and three fine hens to our hosts. I paid him $6. in paper money for them and treated those in the house with them. I myself wished to go back, but *Croesmann* and especially his wife pressed me so to stay with them until I could get through to Philadelphia that I finally complied with pleasure. But I paid for the few days of our sojourn $4. in paper money for myself and the other man, in spite of their refusal Afterwards I let him go and stayed there myself, though sometimes with no little fear of being discovered, first by a soldier who had often waited upon me when with *Nagel* and again by an old woman who lived next door. But I always managed to escape notice until finally on the

7 March. Satur. In the morning some *Leid-Harst* had come out of Philadelphia and, though they did not come so very near here, all the pickets round about took to their heels But I did not like to risk going quite yet so I waited until

8 March Sund. At 9 A M after breakfasting and forcing my last Congress money, about $3. 2 shill and 6 pence, upon them, I bade them Goodbye They made me promise to visit them again sometime The man accompanied me some distance, and then I walked on alone along the straight highway. Not far from *Berenhuhel* Church the road parts, one branch leading to the left to Germantown, the other to the right to English *Ridg Road*. So I took the right hand one as being the safest, most convenient and nearest way. The *Berenhuhl* Church, in which the Rebels had had their watch, looked miserable However I continued my march without stopping, though frequently looking back. At last, having gone no further than two English miles, I saw four women by whose heavy bundles I immediately perceived that they were going

to Philadelphia. Thus I had, in them, good guides, and in a short time they were joined by others. I kept them a short distance ahead of me and in constant view. At 11 30 A M. I crossed, at the foot of a hill, a little stone bridge which was built across a small stream, the name of which I forget, but which empties a short distance beyond the bridge, into the *Schulkill.* At about 2 o'clock I came to a small, poor looking house—(I did not wish to enter a large one, because one could get nothing there). In this miserable hovel I found a poor old Irishman and his wife. They were just at supper and offered me some I did not, however, accept, but only warmed myself a little and made them a present of 2 shills. old Royal Engl. paper money for which they wished me many blessings. Then I went on, but only as far as the next house, which was small also, but very pretty. I went in and found a young German there, a native of the Palatinate (Churpfalz). I immediately got a night's lodging on the strength of my looks. It was very muddy outside. His wife had gone to church in Philadelphia that being only three miles and a half from here. It was not long before she returned with her sister, whose pleasant and amiable manners astonished me. So I stayed there and was pleasantly entertained.

9 March. Mond. At half past 9 A. M. after breakfast, since they would accept no payment, I gave their little boy 6 shillings old Royal Engl paper money and proceeded on my journey with many "godspeeds!" But it was snowing heavily and very muddy. Thus I walked on, arriving at the English fortifications at 10.30. I showed Washington's passes and was then conveyed by a corporal to His Excell. *Genrl. Chef Howe*, in Philadelphia. I did not wish to disclose myself to his Adj^t Gen'r'l. so I only said that I wished to serve in the army, but would take no position excepting with the *Hessen Cassler*. Thereupon I was sent by Capt. *von Munchhaussen*, Adjt. Genr'l. o General *Hau*, with a Hessian *Ord.* Sub officer, to the

quarters of Lieut Gen'r'l. *Knipphaussen.* On arriving there I reported to Brigadier Major *v Dyppy* and told him that I had been taken prisoner by the Rebels and wished to serve here He expressed his regret. I showed him my papers and he went up a pair of stairs to the General After I had waited some time, the General finally came out himself and spoke very condescendingly to him. He said, however, that he could not immediately take me as an officer, but that he would provide a place for me, adding that it would be best for me to serve with the Artillery. I left everything to the graciousness of the General, whereupon I received a written order to Lieut Col. Eudel of the Artillery and gave the same to him, but he regretted there being no position vacant to place me in. He reported this, by letter, to the General. I went there and gave it to Major v. *Dyppy*, who, however, told me that His Excellence the General had given orders to have my name placed in the order for the Field Regiment, if I were willing, and that I was to report the next day at 12 oclock, noon. I thanked him for this and went to the Grenadier Watch (where I had left all the things I had with me) and got my things with the intention of going to an inn. But in two, that I went to, I could get neither food nor lodgings. Finally I went into a Hessian sub-officer's wine-room, drank some wine and ate some bread and cheese with it. Then, as it was getting dark, I left, though without knowing where I would go. I walked quite a distance until finally I met an English carpenter, who was returning from work on a ship, and asked him whether he did not know of some place near by where a man could get a night's lodging. He answered that it was very unlikely I would find such a place, because most of them had failed in consequence of the hard times, but that there were a few left yet. He said, then, that if I had already had my supper, he would accommodate me in his own house and let me share his bed with him. I was content to do so and went with him to his lodgings where he built up a good grate-fire. Afterwards he said he would accept no payment for my lodging, but asked me to treat to a bottle of rum. So I had to decide to do so and pay 1 shill. 6 pence Engl money for it I let him do the drinking and soon went to bed, finding it really a very good one

10 March Tues. At 7 A. M. the carpenter got up to go to work on the ship, but told me to stay in bed as long as I wanted to. It was raining very hard, however, and he soon returned. I did not get up till 10 o'clock. Then I dressed rapidly, took my bundle and went to the Hessian Grenadier Watch. There I stopped until 12.30, and then went to Major *v. Dyppy* who told me that there was a sergeant and ensign wanted in Donop's regiment He advised me, in consideration of the pay, to take the sergeant's position, telling me that Lieut. Gen'r'l *v. Knipphaussen* wished me to rest assured that such a step would not prevent my further advancement. I consented, and Major *v. Dyppy* sent an orderly with me to the Adjutant, Lieut *v. Lepel* of Donop's regiment. Lieut. *v. Lepel* accompanied me to Lieut. Colonel *Hindte*, and finally, after much pressing, I consented to enter Lieut. Col. *Hindte's* company as Sergeant. At the same time, however, I received permission not to report to anyone, until I had been supplied with equipments. He (the Lieut. Col) sent me in the meanwhile to the Sergeant of the company, at whose place I took up my quarters, and that day I did not go out again. Sergeant von Krafft of the Musketeer Regiment of Lieut. Genr'l von Donop and of the Company of Lieut. Col Hinte, in the Hesse-Cassel army, in North America, in the Province of Pennsylvania and other places. At Philadelphia in Queen Street; the Sergeant and Privates quartered together.

11 March. Wed. At 9 A. M. I went with Serg Major *Roemer* to the Equipment Bureau at the quarters of the Lieut. Col. I was given a hat, neck-

tie, buckle, coat, vest and a short sword and hangings. I had to have cloth gamashes (leggings) made at my own expense. That day I staid in the house. At noon Gen'r'l v. Knipphaussen issued the following order, not knowing anything of my engagement. " A man who has been in Prussian service and who can produce his commissions and an honorable discharge and has several good recommendations, who, furthermore, possesses a good knowledge of drawing and the art of engineering, wishes a position as Free Corporal or as other Sub-officer with the Hessian regiment, which Gen. Knipphaussen would like to see him obtain."

12 March. Thur. At 1 o'clock I went to Lieut. Col. v. *Hindte*, reported in my uniform to him, as also to the Company Staff, Capt. v. *Donop*, 2^d Lieut. v. *Losberg* and Ensign v *Lehrbach* In the afternoon I went with the Standard Bearer of the Company, *Emanuel Muus*, a Swedish Pommeranian, to the Hessian Free Yager Foot Corps, to see a Yager named v. *Frihmel*, who was under arrest and was to have been hung the next day, but had obtained pardon, and was to run the gantlet.

13 March. Frid. At 9 A. M. I went to the Lieut Colonel's, to Col. v. *Goose* and Major v *Wurm*, with Lieut. v. *Losberg* (the captain not being present) to be introduced. At 2 in the afternoon I went with the same Lieut. to take the oath at the Col.'s quarters.

14 March. Sat. This afternoon at Capt Donop's with a few officers in company at coffee.

16 March Mond. Company inspection. I wrote a letter to *Croesmann* at whose house in the country I had lodged a short time ago, and gave the letter (in which I requested him to call on me soon) to a woman to deliver.

17 March. Tues. I was placed on the reserve picket which always had to be in readiness (in all regiments) to march out at four cannon shots, or fire alarm.

18 March. Wed. I had a funny adventure. Towards evening I went with the Sergeant Major to a house where there were a company of people. Some Englishmen were locked inside. I listened. One stood outside and asked me why I was listening. It was 8 o'clock; so I answered nothing, but drew my sword and flourished it menacingly at the English Sergeant. He yelled terribly, and, though he had a sabre in his hand, took to his heels, while those in the house jumped out of the windows. I set out in pursuit with my naked sword in my hand (Sergeant Major *Roemer* stood all this while at a distance), but the whole party fled with the greatest possible speed

20 March. Frid. At 9 o'clock in the evening while the Quarter Master of the Company *Denstaet* was sitting with me drinking punch, he behaved impolitely and I insisted upon his going out with me immediately, although it was already as dark as pitch. He wounded me very slightly in the head, as I was about to stoop down to pick up my hat which had fallen off. I wounded him slightly too, in the arm. And all this happened without our being able to see how or where the blows were delivered.

21 March. Sat. I was present at the pay-parade of the whole regiment, which had to march out without guns and march and drill in " wheeling about." I have made no note of the Company pay-parade, because it is a very rare occurrence.

22 March. Sun. I wrote a letter to Lieut. Gen'r'l. *v. Donop* and Maj. Genrl. *v. Juncken*, on the advice of several officers.

23 March Mon. In the morning Capt. *v Donop* sealed my letters with his seal, as I no longer had one, and sent them by his servant to the packet boat which was going to England.

24 March. Tues. Staff Watch next to Hessian Col. v. Goosen's quarters, because the Chasseur Lieut Genrl. von Donop was not with the regiment.

27 March. Frid. Company inspection.

29 March. Sun. On the command in N° 9 on the *Scul-Kiel* with Capt. Shotz of the body-regiment [Leibregiment], 1 Ensign, 3 Sub officers, 1 drummer and 50 privates. A Sergeant received in America as monthly pay 32 shillings Sterling, but from this was deducted daily, for rations, 5 ha'pence, so that he received only 26/- 6 ha'pence when the month had 30 days, and for 31 days 26/- and ha'penny. As rations we received daily 1 lb. salt meat, 1 lb. bread or zwieback [i e buns or biscuits twice baked] peas, rice and *Sprizmehl* for 7 days regularly (allzeit); also 1 quart of rum; at times also *strang-bier*

Pay received in March. 11th 3/-, 16th 3/-, 21st 3/-, 26th 8/- and 8½d—total 17/- 8½d. Ration days in Philadelphia were at first on Thursdays.

— April—In the same quarters up to the 15th inst

4 April—Regiments day, which concerned all the Sub-officers in the regiment; they had to be with the Adjutant from early morning, to carry all orders given by the General to the Staff-Officers, etc, etc

5 April Sund Company's day. In the morning I had a quarrel with the Free Corporal of the Co., *Muus*, because he had gossiped with Free Corp. *Muller* about Maj. v. *Wurm's* Co. But as I was on duty that day I put him off until the next day Capt. v Donop having heard of the affair, endeavored to reconcile us, but even though he seriously forbade the continuance of the quarrel, I told him that I would not submit. In the afternoon I got Corp. *Conrad Schaefer* to take my place for a few hours and walked over with Serg. Maj. *Roemer* to Yager Sergeant v. *Stedenfeldt's* outside of the city From him I heard that Free Corp Muller had repeated the above story with *Muus*, telling it this time in quite a different way. I became so enraged at this that I immediately started off. On the way near a bowling alley I met Muller and accosting him boldly demanded that he should retract in my presence and in that of him to whom he had told

the story. He was very drunk, cursed me and the others, whereupon I demanded satisfaction the next day.

6 April. Mond. Pay parade. At 9 A. M. after drill I went with Muus outside the city towards the Hessian Yager quarters, taking Serg. Maj. Roemer along as a second. In a short time, after I had struck off his (Muus') sword at the hilt and he had taken the Sergeant's, I hit him again across the right hand, whereupon he had enough. I accompanied him to the surgeon's to have his wound dressed Free Corp Muller had the Regiment's *jour* to-day, so he sent me word to have patience until the next day.

7 April. Tuesd. Reserve picket. In the morning after drill I again went out with Serg. Maj. Roemer to meet Free Corp. Muller who excused himself for half an hour on account of his duties, but promised to come after us to the place of meeting. Therefore I walked on with the Serg Major in a different direction from that of the previous day with Muus, waited there a time and finally Muller came with his second, Muus. A whole troop of English officers came riding past, so we had to wait a while. Thereupon we took off our coats and went through four rounds hotly, but regularly, without either having wounded the other. At last Muller asked my pardon and begged me to forgive one who had been drunk and to stop. On the advice of my second I agreed to do so.

8 April. Wed. Short tour. Went out to the bushes (woods), a distance of 3 English miles from the city on the Germantown road, where the soldiers had to get their own fire-wood.

10 April Frid. Ordinary watch Across the *Schul-Kiel* on the watch (the "outermost"—furthest) in a small redoubt with Capt. von Urff of the body regm't. 2 Ensigns, 2 drummers, 5 Sub-officers and 60 privates. On this watch the following novel occur-

rence took place. At 1.30 in the afternoon a man on horseback came from the Rebels, with a white flag, to our out-posts, with 1 Lieut. 1 Sergeant, and 6 privates "commanded Rebels" and brought 15 English prisoners to be exchanged. After necessary report they were admitted At 12.30 midnight a deserter on horseback, with a gun, came from the Rebels; an hour later, another on foot; both were retained until morning, after being taken to the city.

14 April—Company's day.

15 " —Quarters in the same street, but in the corner house on the large street; and, in recognition of my drawing I had only the two quarter-master riflemen (Fourier Schutzen) with me.

16 April—In N° 9 on the *Scul Kiel*.

17 April Frid In the afternoon I was requested by Free Corp Muus to go out with him as his second, which, after long refusing, I finally did. His opponent was a Serg. *Grando* of the Losberg Regt. We went to the place where he had fought with me before Muus could not well use the hand I had wounded and consequently soon received a blow, though a very slight one, in his right arm, which put an end to the duel.

23 April. Wed. Company's day.

27 April —Reserve picket

28 April—Hospital Watch I was placed on the city watch in the 4th street; and on the *Collegia* Hospital watch with Free Corp. Muller of Donop's regm't. and 18 privates of Loosberg's regm't. I found fault with one of these fellows by mistake But when he began to talk back, I gave him a good thrashing The next day, when relieved from the watch, he brought in an accusation against me to his Colonel, von Loosberg, that I had said, "he was one of the infernal Loosberg kind", whereupon his Col. sent to our von Goosen to inquire how the case stood

30 April—At 9 o'clock this morning I was very politely examined by Capt. von Donop in the pres-

ence of 1st Lieut. von Nagel, at his house, and as I could give ample proof against the plaintiff, who was present, he was forthwith sharply reprimanded, and he got a good thrashing in his own regiment, to boot They held that I was in the right

Pay for April 1st 3/–, 6th 3/–, 11th 3/–, 21st 3/–, 26th 11/–3d; total 26/–3d

May. In the same quarters.

2. May. In N° 9 on sharp command.

3 " Company's day. This morning when I came home and had my hair combed, my orderly found a long grey hair on my head.

4 May. At 10.30 A. M. all the Hessian regiments and corps in Philadelphia had to pass in review (not far distant on the Court Square) before General Howe which pleased him so well, that he expressed his thanks in the orders issued that same day.

11 May. Company's day.

12 " Working command. At 12 noon I was on working command at the redoubt N° 1, in the woods till 7 o'clock in the evening Order was given by the English Engineer to make a dyke.

14 May. On sharp command in N° 9.
16 " On the market watch.
17 " On reserve picket.
18 " All superfluous baggage had to be given up and put on board ships.
19 " At 9 in the evening all the English and Hessian regiments received orders not to undress and be prepared to march out at the sound of the first cannon-shot. But everything remained quiet until 5 o'clock in the morning of the

20 May, when we immediately received orders to march, without cannon shot. Of the Hessians the whole Wilwart brigade remained behind in Philadelphia, but ready to follow on the order being given. So we marched off along the Germantown road, not knowing whither. At last, at about a distance of about 9 English miles and above Germantown, at *Bettlehausen*

we marched out (hearing loud cannonading by our and the English Light Infantry and Yagers which had been sent ahead On the left, the English got into the first engagement and we and the Anspachers second, our regiment von Donop forming the left wing. Here we rested until 11 A. M. when General Howe came back, because the Rebels had taken to flight through the *Scul-Kiel* at the mere sight of our light infantry and of the English under the *Leithorst*, leaving much behind them. But only 5 were taken prisoners. Finding nothing more to do we marched straight back to Philadelphia, through Germantown, arriving at 2.30 P. M.

[From 9 o'clock P. M. until 6.30 A. M. of the 23rd inst. under arrest.]. At 9 in the evening while inspecting I got into a quarrel with our army-surgeon After some exchange of words I flourished my sword about his shirt-bosom and then drew it (as he grasped it in the palm of his hand) through his hand so that it was all cut open. Moreover I boxed his ears once or twice and then walked away. The surgeon immediately complained to the Lieut. Col , whereupon my Capt v. Donop himself placed me under arrest in the staff watch of our Sergeant next to the quarters of our Colonel.

21 May. The next day I was not examined, as I had expected to be, because they wanted me to ask for pardon. In the afternoon Capt. Donop came to see me and advised me to write to the Lieut. Col., as the examination of my case had been fixed for the next day at 9 A. M. before Captain Finater So I followed his advice and wrote to him

22 May. Frid. At 9 A. M. I was led by 1 lance-corporal and 2 privates only about twenty paces to the place of examination That I was in the wrong was very evident, besides, the Surgeon had many witnesses According to public declaration I was returned to the watch, and at 12.30 I was put in irons by the provost, the same being attached to the right foot

and left hand; but the rings were so large that I could at any time take out my hand. This continued until the

23 May. Sat. at six o'clock in the morning, when, at the command of the Col., I was "unchained." (N. B. I had to pay the provost 7 pence lock-money). At 7 o'clock the Colonel ordered me to be released from my confinement When I reported to him he reprimanded me very politely, saying, that if it had not been I, degradation would have followed. And so things passed off smoothly this time

All field effects were delivered up to-day. All the old tents had been taken away and put on board the ships yesterday.

24 May. Sund. At noon the former commanding general William Howe departed by ship for England and left the command to General *Klington*. The same day all the cannons were taken away from the outside redoubts and carried on board the ships—a sure sign that we should soon leave Phila; but a field piece was brought by every regiment into the redoubts.

25 May. Mond. Company's day. The inspections fell to me as all the other sub-officers were on duty. In the afternoon at 6, all the sick and the baggage started, in the ships, for New York, the women likewise. But all those women, that were able to march, were compelled to get out of the ship again, and the vessel was directed to await further orders, which were received on the

27 May. Wed. when the ship departed.

30 " Sat. On general watch at the quarters of Gen von Knipphaussen Having the general watch with 24 men at Gen. Knipphaussen's, I had to go to Maj. Dyppy twice. He asked me about my circumstances and reported to Gen. Knipph. who thereupon promised me his aid again.

Pay received in May: 1st 3/–, 6th 3/–, 11th 3|–, 16th 3/–, 21st 3/–, 26th 11/– ½d; total 26|– ½d.

June. In the same quarters up to the 15th.

1 June. Mon. Company's day. In the morning I visited Col. von Goosen and asked him to remember me in Cassel which he promised to do.

2 June. Tues. I sent the above mentioned letter to the Lord Mayor at Falmouth, England, in regard to my things and at the same time one to Cassel to Gen. von Donop and von Junckheim I sealed them with Capt. v. Donop's seal and took them to the paymaster Schmidt—Kings *Cassierer*—whose duty it was to forward all letters by the packet-boat.

Soon after 12 to-night we all received orders to march forth again with " scrip and scrippage " as soon as the first cannon-shot was heard and not to leave the Phila· quarters until the next day at 12 Two English regiments and 100 Hessian foot-yagers had to reconnoitre the first night on account of apprehended attacks, but early the next day they returned without much news.

3 June Wed This morning I wrote to the Saxon Ambassador DuBois at the Hague in Holland and asked him to write to Gen. v. Knipphaussen for me, and gave the letter to Capt. v Donop who promised to send it at first opportunity.

4 June Thurs. At 3 o'clock in the morning 80 men (but only of the Hessian regiments) were sent up the Germantown road, but only a distance of 4 English miles there to make a stand of a few hours and, if nothing hostile appeared, to march back again. We had about 30 Engl. light horse (Leidharst) men with us. The day before I had been in the redoubt. Today I was ordered to N° 10, but was taken along on this expedition At the ruined inn called the *Risin Sun*, to which the command marched, I was detached with 15 men to a hill on the right side of the road where I placed 5 sentinels. At break of day we marched from the rendezvous out of the city; at 8 A. M we marched in again having neither seen nor heard anything new.

At 12 o'clock noon, on account of the birthday of the King of England all the cannon were fired by the ships which were still in the Delaware.

From the 4th of June the rations were given out for two or three days only at one time.

5 June Frid. On reserve picket.

6 " Satur. Some deputies from England arrived here to make peace with Congress.

7 June Sund. Gen. *Cornwalli* arrived amidst firing of ships' guns. In the morning I finished a letter to *von Staff*, Captain in Braunsberg, but as if I were still with the Rebels, and sent him 4d. American paper money to look at

8 June. Mond. After 12 o'clock at night the regiment of Anspach and Beyreuth was embarked in large sloops near the Swedish Church to start for Long Island by way of the Delaware But one command of the same remained behind and went with us on our march from Philadelphia

10 June. Wed. In the morning the Deputies that had come from England crossed the *Schuylkill* in a coach, preceded by an Officer and Drummer of the English *Leid Horst*, to treat with the Rebels; but towards evening they returned.

9 June. Tues. Company's day.

11 " Thurs. We were again ordered to convey all the sick and wounded by sloops to the ships, by 4 o'clock in the morning. It was said that our ship, which had left first with the equipages and sick, was still lying at the mouth the Delaware under cover of the English men-of-war.

12 June Frid. All the royal wagons that had been furnished to the Regiment had to be given up, and were taken across the Delaware to the Jersey side and also the horses belonging to them.

14 June Sun. Church parade of the whole regiment; all the Hessian regiments at the Great Parade Place. In the afternoon all the ships that had been deserted or not finished by the Rebels were

burned not far from the Swedish Church on the Delaware. In consequence of this two stables and a house near by caught fire. Likewise several horses belonging to the *Leidhorst* of this region, such as were deemed no longer capable of enduring hard work, were shot and thrown into the water, at the order of General *Klington*

15 June Mond. In the morning the ships that had not been burned the day before, on account of the strong wind, were all burned. At noon all the baggage had to be transported across the Delaware, also all officers, grooms and horses

At noon came the order to be ready to march at 4 30 P. M. Hereupon the soldiers indulged in a scene which was cruel and ridiculous to behold. Everything in the rooms was thrown out of the windows, and other endless confusion ensued At the appointed time all the Hessians except the Grenadiers came together, also some English regiments. At 5 we marched almost to the end of the city, towards Germantown, where we were at once shipped on board the boats awaiting us and taken across the Delaware. There we waited some time until the whole regiment was together. The place was called *Coppers Ferry*. We marched about $2\frac{1}{2}$ English miles and the greater part of our regiment was directed to camp in a wood It may have been 7 30 P. M when we arrived there. As we had no tents and it was too late to build huts, I lay down under a tree to sleep

16 June. Tues. In the morning order was given to erect huts, because we were to remain here until all had overtaken us from Philadelphia. I went this morning in among the cherry-trees which grew about there, with several other Sub-officers.

17 June. Wed. In the morning Gen'r'l von Knipphaussen, as also all the Grenadiers and Yagers arrived here in the camp from Philadelphia, and there remained in Philadelphia only about 100 Englishmen. The evening before General Stern arrived at the

camp. In the evening at sunset I was on the field picket and was sent out about 100 paces to the front with 8 men, without observing anything. At 9 in the evening orders came to march on at 4 A. M.

18 June. Thurs. We all set out at 4 A. M: and proceeded 6½ English miles until we passed through the little town of *Hottenfeldt* [Haddonfield], where, at about 8 o'clock, we who were on the extreme right camped under huts on a fallow field. At 9.30 o'clock we heard many shots from our outposts on the right and from the Yagers on the left.

19 June Frid. At day-break the whole army, with the equipage, marched past us At noon our regiment had to follow to protect the whole equipage (for the Body-regiment and the Wilwart Brigade followed the next morning); but only about ¾ English mile, when our regiment again camped in a bush to the right in a cornfield and not far from the 15th English Musketeer regiment. This night, during the fire watch, I received 9 soldiers in arrest who had killed cattle, and also 2 English grooms (knechte).

20 June Sat Company's day. At 3 A. M. we marched away again as *Stant Garde,* during a heavy rain. Towards noon we built huts in a meadow near the town of Morristown 6½ English miles to the left. The same night a soldier deserted from us.

21 June. Sun. From 3 in the morning until noon I had the rear guard of our and the English regiment, again in heavy rain. In the afternoon we marched during terrific heat, stopping every minute on account of the wagons, 9 English miles to the little town of Mount Holly. Our Grenadiers and the English, which were in front got into camp about 6 30 P. M., on the right in front of the town, in bush (? huts), again in wheat, next to the Body regiment. I was taken very sick with violent vomiting about 10 o'clock, but got better towards evening. This night there was a terrific thunderstorm and the rain poured down so hard that we in our bush-huts got very wet.

22 June. Mond. At 6 o'clock in the morning the march was continued until we came to the middle of the army. (It is to be remembered here that the English constantly hoped for the extreme rear guard). Before we marched on, our Gen. v. Knyphaussen came and had it made known through the commanders of the regiments that there had been many desertions during the past few days; that we were marching directly to Hesse; that we were to believe nothing else, still less the statements in circulation, that the Rebels would give plantations and houses to those who remained behind. (When I heard this, namely, that peace or at least a march to Europe was to be made, I resolved to resign, because I had no desire to be seen there as a Sub-officer) About noon we again pitched our hut-camp on a meadow at Black Horse [Tavern], 7 Engl miles from our former camp. Very soon after an English deserter who had been caught by the English (by the Royalists) was hanged there on a tree by the road, which caused a dreadful uproar, because the hanged man had many still bleeding wounds

23 June Tues. At 4 A. M. we moved again, in the middle of the army, till towards evening when we again pitched our camp in a fallow field at *Racklestown* 7½ English miles to the right. Here I inquired of our Colonel through Capt. von Donop, about my dismission, excepting if there should not be peace, for, I said, I would never be seen in Europe as a Sub-officer. I received answer that I had better remain, because our march to Europe would probably not take place and I must very soon become an officer, when they returned from Cassel. Besides, I was to receive my discharge, if I wished it, here, or if I preferred on account of the free passage, in England, immediately on arriving there With this I was satisfied. In fact, I did not know what to do.

The same day 2 men deserted from our first

company, and I and Sergeant Heynemann were sent to search in the bushes for them. We came to a meadow where we met some English soldiers with stolen goods. I wanted to take the goods from them, but they told me, if I went but 100 paces further, I would find plenty of Hessian soldiers there in the houses who had done the same thing. I thought our 2 fellows might perhaps be there marauding, which the other sergeant believed too, and therefore we resolved to go there. To tell the truth it was a very rash undertaking, because the Rebels always kept very close to our camp. We went over fences and through marsh and water, certainly for half an hour, when we arrived at a green spot in the midst of dense woods where we saw two houses at some distance from each other. Upon entering the first we found everything lying about in confusion in room, chamber and cellar, the beds torn open and the feathers strewn about, & boxes and chests broken open, but no one was to be seen or heard there. I exhorted the other Sergeant to keep watch that we didn't get attacked. There being nothing to find here we proceeded through a foul swamp about 400 paces to the other house, which was not very large either. As we approached two women and several little children appeared. To my English interrogation they quickly and anxiously replied that no Hessians had been there, but several English soldiers who had taken everything they could find, even the silver shoe-buckle from one woman's shoe. On entering the room I found no less confusion than in the former house. Their husbands had fled because the English soldiers had said they were going to take them as Rebel prisoners to the camp. They begged me to spare them. They were, they said, good Royalists. When I had assured her that I would do so, she said she saw very plainly there was no truth in what people had told her of the Hessians, namely, that they were cruel. She saw that it was the English alone. She asked me to come into the room, but I did not stay there long; for it seemed to me that the woman often looked around, as if hoping for help from the men who had run away, and that such help might possibly come, whereas we were beyond reach of help from the camp Therefore I only demanded some fresh provisions for cash payment and at last received from her 1 rooster and 3 young chickens which had been concealed in the oven. She would not name her price, but I gave her 1 Engl. shill. 10 pence which was all the money I had with me, for which they wished me many blessings and begged me to pick some cherries from the trees in front of the house. But they always seemed to be eagerly looking around for something, so I reminded the other that it was time to go, whereupon these women offered us many good wishes. They went toward the other house, where we espied some people, but on our arrival they were nowhere to be found, having crawled back into the thick bushes again.

With all possible speed we hastened toward our camp and meeting, in the woods that extend nearly up to our huts, some soldiers of our Company who were in search of wood, we strangled the chickens and had them brought after us by the soldiers, because we had to report beforehand. Towards evening we heard, from a distance of a few miles, about 40 loud cannon reports and also some "small fire" which, as we afterward learned, was Genrl. *Klington* with the light infantry against an uncertain Rebel corps, which however, as usual soon took to their heels.

[Marginal note : " On the march, N. B. I was never allowed to carry any of my things or my knapsack ; but whenever I was detached I always took my knapsack and a little box with my papers in it, which I would not give out of my possession." Also : " From this time in the State of New Jersey."]

24 June. Wed. Regiment's day. At 7 A. M. we continued our march again as rear guard to cover

the others. In the afternoon we arrived at a little place called *Wahlsmil* about 6 English miles, or rather just opposite it across a stream and on the other side of a bridge that had been destroyed by the Rebels, but had been rapidly rebuilt, for the passage of the army and baggage, by the English pioneers. Up to this place it was 6 English miles from our former camp. We were soon after again impeded in our march, the Rebels having hewn and cast large trees in our way to prevent our baggage train from moving rapidly. Such tricks were often played on us by the Rebels and sometimes they showed themselves on the hill sides or behind us in considerable numbers. But they never had courage enough to attack us "in our baggage" which at times had become greatly disordered and ill-protected. Nor did they ever stand, when pursued, unless they by far outnumbered us At 9 in the evening we arrived, to the right, at *Emplestown* and pitched our camp in a most beautiful wheat-field Again 4 English miles. The English Headquarters were 5 English miles from here in the town of Allentown.

25 June. Thurs. At 4 A. M. we continued our march in the middle of the army, without noticing anything in particular, except, whenever we passed through a thicket, to miss some who had deserted from us, and to have to endure the most frightful heat. At 7 in the evening we reached, to the right, *Monmos County Frehold Township*, 6 English miles, and pitched our tents on a fallow field.

26 June Frid On reserve picket. At 4 A. M. we again continued our march, suffering from the heat. At noon we had gone 5 English miles and were near the little town of *Freholdt*. When we entered the place almost all the inhabitants had fled and evidently a short time before our arrival, because I found fresh milk in a house where I was ordered to go with some men to fetch water. Every place here was broken into and plundered by the English soldiers.

The church, which was made of wood and had a steeple, was miserably demolished. The city hall, also having a steeple, contained in the lowest story some strong prison cells, in the front one of which there were still bread, beverage, ham and lettuce on a laid table. Also beds and articles of dress were to be found, a sign that these prisoners had been removed in greatest haste. A loaf of bread lay on the floor near the table, which, with much exertion, I managed to fetch or rather draw out by piercing it with my short musket. After staying in the streets there for an hour and a half, while the English soldiers had, in the meantime, been breaking and destroying everything in the city-hall-house, even tearing down the little bell in the steeple (no Hessian was to be seen among them, the commanders of the regiments not allowing it, though many abuses were practised by them secretly) we marched back and, at a short distance away from the place (viz. in front of the town, to the left) we pitched our camp in a fallow field. To-day the Hessians got permission from the commanders of the regiments to take cattle wherever they should find any and kill and slaughter it for the use of the regiment. That evening there was a terrific thunderstorm. Capt v Donop's tent was just back of my hut. I lay in my hut, on account of the rain, leaning on my left arm, together with my orderly, when there was a fearful thunderclap, so that I could not help thinking my hut had been struck. But it struck at a distance of only 15 paces behind my hut, killing one of the Captain's horses—and also 150 paces further to the right, on one side, near a tree, killing another horse and severely injuring several men of Losberg's regiment.

[Marginal note · "This same day the English soldiers set fire to a house outside of the town after having ransacked it, because it was said to be the property of a prominent Rebel."]

Still in the neighborhood of *Mon Mos County Frehold Township*.

27 June Sat. To-day we had rest day About 10 A. M. alarm was given by the outposts on our left wing. A few musket shots and directly afterwards cannon reports were heard The reserve picket had to march out immediately, and when we had gone quite a distance and were in the thicket, just in front of the line, we had to occupy the passes there. I was detached to go on ahead with 6 men, by Lieut. v. Bartenleben who had command of 36 men and 2 Sub-officers of our regiment, and I placed an outpost. Hardly an hour later the Rebels again made an attack, not far from me on my right, but I got nothing to do, as they never showed themselves very long at a time.

[Marginal note "In the beginning of this attack an ensign Werner of the *Rall Battl.* had run away leaving all his men behind him just beyond the picket."]

At midnight another and much more terrific thunderstorm than the previous one came up, with heavy rain, so that we again got wet through. At daybreak we were ordered to leave our post and betake ourselves to the regiment, which, when we arrived there, had proceeded quite a distance. So we marched

28 June. Sund. in the cruel heat, owing to which nearly half of our regiment as also of the other regiments, also of the English, remained behind, often having to stop and repair the destroyed bridges. In the afternoon considerable firing was heard in our rear guard which continued for some time. This was on account of the Rebels some of whom had been so bold as to tear right through the baggage train, and, shooting unexpectedly from a concealed place, had killed a groom and a horse. Towards evening some of them were wounded by our army. At 8.45 P. M. we camped at *Notchwarb*, in the midst of woods and on an elevation in a field of beautiful wheat We postponed building our huts until the next day on account of our fatigue. Company's day.

29 June Mond. One half rest day. In the morning we again heard firing on our right wing (for our

camp was always spread out broad), and the light-infantry, which lay a little way in front of us, had to start out immediately. This morning I went to a little brook, back of the front line, to bathe. I was assigned to the Fire Watch to-day, but exchanged with Free Corporal Muus, agreeing to take his place for him in return. About 3 o'clock in the afternoon we marched again, but stopped to rest, after advancing scarcely one English mile, in a thicket. From there we marched up on a hill from which we could already see the *Raraten River* with many ships. In the meantime the baggage train passed along through a valley to our right. We were obliged to protect it and to wait until it had entirely passed through the thicket in that valley. Then we marched up on a hill, while the left wing, the body regiment and the right wing (also the English light infantry which was close behind us) remained on the *Frehold* road to protect the baggage. No one was allowed to undress or take off his cartridge-box, because, being a *commando*, we had the first outposts and any attack would necessarily be made upon us It remained quiet, however, all night We lay under trees and the baggage not being with us and consequently many things being absent, we felt very uncomfortable.

30 June. Tues. At 7 A. M. we broke up our camp and marched through the borough of *Mittletown*, about 3 English miles, until we reached, two miles further on, quite a large hill where we pitched our camp. I was obliged to help lay out the camp, all the Sub-officers of the Company being tired out. When we arrived at an elevation of land at about 11 o'clock, there were not more than 9 men of our Company and 100 out of the whole regiment together, the rest having all been left on the road on account of fatigue. One man of our Company, Stamberg, a *Hildburghauser* and theologian, had dropped down dead. He was carried to the camp on a wagon and buried in a thicket inside of our front line. Several men were slowly

brought back to life from insensibility. Huts were built, but owing to the heat, it was almost impossible to breath underneath them. Though I had nothing to carry beside my short musket, the rapid marching and intolerable heat and the miserable roads across fields and over hills, often nearly made me faint. My ambition alone fortified me, and by the aid of the Almighty I came out one of the freshest. Towards evening all the baggage passed by us, taking all night to do so. At 5 in the afternoon we already received orders not to undress, but to march at the first signal

Pay rceived in June: 1st 3/–, 6th 3/–, 11th 3/–, 16th 3/–, 21st 3/– and 26th 11/– 3d total 26/– 3d.

On the march we got salt and fresh meat, biscuit and rum, nothing more.

1 July. Wedn. At 8 A. M. I was assigned to the Field Watch for Free Corp. Muus. Towards 10 o'clock we had to march again, but only half an English mile, whereupon we again camped at the foot of a hill and in a large orchard. In the last place we had been obliged to make room for the English. At noon some Rebels again attacked the right wing of our large camp, which caused much single firing from the detached posts. On our left wing a Sub-officer and 12 detached men were taken prisoners by the Rebels without firing a shot or offering the least resistance In the evening Ensign v. Lehrbach had a cow slaughtered, which had been captured. The performance caused us much anxiety and also much fun. We also milked many cows in the neighborhood of our Watch and were lucky enough to manage not to be caught at it Again a rest day.

2 July. Thur. Rest day.

3 " Frid. A rest day. To-day we had an astonishing and continuous rain-storm and as the baggage was obliged to start at break of day and I had only taken my little box and a shirt with me, we had no rest during the night and the next day till noon on account of the wetness. Little to eat and

to drink, and very bad at that, being wet through and unable to rest, innumerable other repulsive and adverse circumstances and my continual damned bad luck, stirred my weeping heart uncommonly. Owing to the many conjectures regarding our future march I felt undecided, as to the present and the future, what I ought to undertake to do.

4 July. Satur. Rest day. Until noon the rain continued unabatedly. After that, however, it was fine weather and the sun shone. After 1 o'clock all the officers' horses had to be brought on board ship N. B. not of the Subaltern officers, none of theirs being allowed to be taken along. At 3 o'clock Generals *Klington*, Knipphaussen and a few others of the generals went away by ship. In the afternoon some of the wagons that had carried our baggage were burned near the river by the army. After 5 o'clock we heard from afar an astonishingly loud and long running fire (Lauf-feuer) of cannons. At 6.30 order came to have all the guns immediately taken on board the ships This afternoooon I had a quarrel with the Free Corporal of the Body Company, Schonwolf, whose tobacco-pipe Serg. Maj. Roemer and I had hidden, which he called a stupid trick. Whereat I struck him on the head with the tobacco-pipe, with which punishment he begged me to be satisfied, when I demanded further satisfaction. This I finally promised with derisive laughter To-day we heard that the Rebels had gone back and were not going to pursue us any longer. Many different things more, regarding our uncertain march.

5 July. Sund. At 5 A. M. we marched forth about —— English miles in the neighborhood of —— where we soon marched up to the water, for we had left the camp by the left flank. Some companies of the Body regiment and also the first two files of the Body Co. of our regiment had already embarked in long boats. Many of these boats were also used for the transportation of animals which were tied to them

so as to swim behind Therefore we went back again and to the right across a pontoon bridge made of boats covered with boards, across which all the English regiments had marched also. We had to follow them to the little island of Sandy Hook upon which stands the Light House for the ships. We had difficult marching through the sand almost as far as the Light House, which is situated at the extreme end of the island. Here we immediately went into the long boats, having, however, to wade through water up to our knees, because it was high tide. From the pontoon-bridge to this place was a distance of about —— English miles, the time of our arrival, after 11 A.M. Our ship, which we and the Body Company had to get to by means of 2 long boats for each, was three-masted, without guns and named —— It lay at quite a distance. We had to row nearly an hour and a half before we reached it and we made a great noise there because there were no provisions on board and no one knew where to get any. Some one was sent to other ships for provisions. The ship-captain was compelled to go too, so that at sunset we finally got our provisions. Never had I been hungrier and consequently I ate my salt pork, with the mouldy biscuit, raw and uncooked. After many entreaties I managed to get some very thin coffee without milk or sugar for a little money, and then I spread out a robe and lay down on the cabin-deck to sleep. In the hold everything was in disorder and there were so many there that I did not want to be among them We would have left that same night, but the sailors of our ship were occupied in transporting the army to other ships. On that account we had to wait and did not know yet whether we were to land at York or on *Long Eyland*. Meanwhile our ship lay between New Jersey on the left and Sandy Hook to the right behind us, and *Long Eylandt* a little ahead of us to the right, while *Staten Eylandt* lay a little ahead to the left. A beautiful prospect in clear weather with the many ships lying at anchor round about. There is yet to be mentioned that, when we were crossing the pontoon bridge, I was greatly surprised that the Rebels did not take advantage of the disorder in our arrangements and crossing, since we were without cannons and even our muskets were unloaded, according to orders received the night before. They undoubtedly would have succeeded since we were too confident. During a momentary detention near the water I dug up some fine large clams on the beach, a thing I had learned from the English, and I immediately ate them with ravenous appetite owing to my hunger. Before we crossed the pontoon bridge all unnecessary horses were turned loose and chased back into the country

6 July. Mond. Not until 6 A. M. did all the troops arrive for embarkation—then a number of ships with men and baggage departed, as some had done the night before, but without knowing where they were going. At last toward 8 o'clock our Captain received orders to start and take us to New York But there was a calm and we had to wait until noon, whereupon we started with a nice fresh breeze Owing, however, to the stupidity of our captain, who did not know how to get out of the way of one of the ships of our large fleet, we got into such danger that we were heartily glad to escape with but slight injury to mizzen-mast and rigging, since we might easily have lost the whole stern of our vessel. The large and fine-looking fleet of 7 or 8 *manuars*, among which was the frigate of Admiral Howe, made a handsome display. In about 2 hours we arrived off New York, but anchored quite a distance from the city, nor did we get off the ship that day. There was a beautiful view round about us here, owing to the small islands lying about, upon one of which were yet to be seen the battered-down redoubts of the Rebels.

7 July. Tues. At 10 A. M. I went into the city of York with Capt. von Donop, where we were met by Maj Bauermeister who told us orders had been given to the ships to land all the soldiers and to march to

camp. Thereafter I went and bought something to eat and among other things 5½ lbs. of coffee for one Spanish dollar and 8 lbs. of brown sugar for one Spanish dollar, which we thought cheap enough. After staying there an hour we went back to the ship where we found that many of our men had already landed At noon we were all off the ship at Fort George and from there we marched to where stood the former English College, at that time turned into an English hospital, where our regiment assembled. Our Colonel Hinte was here again with us, having got well Soon we marched away from there and, according to orders, as far as the 6th English milestone. There was astonishing heat again, so we frequently had to halt Our Colonel missed the right road, so we had to return, not far from a place called *Jonischen* house, where, turning into the right road and going up that way, we finally got to a place a little above the 6th milestone between Harlem and *Bloomendal*, the time being 9 o'clock in the evening. Here, owing to fatigue, we had to content ourselves with lying in the open air. Many of the men complained of hunger, no provisions having been received for that day. At last, though very late, rum and salt-pork, but no bread came, which latter did not arrive until the evening of the following day.

From the 7th inst. we again received as rations rum, fresh bread, salt meat, peas, rice, butter and spruce-beer—later on vinegar.

8 July. Wedn. In the low bushes that grew round about us, some small huts were built. This forenoon the Body Regiment joined us, pitching their camp on our right flank.

9 July. Thurs. Company's day. Some rumors and tales were, as some time ago, circulated to the effect that we were certainly going to Germany.

10 July Frid. In the morning I went to New York for pleasure with 9 orderlies and looked about

me. Towards evening I left the city, taking, however, a circuitous route to the *Jonischen* House to get some cherries and milk and arrived at the camp at the beating of the tattoo.

N. B When we left the city one of our orderlies who was on horseback happened to run against a Sergeant Major of Knipphaussen's, named Schwartz, who was drunk At this the latter began to abuse him terribly. When I arrived on the scene I called the Sergeant Major to account and told him that he alone deserved the expressions of abuse which he had used, and if he thought I insulted him all he need do was to step behind a house with me (to avoid some officers we saw approaching) which, however, he declined alleging that he had some important business on hand

11 July Satur. In the morning I had a tent made of my blanket on account of the wetness of the dew and rain. In the afternoon we received some straw to put in our huts, because the new tents were to be distributed.

12 July Sund. Field Watch I was sent with one Corporal and 18 privates a distance of 3 English miles from our camp to *Yorck* on watch on the road at a place called *Tortellbey*, to guard three powder-magazines. Never until then did I eat so many cherries and oysters as in this place. A very pleasant place. To-day our new tents had arrived and the camp was immediately pitched

15 July. Wedn At 6 this morning I went to a place at the 12th milestone formerly called Fort Washington, but now Fort Knipphaussen, in which *Wisenbach's Garnison Regiment* was garrisoned. Here I looked about me a little and was conducted around by a Lieut. *Bermann* of the *Wiesenbach* regiment Afterwards I went a good half hour's walk further where the *Erb Prince's* regiment was encamped on a hill from which one could see at no great distance across the waters of the East River, *King's Pritsch*

crossing which the Rebels often came into view. I stopped here awhile and then went back past the Yager camp of v. Martenfeldt, arriving in the evening, at the tattoo, at our regiment.

17 July. Frid. In the morning I went with a Sub-officer to *Martins Wurffs* where our provision-house was situated, to get some buttermilk, and a little further on in among the cherry trees. But on account of the intense heat I soon returned to the camp.

18 July. Satur Company's day.

19 July. Sund. On reserve picket. In the morning about 340 or more of those taken prisoners in the *Drentown* affair, and of the regiments of Losberg, Knipphaussen and Rall, and others belonging to various dispersed regiments, having been returned by the Rebels, passed by our camp again Not until this afternoon did I give the already mentioned letter addressed to von Staff to our regiment Adjutant who forwarded all letters (enclosed one to Madame Follert), another for *Fallmouth* to the Lord Mayor, with reference to my things.

20 July Mond. Field watch.

21 July. Tues. In the evening the order came to get up a Company of Chasseurs, for which 2 volunteer privates were to be enlisted out of each Company of the Hessian regiments, and 1 Sub officer per regiment, taking the one who was on sharp command. From this day on we again received rations for 7 days, excepting rice instead of bread for 2 days. The day of issuing was often changed.

22 July. Wed. At an early hour I made it known to Capt. von Donop that I would like to join the Chasseurs. He informed the Lieut Col. and it was granted me I reported to all the Staff and Company officers who extended me their congratulations. I and all the other detailed men were obliged to be ready to march out at the first order. I sealed my papers and gave them in the care of the Captain. The Chasseurs of our regiment were relieved from further

service. In the afternoon I went in among the cherry-trees with the Company Commissary Denstadt. We lost our way in the woods and arrived at some huts, in which and in the adjoining little gardens many things, but no people were to be seen or heard. Presumably it all belonged to negroes. We left everything untouched. Everything seemed to me as if belonging to housed hermits. I am about to enter on a new undertaking; it being always perilous, I pray most fervently to God the All-merciful. to protect me from all misfortune, to give me discretion and fearlessness and to help me regain my lost rank—and finally that I may receive God's mercy and pity by being kept well in body and soul. I hope for this. God strengthen me.

23 July Thurs. In the evening it was commanded by an order that the Chasseurs should be ready to leave early the next morning. This night I was taken uncommonly sick, to wit, with such a stomachache that I apprehended death But I was better towards morning.

24 July Frid. I received, for the privates of all Companies, [die Grund und Rangier, die Armatur und Muntirungs Listen] I gave my papers sealed up to Capt. von Donop and received from him a very good letter of recommendation to the new Captain of the Chasseurs, who was an Englishman by birth and of the highest rank. He had studied in Gottingen and was called George von Hanger.

25 July Satur At 8 A. M. I marched with 10 privates to what was called the Morris House where his Ex'c'y. General von Knypphaussen lived and where the Chasseur Company was to rendezvous. The Company was formed out of the 11 regiments on *York* island, viz : Leib Reg't, Erb Prinz, Prinz Carl, Donop, Mirbach, Trimbach, Losberg, Knyphaussen, Woellwarth, Garrison Regts of Wiessenbach, and of Seitz, and consisted in all of 4 officers, 12 sub-officers, 3 drummers and 100 privates. General

Knyphaussen instructed the Hessian officers and then we marched to a hill called *Spakent Hiell* opposite *Indepentence* near *Courthland's* House, 9½ English miles from Donop's camp, where the Yagers were stationed. I was obliged to be commanding sergeant and Lieut. Col. von *Wurmb*, who commanded the whole Yager Corps, promised me his aid. We had to build huts here and at first I had a great deal to do, with little rest day or night and not being able to undress. That is the way it was with us, without anything special happening, on the 27th, 28th, 29th, 30th and 31st of July. We had a hard time with our provisions too, getting neither beer nor vinegar   From this day on until the 15th of November I was with the Chasseur Company of Capt. von Hanger's, in camp at *Spaken Hull* (Spuyten Duyvil Hill).

Pay received in July, 26/– ½d, in August 26/– ½d, in Sept. 26/– 3d, in October 26/– ½d

1 August. Sat.   At daybreak we and all the Yagers who were not on watch or picket had to patrol. We Chasseurs had the middle of the Corps.   We marched a distance of about 4 English miles, when we arrived at an elevation, where out of the near lying bushes three musket shots were fired.   The bullets killed the horse of a Yager who was riding on our flank.   We immediately marched up to the place and several more shots were fired   Standing a little lower down now we could hear the bullets whistle over our heads   We could see nothing.   It was very hazy and one could not see 50 steps ahead.   Some mounted Yagers who had been sent forward came back and brought the news that a considerable number of Rebels had made a stand on another height and had fieldpieces with them   At this news we retreated in good order without firing a shot   Our corps consisted of 5 foot and 1 mounted Yager and our Chasseur Company, and 2 three lb. *Amazetten* which had been given to the Corps by the English.   Around these several Yagers constantly remained with muskets and bayonets.

2 Aug. Sund. Towards evening a loud alarm was given in our camp, because some Rebels showed themselves near the outposts. We all had to turn out, but only to advance to the front of the camp. Nor did we stay there long, for it soon grew quiet again.

3 Aug. Mond. In the afternoon we saw from our camp a great fire which reduced nearly 64 houses in York to ashes, among them provision and bake-houses. Some few suspected persons, among whom were also Frenchmen, were arrested on account of it.

4 Aug. Tuesd. At 2 o'clock this afternoon when I was in the Erb Prinz camp a terrible thunderstorm with heavy rain again came up. The lightning struck a schooner which was lying off New York, set fire to it and was the cause of its blowing up with 260 bbls. of powder The pieces of iron that were scattered about did damage to adjacent houses.

5 Aug. Wedn. Some deserters came in from the Rebels. They were Brunswickers who had been taken prisoners with General *Borgonne.* They told us much news, for instance, that the Rebels received much and frequent help from the French. The French fleet which did not yet act in open hostility against us was eagerly expected. We passed many nights in this neighborhood without getting the slightest rest (owing to the great number of mosquitoes) and we suffered by day from the swarms of flies.

6 Aug. Thurs. Towards evening we had church parade under the apple-trees at Courtland's House with Superior and Sub-officers.

7 Aug. Frid. In the afternoon I went with *von Martefeldt* to the 52 English Musketeer Regiment which was not far distant from us at King's Bridge In this regiment there were said to be two noblemen who were, like myself, Sergeants and had been before in Prussian service. One was called *von Schauroth* who had been in the Fusilier Regiment of *Lossow's* as 2nd Lieut, the other *von Heyden* who was said to have been in the regiment of the Prince of Prussia as "*Porte*

épée Junker." The latter of the two was a fine-looking man and pleasant to associate with and I often had friendly talks with him. In the month of September this regiment, which was not complete, was reduced and the officers and sergeants were sent to England to recruit again.

9 Aug Sund In the morning we had church parade again with upper and under musket [Ober und unter gewehr).

10 Aug. Mond. I wrote to *Fallmouth* again about my things, as a packet-boat was about to leave

11 Aug Tuesd. Ensign *Kleinschmitt* of our Company and of Regiment *Woellwarth* deserted on account of his debts, while under leave of absence from N. York.

19 Aug. Wed. At daybreak this morning our whole Corps again made a patrol forwards, as far as the last time, only a little more to the right. I was only permitted to go along when the whole Corps went I managed to get detached to the side with 4 men I proceeded according to given orders, took my stand on a height, but like all the rest I could see nothing.

22 Aug Sat. The Yagers almost mutinied on account of being kept three days without provisions. There was a constant calling for them. We Chasseurs got our rations separately and usually on time.

23 Aug Sund. Church parade [mit Ober und Untergewehr]. To-day I could stand it no longer. I had been having the diarrhœa very badly which finally developed into bloody flux, and from day to day it grew worse so that I almost believed that I would die. I continued in this condition, saddened by many other sorrowful incidents, until

2 September. Wed. when I at last began to get better, but only very slightly. However, I began to walk about again.

10 Sept. Thurs I found a Spanish dollar in the camp without hearing who had lost it.

11 Sept Frid. Although I had not entirely recov-

ered from my sickness I returned to duty again. It was my first sickness since leaving Prussia.

22 Sept. Tues. Late this evening order was given for the whole Corps to be ready to march by 6 o'clock the next morning, to take as little baggage as possible, and for the sick and unfit to stay behind.

23 Sept. Wedn. At 6 A M. we started, taking our two *Amazetten* [amuzette, throwing 1 lb. iron bolt] with the woolen coverings, also one shirt and bottles and kettles. As we had wagons I was only allowed to carry my short musket. We had marched hardly an hour when it began to rain very hard, and as it did not stop and we were near what was called *Philipp's House*, we opened the pretty church there and quartered ourselves in it—but only the Chasseurs and Amuzette-Yagers, in all about 30 men. Finally a search was begun and a large potato-field was cleaned out and many other luxuries brought in. Fowls, pigs and beef were slaughtered, although everything had to be done secretly. As usual when on the march we received nothing but salt pork, crackers and rum for rations. In short we led, as the Hessians termed it, a Hussar life. The rain continued with surprising violence so that we were glad to have got into such nice dry quarters We gathered hay and straw and made ourselves good beds. For a mattress I had a cushion covered with green cloth, the covering of which I took with me when we marched away, but disposed of it. The Yagers lay in their camp above Philipp's House very wet, because they had only been able to build huts to protect themselves against the rain. Constant complaints were made to the Yagers and to us that cattle had been slaughtered ; but the matter was not very closely investigated by the Staff and other officers So we had good night-quarters here. The rain stopped during the night and it became clear again.

24 Sept. Thurs. At 8 A. M. General Kniphaussen and also the foraging sharpshooters of the Grenadiers

arrived; after them came the regiments of *Erb Prinz* and *Donop*, the *Leib Regt*, the Garrison Regt. of *Wiesenbach* and a few English regiments. We had to break camp immediately to make room for them. We marched and came up with the Yagers again remaining with them for two hours. Thereafter we started together and marched to the 20th English mile-stone, keeping to the right of it and ascending a height. Here we were obliged to build huts to camp in until further orders. The foraging commenced again immediately, during which some of the soldiers began to plunder. Many of the houses, which I saw afterwards, had been left in a deplorable condition and the soldiers had made a good haul We were not forbidden to get provisions, but very strictly admonished not to take anything from the people in their houses. However, even when they were caught in the act, the punishment was not equal to the prohibition. For a few days we had an abundance of good food and this was my only booty. The English General *Erskine* had crossed the Hudson River on our left with a few English regiments. He also sent over large numbers of cattle and other provisions on boats every day. He also often came in collision with the Rebels, which we conjectured from his firing and from prisoners being sent over. We Hessians, however, stayed there and undertook nothing, which was unendurable to me with my ambition and the tedium of our life.

25 Sept. Frid. Rest day. Opposite our flank, a little to the right, across the water of the East River, stood *Emmerich's* Corps. A few short distance patrols to the front were made by us.

26 Sept. Sat. Again rest-day.

27 " Sund. In the morning a patrol went out from our Corps, of about 300 men. They had met with some Rebels who, however, fled rapidly. They brought back as prisoners three officers of the militia, of whom one was called a Captain and who had an

astonishing goitre, who, however, declared that he would never cease to fight for his freedom. They were placed in the prison-house in New York. In the afternoon Capt. *Ewaldt* was sent out on patrol, to the right, with 2 Subalterns and 160 Yagers. He came back on the 29th without having effected anything. On his arrival a Yager threw his musket, out of impatience, upon the ground. It went off and the bullet hit another Yager, who was standing with some others to get some brandy, in the back of his neck and came out of his breast, so that he straightway fell dead to the earth. The wrong-doer was put under arrest, but after a few days was let off with a slight castigation.

28 Sept. Mond   We heard a loud but not long continued firing on Jersey and in evening over 100 prisoners were sent over. They were Rebels and were sent to New York   We Hessians had rest day again

29 Sept Tues.   Rest day again.

30 Sept. Wed   At daybreak this morning we sent out another patrol of about 80 men. We Chasseurs had our sub-officers and 10 privates among them. Capt. v Donop of the Yager Corps commanded himself   But he had not gone more than 2 English miles when he was surrounded by the Rebel Light Horse and Infantry, some 100 men   Our mounted Yagers, some 12 or 16, under command of Lieut. Mertz, had led the advance too far from the infantry and therefore they were soon overcome and separated and Lieut Mertz, himself severely wounded, was taken prisoner, besides one Quarter Master, one bugler and 8 mounted private Yagers, and 7 foot Yagers were also taken prisoners, though almost all of them were wounded. Capt. von *Donop* found a hole through which to retreat. We heard the firing and our few mounted Yagers were despatched there directly to their assistance. The whole Corps stood ready to follow at the first signal   The Rebels however had im-

mediately disappeared with their prisoners Two dead mounted Yagers were brought into our camp, who were terribly disfigured by wounds and one mounted Yager, also wounded, was brought in. One arm and one leg had been shot in two. One foot Yager sub-officer was also brought in seriously wounded The last two were cured again, but were incapable of further service.

1 October. Thurs. At half past nine at night order was given to be ready to march. We marched. The men were not permitted to have anything but their blankets. One amuzette was taken along but without powder wagon, with only about 30 rounds. Whoever was not able to march well had to stay behind. All silently, without speaking a word, our march was continued, which therefore seemed made for some grand undertaking. We Chasseurs gave 40 men to the advance guard, whom I voluntarily joined We marched on through the darkness through woods and over stony roads without stopping. Behind us as the advance guard came the Anspach Capt. von *Wallenfels* with a new picket, then the amuzette and finally the Corps, when we marched on thus quietly, but with good step, and one almost fell asleep At about 3 o'clock in the morning *Hartong*, formerly a student, now the *fourier* of our advance guard, who had been detached and was assisted by 10 men, was suddenly and unexpectedly challenged. He was not resolute enough, so six almost invisible Rebel Light Horse, holding guard, fired and galloped off Lieut Andresohn had the first and I the second platoon of the advance guard. The men, however, were so eager for the spoils that they could not be held in order, and it being dark they nearly shot down each other. I endeavored to keep my platoon together by beating them, and it would have been very bad for us, if we had had an observant enemy before us. The Yagers did so also. It being dark, an old woman who was coming out of her house was unknowingly shot through

the leg by one of our men. Some of the men had got
as booty handsome blankets and woolen coats left
behind by the Rebels. Finally we got our ranks closed
up again and took possession of a height close behind
the house to stay there until day-break. Then we
left and marched further on and, at the break of day,
along a high hill on our right across a valley there.
More than 40 musket shots were fired at us from the
hills accompanied by the usual wild shouts. We
being so low down could hear the bullets whiz over
our heads, although it was a distance of 600 or 700
paces. We, the advance guard, ran with utmost
speed to attack their flank, but we were ordered back
and as it now became light day we were obliged to
march to the right again upon a height, then again
to march forward to what was called *Weit Blene.*
Here we halted at a pretty house. Many of the men
of our Corps went about and snatched up all the fowls
and pigs, which was not forbidden them. I was thirsty,
so I went into the house to get a drink It was quite
full of soldiers and everything was in confusion, but I
heeded it not. The people lamented greatly. If I
had gone out with bad intentions I would have demanded much. As it was, however, I only took my
fill of milk and a soldier gave me a good big piece of
fresh butter for which I took an earthen plate and then
went away again. Finally, while we were still there,
we saw a large body of horsemen and footsoldiers approaching us. We immediately prepared to fight, but
when they drew nearer it proved to be Emmerich with
his Corps, besides a few hundred of the English infantry. So we proceeded a little further together.
But nothing was to be met with, so we turned back
again to where animals could be found—living or dead
they had to join us. We also took all the field fruit
we could carry. Most of the soldiers and Yagers,
going in couples, had a stick between them for carrying meat and chickens So we marched on and from
out the bushes and the hills on the way the farmers

frequently fired upon us, when our men showed themselves with their pigs and chickens.

2 Oct. Frid. At 2 o'clock this afternoon we arrived, almost entirely worn out, at our old camp. Many, however, arrived much later.

3 Oct. Sat. Rest day.

4 Oct. Sund At daybreak the whole Corps again advanced on patrol, but not far, it being dirty, rainy weather. We had to make this patrol owing to the lack of forage and to protect the foragers. We had no amuzette with us. In a few hours, when our foragers had loaded up, we went back again.

5 Oct. Mond. Rest day.

6 " Tuesd At 2 o'clock A. M. the Corps had to advance again without amuzette and further than the last time, on account of the foragers, for everything within 2 or 3 English miles had been gathered in, and the same was the case with our provisions. We had to be content with the provisions furnished us, though we were half starved. On this patrol we lay quiet, without those who had been sent ahead, and waited until our foragers had finished. In the meantime we enjoyed ourselves exceedingly among the many fine chestnut-trees, the nuts being ripe and very good to eat. About 7 in the morning we marched back again.

7 Oct. Wedn. At noon some of the men went marauding with my knowledge, but they were so unfortunate as to be taken prisoners by the Rebels who lay in ambuscade, though it was hardly 1½ English miles from our camp. The men were 2 privates of *Donop's* regiment and one of the *vacant* regiment of *Woellwarth* I duly reported this at once, as if they had gone off on their own own account without my knowing where they were going and I had approved of it. These three were entered in the reports as missing.

8 Oct. Thurs. Rest day. At 8 o'clock at night order was given to be ready to march with all the baggage.

9 Oct. Frid. At 10 A M. while the rain was fall-

ing in torrents, we drew in our pickets, sent our baggage ahead and followed the other regiments, which had already marched off, until we arrived in good order at our old camp near *Courtland's House*, impeded by nothing but the astonishing showers of rain, which wet us through and through Owing to the moisture no fire could be kept alive and therefore we had to freeze to-day and the next day too on account of the continuous rain. But we were quite content at being away from the former camp where we would have had to endure much more and besides go hungry

11 Oct. Sund. At noon some Rebels unexpectedly rode up from Courtlandt's House and finding our outposts, to wit, a mounted Yager who had dismounted and a foot-Yager, both asleep, stripped them of their weapons, gave them, in derision, a sound drubbing and then let them go, but without horse or arms. The Rebels then ran off again. Our whole camp took the alarm, the Rebels were pursued but were fortunate enough to escape, thus leaving us ashamed at this affair and at leisure to cogitate over it The two outposts, understanding how to excuse themselves very cleverly, were punished with only a few days' arrest.

12 Oct Mond. At 8 A. M. our whole Corps, but without cannons, had an advance patrol, but only to within a short distance of Philipp's House. We marched up there behind the fences, halted awhile, some of our mounted Yagers reconnoitered with *Lieut. Col. v. Wurmb* and then we returned without any further observations.

16 Oct Frid. At 10 A. M. I got leave of absence to go to New York, but I remained that day in Donop's camp near New York. Dined at Lieut. Col. *Hinte's,* in the evening with Capt. von Donop. I slept there that night, and not till the next morning, to wit

17 Oct. Satur at 8 oclock did I go to York. There I bought some things and sent them back to the Chasseur camp by two Chasseurs whom I had taken with me I stayed until about 3 P M. when I

went back as far as Donop's camp. I slept here again and went in the morning.

18 Oct. Sund. at 7 A. M. back to our camp where I arrived at 9.30 o'clock.

19 Oct. Mond. From the 19th inst until the end of the month, alternately however, I did not feel well, because whenever I ate or drank anything I felt sick and vomited.

22 Oct Thurs. From 1 o'clock at night until 2 I (like all the other commanding Sergeants) had to patrol with 8 Chasseurs, a distance of about 1½ English miles, back of Courtlandt's second house and across the water. I stationed our post at a crossing of roads where I assigned good positions to my *commando* and the sentinels. Remained there one hour, then marched back as quietly as possible, we ahead. This had been ordered, because an attack was feared, as had been revealed to us.

23 Oct. Frid. At 9 A. M. an alarm signal was given " with the half-moon", because some Rebels had been seen at our outposts. All our companies had to hasten to their alarm positions, but, as everything soon grew quiet again, we marched back to our huts

26 [4] Oct. Sat. At 8 A. M. the whole Corps, as soon as the half moon had been sounded, had to turn out to go on patrol, almost as far as Philipp's House, because some Rebels were reported to be there. But we saw none. I was detached with 12 men to reconnoiter. After standing there in vain and watching and on the return of our reconnoitering party we all marched back to the camp. Such patrols at night time and frequent alarms were a common thing and all the wagons were hitched up.

29 Oct. Thurs In the morning the 1 Corporal and 7 privates of v. *Woellwarth's* regiment and the 1 Corporal and 9 privates of v. *Wiesenbach's* Garrison regiment, that were in our Chasseur Company and were to go on board the ships for West Florida. the next morning, were sent for to go with the regiment.

30 Oct. Frid. In the morning our 3 marauders, who had been taken prisoners above Philipp's House, and had been released, came back. They were put under arrest in our Camp Watch, but only until the next morning when they were released without further punishment. This, however, only took place at my instance, because I felt myself (after them) most to blame for it all

1 November, Sund. At 10 P. M. a Yager deserted from the picket and his post, immediately our mounted Yagers had to start out in pursuit, but it was without result. From a distance some shots were fired. We all had to turn out, but only as far as to the front of the Company camps. In a short time after the return of the detachment that had been sent in pursuit, all was quiet, and all marched back into their huts. Hardly a quarter of an hour passed before *Lora* was again called out and all had to turn out again Soon all grew quiet and then we slept without disturbance until

2 Novem. Mon About 7 A. M when the Half Moon was sounded, and the whole Corps, though without cannons, had to turn out to go on patrol. I staid behind because I had to make out some lists, which were to be sent to the regiments, in regard to equipments for our men. Emmerich's Corps marched on the other side past the redoubt called *Indepentence*, with some cannons, advancing a short distance. Our Corps marched there too, crossing the water at the second Courtland House and then keeping to the left of Emmerich. We stopped on the right above Philipp's House and after a time returned again without having seen or accomplishing anything.

5 Nov Thurs Capt. v. Hanger being pleased with my writing gave me 2 *Ginees* for my pains and ½ *Ginee* regularly every month for the future in addition This day we received the assignment of our winter-quarters But no time was announced yet for our departure.

6 Nov. Frid. Different rumors were circulating, to the effect that the Chasseurs were going to be taken back to their regiments, which suited no one and me least of all, though I had no rest night or day and no longer knew how it felt to sleep with my clothes off or on a soft couch, so true it is that one can get accustomed to anything. On the other hand my hardships were made a delight owing to the greater freedom I enjoyed. I liked the extra pay too and resolved to save it and, in case I should not be an officer by next spring, to send in my resignation, and use the money for my journey. I must wait and see how it all ends. May God help me!

8 Nov Sund Never have I been permitted long to enjoy commenced comfort Hardly had I hoped, after so many troubles, to feel somewhat reconciled again in my winter quarters with the Yagers and through the generosity of Capt v Hanger, when the order was given this afternoon that we were to be ready to march. Later we were informed that we were to occupy the redoubts back of our camp where the Erb Prinz regiment had been stationed, as garrison The latter marched the next morning at 2 o'clock A. M. into the winter-quarters assigned to them.

9 Nov. Mond. At 5 A M. we started with scrip and scrippage for the Erb Prinz camp. The regiment was still there, but left at 7 o'clock Ensign Zimmermann, I and 4 Sub-officers and 50 privates were placed in *Number 2*, as watch 1 Sub officer, 1 Free Corporal and 12 Privates. In *Number 1* was posted Lieut von *Andresohn* with the remainder. *Number 3* was garrisoned by some of *Number 2*. I lodged myself with several others in the little huts of the Erb Prinz near the redoubt. Towards noon we received 3 days' rations Thus we were here and nobody, not even the Captain himself, knew what our further destination would be. This afternoon Donop's and Trimbach's regiment advanced up before Fort Knipphaus-

sen into the huts of the deserted camp of the 3 regiments of Knipphaussen, Loosberg and Wollwarth. They were to stay there to garrison the fort and the surrounding redoubts.

12 Nov Thurs. In the afternoon I went into Donop's camp but did not stop there long, as I had gone away without telling any one anything about it. At night we received orders that, after being relieved we were to march back the next morning at 3 A. M. to the Yager camp and at 4 o'clock to advance on patrol with the whole Corps. But we were not relieved, so they were obliged to patrol alone In the meantime the Yagers deserted in large numbers on account of bad camp (just like ours) and poor rations, namely (like the whole army) scarcely 5 lbs of bread in 7 days and for 2 days rice instead of bread. How often, under such circumstances, the pieces had to be cut thin!

13 Nov. Frid. In the evening when it was very dark and raining too I took a notion to go to the Body Regiment which was encamped on the other side of a stream called ———— on the hill at King's Bridge, where formerly the *Koehler* Grenadier Battalion had been stationed. This walk, however, nearly cost me my life. I stopped hardly an hour at the camp. In the meantime it became pitch dark and rained very hard, I was enjoined to stay, but no! I could not see one step ahead of me and fell several times. When I reached the embankment leading to the bridge across above named stream I fell up to my waist ("up to half my body") into the water. I managed to scramble out again and continuing to fall very often I at last arrived, very wet and muddy, at the camp. That night there was a "cruel" stormwind and rain, so that I thanked God as having escaped as I did.

15 Nov. Sund On command d'honneur. At 10 A. M. we were relieved by a detachment from the 3 regiments, Body Regiment, Donop and Trimbach, 1 Captain and 1 Subaltern, and we went back to our old

camp of the Yagers, most of the huts of which had, however, been torn down. It was very cold, snowing, and therefore we had a rough time of it. At about 2 o'clock in the afternoon the Yager Corps received orders to march the next morning to their winter quarters on *Long Islandt*. The Chasseur Company, however, were to get ready to march to their regiments. It was pleasant to none of us, but it had to be. Capt v. Hanger expressed his thanks, and especially to me, for the good order I had kept and gave me $\frac{1}{2}$ *Ginee* with the promise to recommend me especially to Colonel v. Goose. We immediately marched away and towards evening arrived at the camp of our regiment at the 11th milestone below Fort Knipphaussen. I received my pay up to the end of the month

17 Nov. Tues. At daybreak this morning I went on furlough to New York to buy some necessary shirts. I stopped at a German's house, who was a lamp cleaner in Robinson street near the Colleges which were now used as an English hospital

18 Nov Wed. In the morning I saw for the first time two sailors, on an English man-of-war, hoisting up a yellow flag between the masts until it had reached the very tip top—the common sign that a person has to lose his life on account of some crime. At 3 P M. I left New York and reached our camp, which was 11 miles distant, at sun-down Our camp there was very poor, because many of the huts which lay around the foot of the hill, among them mine, got full of water whenever it rained The drinking water was also very bad, and in every respect matters were in such a state, that if no change is made, diseases must unavoidably arise.

20 Nov. Frid. Tent-coverings, iron pegs, axes, saws and divers other articles were furnished, which were very serviceable to protect us against the cold

23 Nov. Mond. Company's day.

24 Nov. Tues. At 5 o'clock this afternoon the Body Company and ours, being Lieut. Companies,

received the order to move to the camp of the huts of Trimbach's regiment, which was contiguous to our camp on a height towards Fort Knipphaussen. The Trimbachers were to march into the barracks at Fort Knipphaussen to have winter quarters there. The workmen on the barracks did not complete their work, so our change was postponed.

27 Nov. Frid. I was detached with 12 privates on sharp command to a hill called, in English, *Nord Rever Hill*, not far from *Spaken Hill*. Here there was a fine redoubt with 4 eighteen pound iron cannons, for whose firing 3 Hessian cannoneers were relieved every 7 days. The command, commencing with to-day, was relieved every 4 days, though it had previously been only 2 days. So I was posted there till the morning of Tuesday the 1st of December A very good command this was, very comfortable, pleasant and undisturbed, because no Staff-officer ever troubled himself to come up there on account of the height, etc. etc We were relieved at daybreak.

Pay received in November 26/– 6d

December. In camp at 11th English mile-stone under Fort Knipphaussen

1 Dec Tues. On active command on North River Hill When I returned from this command we moved, as above mentioned, into Trimbach's deserted huts, which turned out to be so small that they all had to be enlarged In consequence thereof and of the cold weather there were many vexatious occurrences and one was compelled to shift for a few days, as best he could (which was miserably enough), before any improvement could be brought about. My intentions now began to shape themselves as follows. If I could not be certain, by promises made to me, of having an officer's rank by next spring, I resolved to hand in my resignation and then to choose among different opportunities the best course for my future welfare. My thoughts occupied themselves with a thousand different plans

2 Dec. Wed. On reserve picket In the morning I ordered my 7 tent soldiers to begin to enlarge my tent by adding one to it that had been torn down. In the meantime I had the absent field chaplain's hut to live in, which Capt. v. Donop and the Adjutant permitted me to do, on account of the bad weather, until the field-chaplain should return from New York

3 Dec. Thur. On field watch. While I had the field watch an astonishing number of boats, small and large, some of our frigates, sailed past us during the night, coming from New York in order to follow the regiments which had been ordered to advance to get forage and some fresh provisions. Of the Hessians no one was detached thither except Mirbach's regiment, the others all being English. Most of the Generals were also English To-day the whole army again received bread instead of rice, 7 pounds for 7 days

5 Dec. Sat Company's day.

6 Dec. Sund. In the afternoon as well as Monday morning all the detached men returned, as also the ships. These had not gone further than the regiments had been before them, without having accomplished much.

8 Dec. Tues. At daybreak this morning I had to go with 10 privates of our regiment on work-command across King's Bridge between the two redoubts King's Redoubt and Number 7, near a new log-house, beyond the pickets Directly in front of this log-house there stood opposite to each other two gallows on which two English Royal *Rehentschers* (Rangers) had been hanged for murder. Every three men got regularly 1 *Tschille* (gill) of rum before work. We were obliged to stay there in a cruel wind and rain until 2 P. M

9 Dec. Wed. At sun-set this evening I was on active picket with 6 privates in Number 1, back of what was called General Knipphaussen's quarters, Morris House, at the water's edge, and not far from our regiment's camp.

10 Dec Thurs. There was such a cruel rain and wind, that it looked very bad for us in the huts, because the water leaked through everywhere. Besides it was very cold, but one could not keep a fire on account of the smoke from the wind and the water, nor was it possible to sleep dry under our blankets. May a special mercy of God keep me amidst so many evils (and all the others too) in good health.

11 Dec. Frid. Regiment's day. Towards morning we had the first and quite a heavy snow-fall, with heavy frost.

13 Dec Sund. There was again astonishing wind and rain and some of the huts caved in owing to the bad ground.

14 Dec. Mond. Company's day

15 Dec. Tues *Spruse bier* was again furnished us from New York, each man receiving 1 canteen full But we did not get it from the Storehouse for our regiment before the 19th inst., for which the regimental Quartermaster was to blame

19 Dec Sat. We did not get our beer till today. On reserve picket.

21 Dec. Mond On field picket behind Morris House.

22 Dec. Tues At daybreak this morning after leaving the picket with my 6 men from Number 1— it had been snowing all night so that one could not find any foot-path—I fell several times into large snow-covered pools of water, and finally into what had been a cess-pool, but fortunately only a little above the knee of my left leg. Both of my big toes were almost frozen in my linen stockings.

23 Dec. Wed. Rations were supplied with great irregularity. We received 2 English pounds of fresh beef which was deducted from the remainder of our rations But this time we got nothing more than butter, meat, rum and peas, of which however the fresh meat was deducted from the whole. No bread, however, and no flour and, in fine, nothing at all Innum-

erable reasons were advanced that were said to be the cause of this, such as that the provision fleet had been captured by the French. Only a small supply was left in the provision houses The river was frozen over so that we could get nothing from New York by that way. It was possible to go there with wagons to get something, but this was not done, no one knowing the reason. In this manner we had to do without bread until Dec. 25th.

24 Dec. Thurs. Company's day

25 Dec. Frid. First Christmas holiday. I was detached, without bread, on active command on *Nord River Hill*. No bread could be procured, not even for money. I also had Company inspection and therefore wished to wake the men early that were under my command. When, in the act of doing this, I had got to the Sergeant Major's hut, I accidentally stepped upon an iron barrel-hoop, fell over a log of wood and cut my left shin on it. It made quite a wound and they advised me to give up the command and remain behind on account of the cold. But not wishing to do so I only put some rum and soap on it myself. To-day my leg swelled so much that I had to take off my gaiters. On account of the lack of bread I sent an orderly over past the King's Redoubt to the English bakery and there he bought me a loaf of white bread weighing a little over a German pound for 1 Engl. shill. $5\frac{1}{2}$ pence, and also some potatoes. In order to get the latter, however, he had, out of attachment to me, braved the danger of being caught by the outposts. So this was the good cheer of my Christmas holidays—and yet I would have been contented, if my leg had only been well, which, however, was visibly swelling and gave me much pain.

26 Dec. Sat. My leg got worse. I did not know what to do, nor did I wish to send to a surgeon. I could only hope for the best. It was surprisingly cold, and this was greatly increased by an unbearable wind, with heavy snow. The watch house here on

North River Hill was the best of all those near York, and there was also an ample supply of wood near by, and we consequently had enough fire to be almost roasted—yet we nearly froze on the side away from the fire The snow found the smallest crevices in the roof and it lay a hand high right near the fire without melting. We had no bread and little of anything else to eat, so any one can easily imagine what meditations this caused I tried in every way to lighten the duties of my 12 men On my leg I noticed, with thanks to heaven, signs of healing

27 Dec. Sund. This morning I sent two orderlies to the camp to see and ask whether we were not going to have some bread soon and to get me a plaster for my leg from the Company Surgeon—My leg was beginning to get better When the orderlies returned I was comforted by the information that I with my detachment would get bread in good time next morning. Flour, which was half oat-grits, had already been sent to the bakery to be baked. Likewise every man throughout the whole army received 1 gill of rum and some peas. There was even then a commotion among the soldiers—So that, if bread should fail for a few days more, a general desertion would be inevitable. This afternoon the weather grew very fine, the wind having fallen. Still it was quite cold, though calm.

28 Dec Mond. Towards evening as I was yearning for bread and was about to send after it, a soldier detached from the regiment came and brought us some; but, my God, how frightened we all were when we saw it and what terrible stomach aches we had after eating only a little of it; for it was nothing but oat-grits, which it had been impossible to bake through. It weighed very heavy and with the same weight it lay in our stomachs. Great as our delight had been to get it, equally great were our pains and curses after eating it If we were to have bread of that kind much longer disease and desertion

would inevitably soon break up the army. I comforted myself a little with the improvement of my leg and hoped the best for the future. My prolonged damnable fate is making me less sensitive.

29 Dec. Tuesd. In the morning on my arrival in camp the men of the regiment had only just received their share of the miserable bread and, like all of us, little enough. Nor did they know, when, what and how the rations for the next provision day would turn out. I had my leg bandaged by the surgeon and therefore could not go out, but was reported sick. From this day (until 19 Jan. 1779) sick in camp under Fort Knipphaussen, being injured on my left foot by a fall.

30 Dec Wed. We got oat-grits again, namely, 3 measures of grits and 1 of corn-meal, with which to bake our bread. It was a shame, the stuff being already half spoiled and hardly fit to eat. All the provision houses were empty. A report was circulated, that the fleet with the money and provisions for the army had been captured by the French The New York merchants had already advanced some money to the army. Likewise the bakers in the city were commanded to stop baking and keep their flour for the army. In every way there seemed to be much distress and trouble in preparation for us

31 Dec. Thurs For the last day in the year it was as beautiful a day as ever it could be in Spring. All the worse however for the stomach, because there was little to be procured for it. Just as I was writing this we heard the joyful news that the provision fleet had at last arrived at New York. Some of the ships, however, were said to have been lost in the storms; if they do not come in later.

Pay received in December 26/-½d.

(End of 1778.)

1779.

1779.—January. Still in camp under Fort Knipphaussen and laid up with my injured left foot.

1 Jan. In the regiment the Sub-officers received the small sum of 4 Hessian Reichs Dollars yearly for equipment money. But I remained almost 3 English shillings in debt as Lieut. Col. Hinte had advanced me 2 Spanish Dollars in Philadelphia. I had also taken as advanced payment, a pair of shoes out of the [cammer] because I got them there cheapest.

3 Jan. I finished the letters which I had already begun to write to Braunsberg to *Herr von Rath* and enclosed one to Madame Fallertin, but I wrote to them as if I were still with the Rebels I wrote a letter also to Falmouth, England, with reference to my things. These letters I wished to send by the first packet-boat that left New York.

17 Jan. We again received white wheat bread from the English fleet, which arrived ship by ship; and this will, I hope, lessen the beginning of much deserting. We also received some rice, after having, until now, been obliged to eat that miserable oat-grits bread.

19 Jan. I got myself restored to the regiment for service, though the wound in my leg was not yet healed.

20 Jan Company's day. A few letters had again arrived from Germany and I received from Lieut. Gen. von Donop a compliment and many assurances of early promotion (in a letter to Capt. Morhardt who had command of the Body company). But this did not deter me from insisting upon my discharge.

21 Jan. Sharp command, to New York on Baggage Watch until the 28th inst. N. B. As I desired to go to New York to buy something I asked the Adjutant, Capt. von Leppel, to be assigned to the regiment watch in Cherry Street, because it was accounted as a

command to command. It had to stay 7 days until the 28th inst.

23 Jan. In the morning went to the watch-cellar in New York. An Englishwoman came and asked me for some breakfast.

24 Jan. In the evening I took a walk in New York and, on account of the flagrant excesses occurring there, took with me 2 soldiers which I had follow me at a little distance. After some little amusements I passed by a soap-boiler's shop on my way back and stopped there on account of the racket. Directly a man came out of the door and when he caught sight of me he called on me for help. I went inside where I saw a pretty young woman sitting with a baby in her arms. She addressed me excitedly, but so confusedly that I could not make out what the matter was. Meanwhile the man ran up a flight of stairs and made a terrible noise up there. Just as I was about to go up, he came stumbling down with a musket, making great and ridiculous efforts to fix the bayonet. With the butt end of his musket he was chasing before him an old woman who was crying piteously. By seeing and hearing and finally from the words of the young woman I found that the man was drunk. I brought him to silence, whereupon the young woman thanked me politely in English, and I went away laughing.

30 Jan. Company's day.

Pay in January:—1st 3/–, 6th 3/–, 11th 3/–, 16th 3/–, 21st 3/–, and 26th 11/- ½d;—total 26/- ½d. sterling.

With the Chasseurs I had received pay semi-monthly, but with the regiment I got it every 5 days as usual.

February. In camp under Fort Knipphaussen.

3 Feb. In the morning I wrote an answer to Gen. von Donop, in Homburg Hesse, rendering my thanks and commending myself to his further interest. Gave the letter to Capt. Mohrhardt to be mailed. Now (one can see how much reliance there is to be placed on one's resolutions) I am uncertain what to do in

reference to my discharge. I will wait a short time and then time and circumstances will bring me to a decision

4 Febr. On short tour. Rations had to be taken to the men who had been ordered to the redoubts, and a Sub-officer was sent to superintend the matter. I went with him as far as *Spaken Hill.*

7 Febr. Sent the above-mentioned letters for Braunsberg and Falmouth by a drummer to New York, to be properly mailed to Europe.

9 Febr. Company's day

12 Febr. On picket. In N° 1[1] on East River remaining all night N. B. I had to stay with the picket on the East River till the afternoon of the next day at 3 o'clock, because, before, the picket huts had always been burnt down.

14 Febr At low-tide this afternoon I went to the East River[2] for oysters, where I had a delicious feast on them.

16 Febr. Company's day (and) Church Parade.

17 Febr On Fire-watch.

22 Febr. At 1 P. M. at Fort Knipphaussen, our regiment as well as all the Hessians, were mustered by an English Colonel, the weather being dreadfully rainy. The previous night the rain had poured so much water into our huts that we had to bail out many camp-kettles full. From this time, since Philadelphia we had to wear hair-locks [queues] again.

24 Febr. During the night a loud alarm was made, because General *Klington* had crossed with several English regiments from New York to New Jersey, where he intended to make several expeditions. Our regiment was relieved from the redoubts by the regiments of Losberg and Knipphaussen, as the present Brigade of Gen. von Bose.

25 Febr. In the night the Hessian Body-regiment, besides several English regiments, marched under the

---

[1] *This* "No 1" was a redoubt back of *Morris House*
[2] Harlem River Its oysters were excellent at that time.

English General Tryon some 30 English miles on the road past Phillip's House¹, during which time Donop's and Bose's (previously Trimbach's) regiments had to be ready to follow at the first sign.

26 Febr. Regiment's day.

27 Febr. Company's day. In the afternoon Gen Tryon came back with the English regiments and the Body-regiment of Hessians which latter had only one wounded wagon-driver, who had been obliged also to give up the powder-wagons of the regiment. The English had a few dead and wounded, but they brought 28 Rebel prisoners besides 2 iron cannons. General *Klington* had returned from New Jersey on the 26th inst with somewhat greater loss and less success.

Pay for February, altogether 26 – 3d.

March. In camp under Fort Knipphausen.

1 Mar. I took a furlough to New York and wanted to make application to join a newly organized Corps of Hussars, whose originator was an English lord called Lord *Simko*. I applied through my Capt v Donop to Capt. Thumer, a Hanoverian in the English service, who told me that all commissioned officers were paid according to rank 4 or 500 guineas. I could only be engaged as *Voluntair* with lowest advancement and with a good and certain douceur, which I declined in spite of much persuasion, and so changed my intentions. In the afternoon, as I sat at a table in the above mentioned place—New York—a drunken English soldier came into the room He had a piece of dead horse, that is frequently seen lying about here, and offered it for sale. Upon his constant pressing and at the sight and the fearful stench I felt obliged to kick him out of the door, and I would have liked to give him a good thrashing, if the stench had not prevented me from having anything further to do with him The room had to be fumigated a long while before the stench vanished. I could narrate many and very

---

¹ The Manor House in Yonkers, now City Hall.

frightful occurrences, of theft, fraud, robbery and murder by the English soldiers, which their love of drink excited, and as they received but little money, they used these disgusting means.

2 Mar. I left New York to return to the camp.

(Continuation of Service-Table and Notes for 1779)

4 Mar. Thurs. This afternoon I went with Free Corp. Muus across King's Bridge into the camp of Lieut Col. Emmerich's Free Corps to call on the former Free Corp. Muller, who was a Lieut. there. On my way back, when we had almost reached the Hessian Body regiment's camp, we noticed that in a tumult, which arose a little behind us, a German soldier of the Hessian Body regiment was being badly beaten by the Green Pennsylvania Provincial *Leid Horst*. The Englishmen were drunk and would not listen to our questions. We drew our swords, rescued the beaten man, but we were outnumbered. Free Corp. Muus received some hard blows, but I cut my way through successfully, though I was, owing to their number, several times thrown into the mud. I had so well managed, although I had not struck sharp, that it was well for me that they did not know, with certainty, to what regiment I belonged.

(On New York Island in camp near Fort Knipphaussen)

6 Mar Satur On picket in N° 2 remaining there over night. Not feeling well I had myself bled in the right arm whereupon, praise be to God, I felt well again.

7 Mar. Sund Each man of the regiments received Spruce Beer which was taken daily to every hut in a camp kettle

10 Mar. Wed. On Fire Watch

12 Mar. Frid. Company's day.

14 Mar. Sund. Up to Saturday the 18th inst, on sharp commando in King's Redoubt across the East River and King's Bridge near Emmerich's Camp with 12 privates. In the redoubt there were two 9 lb. iron

cannons An insurrection was now disclosed in New York by a negro. The band was said to consist of several hundred Rebel conspirators who intended to set fire to the city. Some of them had been arrested In consequence there was much anxiety among the soldiers in New York. They were not allowed to undress at night until several days later when it grew quiet again. 20 March. Company's day. 21 March. Church Parade. 22 March. Company's day. 24 March on picket in N° 1. 28 March. Fire watch and pay parade.

29 March. Mon. In the afternoon I went hunting with the Yager of Lieut. Col. Hinte, not far from our camp, and shot some black-birds.

30 March. Tues. Ditto in the afternoon.

31 " Wed. In the afternoon I went to N° 3 (the Redoubt) on *Spackent Hill* to call on Free Corp. Muus who was detached there in command. This day was unusually hot and for the first time this year.

Pay in March altogether 26/- ½d.

April. In camp under Fort Knipphaussen.

2 April Frid. Church parade on Good-Friday.
4 " Sund. Ditto on Easter
5 " Mond. On reserve picket.
6 " Tues. Company's day.
8 " Wed. In the evening I went to the English Provost Capt. named *Mr. Fiva*, by birth a Swiss He had a Company in the English Reg'm't He was a favorite of Gen'r'l. *Tryong*. My Captain von Donop had strongly recommended me to him to be spoken of to the General, because I was inclined, under advantageous circumstances to go over into English service He promised me with certainty to speak favorably of me to the General and to let me know about it.

9 April. Frid On short tour. At $7\frac{1}{2}$ A. M the General-in-Chief ordered that all the regiments should begin to drill.

11 April Sund. On picket. *Nord River Hill* till the 15th inst.

16 April Frid   Company's day.
17   "   Sat.   On picket N° 1.
18   "   Sund. I was in the little town of Harlem not far from where our camp had formerly stood. There were no inhabitants in it. All had left and at that time Mirbach's regiment had their quarters in the few houses
20 April. Tues.   On Fire-Watch.
[21   "   Wed   On reserve picket.
25   "   Sund. Company's day
26   "   Mond. At 6 A M. (as regularly henceforth) I was detached, since I knew something of drawing to assist at the redoubts which were being completed on the hill—*Lourall Hill*—opposite Fort Knipphaussen for which the Ass't English Lieutenant of the 16th regiment, *Mr. Spraul*, promised me 1 / – 6 sterling per day besides my pay and daily a gill of rum. In the regiment I had no further duty

27 April. Tues.   I received 9d 1 copper winter *douceur* as did all Sub officers and privates.

[From the 26th on I was engaged upon the fort on Laurel Hill assisting the Engineer and till the end of May on the directly opposite *Forsed* Hill.] Pay received April 26/– 3d.

2 May. Sund   In the afternoon when I was about to return from the working detail *Col. von Goosen* who lodged under the Fort and was dining with Col. von *Buschhaussen* of Maj Gen'r'l v. *Bose's* regiment, sent for me and said that he was expecting there would soon be promotions in the regiment and that as he wished to forestall a possible appointment from without he would write for me to the General and send along a copy of my resignation which I was enjoined to bring the next day in good season.

3 May Mond. In the morning I did so and received many promises. I do not trust my flattering luck, but I will wait a little before I decide on anything else

5 May. Wed. A very unpleasant joke happened to me, which might have caused me much injury. While

I was giving orders to the redoubt workmen on Laurel Hill there came from von Bose's regiment a Surgeon whom I knew and who was shooting below at the foot of the hill. He aimed at me and I jokingly called out to him to fire away. He rashly fired believing me too far off to be hit. He hit me however with several heavy shot on the right knee and other parts of my leg from which I got blue spots. Several orderlies too got some of the charge and the surgeon would have been terribly flogged if I had permitted it. If I had not happened to be on the height when a strong wind was blowing the shot would certainly have done harm.

15 May Sat. I had to leave Fort Laurel Hill early on account of a tooth-ache and I had the Company Surgeon pull out the tooth which I had broken in January '78 At 2 o'clock I returned to work.

18 May. Tues In the morning I was detached to assist the other Engineer, Lieut. *Marchall*, to erect a battery of 6 guns on the top of the hill of Fort Knipphaussen to which the circumvallation line from Laurel Hill extended. For this work I had men of the Hessian Body regiment of Donop, English of the 17th reg'm't, of the 57th and of Roberson's Corps.

19 May. Wed. In the morning it began to rain astonishingly hard and kept on more continuously than I had yet seen, since I had been in America, until the 22nd Sat. when it again stopped The next day, however, no work was done until it got drier

27 May Thurs. In the morning the redoubt work was changed as follows. From 5 o'clock A M until 11 (with a pause from 8–9) and from 3 P. M. to cannon-fire.

26, 27, 28 till 30 May. Sund. The English Light Infantry and a few other regiments had marched, of the Hessians, the Yagers, (the English Light Horse) regiment von *Bose*, the Grenadier Battalion v. *Lengecke*, von *Munchenroth*, v. *Linsing* and *Koehler*, which was now called v. *Graff*, a Garrison Guard Battalion of the regiment *Prinz Carl*, English and Hessians together comprising a little over 6,000 men. Their real destination was not exactly known. The camp was pitched in the neighborhood of Phillip's House, as a year before, but they were immediately taken across the river to Jersey In a few days they returned without having achieved any success more than to take a few little redoubts. But they remained stationed in the neighborhood of Phillip's House, (in which the General in Chief, Clinton, lodged) but for what reason, must be left to time to teach, it being idle to waste words in such cases

June. During June—on *Forsed* Hill

1 June. Tues. Towards evening our regiment, also Morbach's, was divided into companies to pitch the camp on the north side. Our company remained in the old place. I remained by permission in my hut with my orderly, to sleep.

16 June Wed I gave my papers and money sealed up in a box, besides a silver bordered writing tablet to Lieut. Col. v. *Nagell*, Jr, to take care of, because I trusted him most. Pay in June 26/- 3d.

July. During July engaged on the Fort.

10 July. Frid. I wrote a letter to the merchant *Follert* in Braunsberg and enclosed one to his eldest daughter *Lohnichen* (Helen), but as if I were still with the Rebels. The above-named regiments, likewise General *Tryon* with the 23rd Eng— Guard Regiment and several other regiments also the English *Fennings* (Fanning's) Corps and the Hessian Regiment von *Landgraf* which had been stationed on Long Island, having marched to *Connecticot* and then to Virginia, one heard daily different rumors about them, constantly contradicted by new ones, nor was the truth ever known. About 30 English miles in front of the lines, on *Verplank's Pint* some fortifications were made by the Assistant Engineer—*Marchall*, Lieut. of the 60th regiment. For the protection of the same some English regiments were stationed there. Across the North River, on *the Jersey*, was also a fort *Stony*

Pint in which the 17th Engl. Regiment, a few Scotch and some 50 men of Robinson's Corps were stationed as garrison.

16 July. Frid Towards day-break the Rebels had arrived in quite large numbers, treasonably led by two deserters from their posts. They had found the posted picket not awake and had therefore overcome it and then, penetrating into the fort, had killed nearly 60 men, although the English, in this unexpected attack, defended themselves right bravely encouraged by their Colonel, *Jahnsen,* a handsome young man who was already severely wounded. Of the English not more had escaped than 1 Lieutenant, 1 Reg'm't'l Quarter Master and 6 privates. The others were all taken prisoners, and nearly 40 were wounded. In the fort there were nine iron 9 lb. mortars and 3 or 4 other heavy guns, which fell into the hands of the Rebels, besides a handsome supply of ammunition and provisions. This event caused great excitement. Different movements were made by General Clinton with our small army, the purpose of which the future will show.

18 July. Sund. This morning the workmen were ordered back and ordered to take part in garrisoning the redoubts until further orders. The army had marched further forwards and in the afternoon we heard loud cannonading which came from the recapture of *Stony Point* Fort by our troops, which, however, the Rebels had immediately deserted, having first removed the guns and everything else and destroyed much of the fortification.

20 July. Tues. Again 15 men from each regiment were ordered to work on *Laurell* Hill to complete the circumvallation line already begun Since May I had always worked with Donop's regiment on *Forsed* Hill of Fort Knipphaussen and continued at it now until the work of the carpenters was completed. To-day I wrote a letter, for amusement's sake, to Miss *Weinstockin* at Braunsberg and Madam Follert. I mailed these letters in the month of March 1780.

— July — General Cornwallis had again arrived from England and had assured us that in a short time a fleet with 5,000 men would arrive here and 2,000 in West Florida.

23 July Frid. Again, as before, a strong working party was formed and the number of men under arms in the redoubts diminished, since, the night before, our army had returned from their march and taken up their old camp again near Phillip's House

24 July Sat. In the afternoon the block-house on Laurel Hill was taken down and was to be put up again at Stony Point, whither it was taken by ship.

26 July Sund. In the morning our army, with the exception of a few regiments, returned through pouring rain. The regiment of Landgraf, formerly of *Wottgenau* was quartered in the huts of the captured 17th English regiment, and the other three English regiments that had come with them were placed in a better camp in the city.

29 July. Thur. In the morning our separated companies came together again in their former camp, to make room for those regiments of the returning army which had arrived

30 July. Frid. In the evening I had to leave the redoubt at an early hour feeling sure that I had an attack of fever. I had to go to bed immediately, and after taking a dose of rum and pepper I felt a little better, so that, with hope in God, I went out again.

31 July. Sat. This morning the remaining portion of the whole army that had been sent out in front, returned and encamped in different places. The Hessian regiment von *Landgraf* had to make room for the English *Lord Radens* Corps in the camp of the captured 17th regiment, and pitch their camp at the Charles Redoubt where, a year before, first *Koehler's Grenadier Battalion*, afterwards the *Leib Regiment*, had been stationed   Pay in July 26/- ½d.

August   During August still engaged on *Forsed* Hill.

1 Aug. Sund. In the forenoon I again had a strong attack of fever, so I left the redoubt and went home. I lay down feeling very weak. My uncertain destiny forced many silent tears from my eyes. I returned to duty in the afternoon, though feeling very weak.

2 Aug. Mond. In the morning I stayed from work and took an emetic which was quite effective, driving off much gall; but not feeling well all day I remained home and did not do any work. The detachments in the redoubts had been strengthened, since the army had returned; but they were relieved daily, as before. For the redoubt-work the Leib Regiment; Landgraf; Prinz Karl; Donop and Bose gave each 36 men and 1 Sub-officer a day—all together each day, after the *tour*, 1 Captain and 1 Subaltern.

English. the 44th and 57th regiments. The 57th gave 35 men and 1 Sub-officer, being stronger than the 44th regiment. The 44th gave 25 men and 1 Sub-officer.

3 Aug. Tues. This morning I went to the redoubt, but had to return very soon, because I felt sick again.

4 Aug. Wed. This morning I felt so weak in all my limbs that I apprehended the severest illness. I lay in bed almost all day. From the way I feel physically I fear my death is nearing My sighs can no longer move God. I would be glad to die, were it not that I must die a sub-officer (that worries me, on account of my relatives, even at the brink of the grave. I despair when I think of my former happiness.)

5 Aug. Thurs. My fever has left me entirely. God will guide further events kindly for me. But I cannot understand the circumstances in which I now find myself I am obliged to go through all kinds of misfortunes, even the most disgusting. I am in the saddest spirits. All my actions are at variance with my heart's feeling. My own self-examination and my mind are discontented with this A thousand different moods seem to conflict within me and trouble me.

Then I become vexed at myself and disagreeable to others. How often do I deplore the harshness of my fate, and I am beside myself when I think of the consequences, namely, that I am to be unhappy and unsuccessful without having a bad heart

Much news was given us by papers and oral communications. The French were reported to have taken two islands in the West Indies, namely, St. Vincent and "*Cranada*"—There were also unpleasant rumors about our long-expected fleet, which the future will determine. Even here in our neighborhood one hears and sees nothing good. The English soldiers, especially those of *Lord Raden's* Corps, perpetrate daily the grossest highway-robberies and even kill. One night some English soldiers attacked a Hessian Grenadier Sergeant with their bayonets, wounded him in many places, robbed him of everything and left him lying on the spot, where he soon after died. Innumerable like incidents occur, even in the day-time

8 Aug. Sund. I took back my money and papers from young Lieutenant *Nagell* to have them in my own care, for which purpose I had the English carpenters make me a box with a lock.

16 Aug Mond. I got a receipt from the assistant engineer for the time that I had been engaged in work, because the day before an order had been issued by the General to the effect that the regiments were to distribute the work-money from the time of beginning down to the end of June of this year. I handed in my receipt to the regimental Quarter Master (who was just going to the city) to take to the cashier, and I awaited my money

This same day the guns were removed from Fort Independence.

17 Aug. Tues. This morning the powder-magazine at Fort Knipphaussen was torn down and the woodwork used on *Forsed* Hill. Likewise the woodwork of Fort Independence and King's Bridge, which was transported on wagons.

18 Aug. Wed   This morning I received my work-money from our regimental Quarter Master *Zinn*, for 69 days at 1 shill. 6d. a day, total therefore 5 £ Engl. 3/– 6d.

19 Aug. Thurs.   Towards evening those of our watches that were stationed nearest New York heard loud musket firing and the next day we heard the following news, very sad for us, but the affair had been cleverly planned and executed by the Rebels. On the little island of *Pauli Hoock*, situated near New York to the right of New Jersey, a detachment of our men, numbering 100, was constantly stationed, to observe everything on Jersey. And this morning an English Colonel with 150 men had been commanded to destroy a Rebel picket on Jersey. As yet no one knows whether it happened through treason, calculation or mere chance that the Rebels, at the very same time, made an attack on *Pauli Hook*, surprising the 100 men stationed there who belonged to the Erb Prinz, Knipphaussen and Lossberg regiments, and capturing 1 sub-officer and 15 privates. As soon as the firing was heard, two Companies of the Hessian Erb Prinz Regiment were immediately ordered from New York to re-inforce *Pauli Hook*, but they were not able to do any great harm to the Rebels owing to their careful retreat with their prisoners, and were obliged, besides having a few more killed and wounded, to watch the enemy march off. In the meanwhile nothing was heard of the English Colonel, because he had not yet returned. Very late, however, he did come back, but without having accomplished anything.

21 Aug. Sat.   As it was my birthday and rained hard I remained home and in solitude, drank a bottle of wine—but my contemplations made my heart heavy.

22 Aug. Sund.   I received additional 2 *Ginues*, 3 English shill. and 11 pence arrears of work-money which had not been payed out simultaneously with the other owing to a mistake of the Commissary. Accord-

ing to that the last days of April, May and June were paid me in full.

23 Aug. Mond. This morning the 44th English Musketeer Regiment marched out of the huts on *Laurell* Hill to *State Island* and 3 Companies of Prinz Carl's Hessian regiment (which, since the return of the army, had not been far from there) came into the huts.

25 Aug Wed. This afternoon the 57th English Musketeer Regiment marched out of the barracks of Fort Knipphaussen (into which the 2 companies of Prinz Carl's Regiment meanwhile came). The 57th regiment was ordered to New York until further orders

To-day a large fleet had arrived at New York with provisions and soldiers, numbering nearly 100 men, but all of them English recruits The Hessians were with the second division,—which was also shortly expected. Up to date we have had a surprisingly large number of sick, which increases daily I was, as above mentioned, rid of the fever, but felt weak in all my limbs.

31 Aug Tues. A little *Flasche* of ——— cannons was commenced on Forsed Hill on the north side Pay in August 26/- ½d.

September. During September on Laurel Hill works.

1 Sept. Wed. In the afternoon after promptly completing the work I had to attend to on the redoubts, I went into the Hessian Yager camp to see v. Martefeldt whom I have already mentioned and who returned with me towards evening and remained until the next evening. To-day it was made known in the order that Emmerich's Chasseur Corps was to be distributed among the English regiments, but the officers, with few exceptions, received free passage.

2 Sept. Thurs. The Hessian regiments stopped sending out so many on *sharp command*, and set only 28 privates a day to work, because the number of fever-stricken was increasing daily

6 Sept. Mond. At 10 o'clock this morning our regiment was mustered in regular order by an English Commissary and we alone had over 200 sick superior officers, sub-officers and privates. I did not take part in the mustering.

8th Sept. Wed. On account of the large number of fever cases (especially in Donop's and Bose's regiments) we could not spare more than 20 men per regiment for work There was a veritable epidemic here and the inhabitants and Rebels also were frequently visited by contagion. This morning there departed also, the two English Regiments, namely the 7th, an English Fusilier regiment and the 23rd, a Fusilier regiment which had been encamped on *Spaken Hill*—by ship, on the north side, for New York. The 23rd went directly to *State Island*, where the 44th regiment of the English passed to and fro on ships, and departed the very next day, though no one could tell from the many different conjectures what the real object of their journey was.

Likewise Knipphaussen's and Losberg's Hessian Fusilier regiments had to join this expedition under the command of the Hessian Colonel von *Loose*. But a short time after, Col. von Loose, with a few men of von Lossberg's regiment, came back again. Knipphaussen's regiment had been scattered by the storm, for the greater part captured by the Rebels and taken to Philadelphia. Nearly all of the 44th regiment returned again, although very much injured.

9 Sept. Thurs. This morning the detached men in the Rebel redoubts had to help the carpenters tear down the redoubts and the same evening the detachment which was usually stationed there went away

10 Sept. Frid. No. 7 was torn down and 8 men of every regiment were detailed to do so. Their destruction was undertaken because the sick increased from day to day and the regiments could not endure the service.

11 Sept. Sat. I had to go from *Forsed* Hill over to

Laurel Hill to assist at the line of communication with the former, the Engineer being sick, To-day N° 6 was also torn down.

12. Sept. Sund. Independence was begun to be torn down.

14 Sept. Tues. An order was issued for the following day being the 15th of this month, directing that the work was to commence at 6 A. M. and be suspended only from 11 to 2

16 Sept. Thurs Part of the abattis from the redoubts, so far as they had been demolished, was taken to N° 8 for its repair, which latter redoubt was now strongly garrisoned, 1 Captain, 1 Subaltern and 50 privates. This afternoon the Landgraf's regiment marched from Charles redoubt back to the camp where Lord Raden's Corps had last stood. This Corps now took position on *Spaken Dubbel* near the Hessian Yagers

17 Sept. Frid. The half-stone watch house of the King's redoubt was torn down

18 Sept. Sat. In the morning all the workmen were brought together, consisting of 1 Captain 2 Subalterns, 10 Sub-officers, 2 Drummers, and 172 privates, which I had to distribute for demolishing N° 4, N° 5, King's Redoubt and the remains of the powder magazine in Independence We were through at about two o'clock in the afternoon.

19 Sept Sund. The order already having been given for certain English and Hessian troops to be in readiness to go on board ship at the first order, a few ships went, later on, to *Stony Pint*, on the North River, to get the English garrison and everything that was there, and to garrison the fortresses with but few men From to-day, since everything had been torn down on the right hand of Laurel Hill, the workmen formerly detailed by the regiments for that work were given among the workmen employed in building, that is, daily per regiment 36 privates, 2 Sub-officers, for the whole, however, 1 Captain, 2 Subalterns and 1

Drummer, although there were always some wanting on account of the still prevailing sickness.

20 Sept. Mon. Towards 9 this morning the Queen's Rangers left their camp at King's Bridge on horseback and on foot for New York in order to embark there. This afternoon the English soldiers, who had been in Fort *Stony Pint* and *Verplank's Pint*, came back, to wit Pfenning's Corps, 23rd Regiment Musketeers, English 64th, 63rd, 42nd, some of the 71st and 81st regiments and Robinson's Corps. Until further orders those forts remained garrisoned by a few English regiments. But some time after they were demolished by the English. The embarkation of the troops was daily expected, though no one could foretell whither they would be bound Of the Hessians the following were ordered to go· Grenadier Battalion von Linsing, v. Lengecke, v. Munchenroth, besides the Grenadier Battalion Graff and 200 men of the Foot Yagers.—of the English. all the Grenadiers that were here, the Light Infantry, the 7th, 23rd, 33rd English Musketeer and 37th ditto regiments, 54th ditto, 57th ditto, Pfenning's Corps and the Cavalry and Infantry of the Queen's Rangers and Lord Raden's Corps.

22 Sept. Wed. This morning Lord *Raten's* Corps. or the Irish Volunteers, marched out of their camp to New York. And the 64th English Musketeer regiment which had moved first from Stony Point, then Harlem, and finally into camp near N River Hill, now gave daily 20 men and 1 Sergeant for work.

Half of the Irish Volunteers had been stationed some time ago on Long Island, and were there now.

To-day ships had again arrived from England and in them were our already announced 900 and some 20 recruits, together with several officers and Sub-officers.

24 Sept. Fri. Owing to the great number of sick our regiment did not furnish a single man for work, and Bose 10 men more. The fever increases every day and is now commencing in the other regiments as well as all over the island.

25 Sept. Sat. We received our share of the arrived recruits consisting of 38 men, also 35 men for Trimbach's regiment. The latter were to do duty with us, now that their regiment was absent, until a favorable opportunity came to join it. The recruits for all the absent regiments had to do the same.

28 Sept. Tues. This morning Bose's regiment marched for New York. They had to draw lots with our regiment and, winning, were ordered to assist in the performance of military duties in the city, as soon as the Grenadiers should leave.

To-day the Hessian regiments received the new articles of equipment which had arrived with the fleet, but they were not yet distributed. The previously appointed and above named English and Hessian Regiments had now gone to sea with the ordered ships under command of the English General *Cornwall*, the others waited for further orders.

29 Sept. Wed. A ship brought in to New York the sad news that Lossberg's and Knipphaussen's regiment had, on their journey, nearly all been wrecked and then perished in captivity. We could not with certainty determine the extent of the loss

Pay in September 26/– 3d.

October. Still on Laurel Hill until the 26th Oct.

3 Oct. Sund. From assistant Engineer Lieutenant *Sproule* I received my receipt for two months, to get my money from the Chief Engineer *Mercel*. I gave the receipt to the Adjutant Lieutenant v. Lepel who received all monies, the regimental Quarter Master being sick.

6 Oct. Wed. I was detailed with 50 men, Hessians, with Engineer Sproule, to repair N° 8. And so it was finished on the 6th, 7th and 8th. Then I continued work on Laurel Hill.

7 Oct Thurs The hut-money was payed out to the soldiers and I, as Sub-officer, received 1 Spanish dollar, like all the privates

9 Oct. Sat. I received from Lieut v. Lepel my

work-money about 20 Spanish dollars, for 2 months, to wit : August and July.

23 Oct. Sat. In the afternoon our regiment received the order to send all the sick, next Monday, into the city and for the whole regiment to follow on Tuesday, to get into winter-quarters early on account of the large number of the sick

26 Oct. Tues. At 6 this morning the regiment marched not to New York, for, as late as 9 o'clock Monday night the order had arrived to march to Long Island. Captain Donop was to arrange the quarters. He took me with him. So on Tuesday morning at about 3 A. M. I went, accompanied by one private, to the river near Martin's Wharf in order to cross the ferry not far from the so-called *Holli Goett*. This I did at 4 A. M. and then we left this perilous whirlpool, which wrecks many ships, of which we saw traces on our left. Here I came across several foraging sharpshooters which I took along with me. We marched on the road to *Buschwig* and arrived at the church there at noon-time. The houses there being very spacious Captain Donop himself hurried about to arrange the quarters But afterwards when the regiment arrived at 4 o'clock in the afternoon, the confusion was so great that no quarters could be found. Even I had to arrange quarters for our company on the East River, not far from New York, lying opposite, so I had my hands full till late at night and had my quarters temporarily at *Franz Titus'* The Sergeant Major of our Company was taken sick, so I had to attend to his duties and in consequence I had for several days hardly more time left than for eating and a few hours for sleep.

29 Oct. Frid. The quarters having been changed I took mine two houses further, at *Thomas Killmann's*, also a Hollander, as most of the inhabitants around here were.

Pay in October 26/– ½d.

3 Nov. Wed. I lent Captain von Donop, at his

earnest request, 3 *Ginues* on his soon to be received *douceurs*.

5 Nov. Frid I was again appointed *ad interim* by the Colonel and the Lieutenant Colonel, the regimental Quarter Master being very sick, to transact his duties and I was excused from my Sergeant's duties.

6 Nov Sat. So I had to give out the bread for the whole regiment, in the bakery. And . . . . .

8 Nov. Mon. I had to receive in *Brockland's* Ferry, just opposite New York, on Long Island, forage for all the regiment's horses. From the *Buschwicker Church* to there was about 6 English miles ' This took place every Monday.

11 Nov. Thur. I had to receive, at the above named place, the provisions for the whole regiment. This recurred every Thursday.

13th Nov. Sat. At day-break this morning I received, by order of Col. v Goosen, a horse to take wood to all the houses that were designated by the Militia Colonel *Wil. Axtell* for Donop's regiment, we being in need of it. The distance amounted to about 40 English miles before I had completed the circuit. Yet I had to distribute bread to the regiment at 4 o'clock in the afternoon.

16 Nov. Tues. This morning, taking two orderlies along, I went to *Broklin*. From there I had myself ferried across to New York in a royal boat, free of charge, and having bought some things for myself I returned the next morning—viz.

17 Nov. Wed. to *Buswig*, without having met with anything unusual.

19 Nov. Frid. This evening, after sundown, there was loud firing to express the joy felt at some great advantages which the English were reported to have gained over French and Rebels in South Carolina.

20 Nov. Sat. This morning, having no time to spare myself, I sent an orderly, with the permission of Col. v. Goosen to New York with a power to get

from the Chief Engineer Captain *Mersel* (Lieutenant Sproule was still dangerously ill with the fever) the money still due to me for my work on the fortifications on Laurel Hill for the month of September and up to the 26th. Oct. of this year, @ 1 sh. 6 ps. sterling per day. This was sent to me in cash, in the amount of 18 Spanish dollars

November pay, 26/- 3d.

2 Dec. Thurs. While I was on my way to get the regiment's rations (it was pouring with rain) I came very near getting into serious trouble again. The Colonel's groom addressed some very impudent words to me concerning fresh meat, and, having no stick with me, I took my sword with the sheath and struck him several times. But the sheath unexpectedly slipped off and the groom throwing up his left arm, I dealt him a severe cut below the elbow through to the bone. I was in anxiety myself, though I had done it unintentionally. I went to Colonel von Gosen, told him the whole story myself and he pardoned me without any reproachful remarks, even in spite of the earnest complaint of the groom For some weeks the groom suffered intense pain, but was not lamed.

10 Dec. Frid. Chasseurs were again to be levied. Colonel Goosen asked me whether I had a desire to enlist again. But no, my heart was full of a thousand resolves without feeling anything definite. Considering my character I am now doing quite well Heaven seems to be more propitious towards me and in this hope I am daily expecting the promise of a better lot —from Hessians.

16 Dec. Thurs. I had to go to New Town for provisions to-day, about 4 English miles from *Bushwik* church. The same afternoon we received, at a late hour, the order that our regiment and the Body Regiment were to march to New York to be garrisoned there, as soon as the already appointed regiments should have left on the ships, and in the meantime to be ready to execute this order at any moment.

This was very disagreeable to me and caused me many melancholy hours for many reasons.

18 Dec. Sat. At 1 o'clock at night our regiment received orders to march to *Brokl. fery* at 8 the next morning. I was very sad at this, because I had been having a most pleasant time here and unfortunately my heart felt itself in love with the daughter of my host, a girl that could not but please (without explaining why, here). Her name was Sally, age 14.

19 Dec. Sund. So at the appointed time we left, I, for my part, feeling very melancholy. At noon we arrived at the ferry, but the wind blew such a gale that we could not cross in boats to New York. Therefore we left all our baggage in charge of a watch and marched back to *Buswick*, with the order to be ready to march again as soon as the storm subsided. My love gave me wings to fly back and, as I was always allowed much liberty, I did not march with the regiment, but took a shorter way. It was astonishingly cold, but the affectionate welcome made me proof against the weather

20 Dec. Mond At 3 in the afternoon orders were again issued for us to march to the Ferry (to me always most detestable orders, for otherwise I never left my pretty room. Ah! only one who loves can truly understand how mere nonsense can charm us, when we love and are loved again, though innocently) It was snowing again and very cold. Before we reached the ferry it was nearly night. Then orders were dispatched to march back until the following morning. I did so with the same joy as before and was again pleasantly received. It is certain, if I could make up my mind to forget Europe and my position, that I would have turned my thoughts to nothing but my happiness with this girl. My own knowledge of the shortlived spells of love that I am constantly subject to gave me hopes of forgetting her in the future My Colonel, however, gave me a commission to remain behind tomorrow and to superintend the transporting of the

bakery, the sick and the regiment's baggage to New York on the following day.

21 Dec. Tues. The regiment marched at 2 o'clock in the afternoon and got over to New York, though at a late hour. Then went into barracks on the large square not far from the fresh water (near the new *Scheel*). Landgraf's regiment and the Body regiment were put in houses on the other side of the barracks where the Hessian Grenadiers had been stationed. By the way, there were still in New York the Anspach, the Bayreuth, the 80th and 43rd English, and the Scotch 76th and 40th (42, 46?) regiments. *Prinz Charl* had remained near Fort Knipphaussen, the *Erb Prinz* regiment had occupied our huts and the Yagers were where Bose's regiment had been (nearer to New York). Mirpach's regiment in huts near *Martin's Worft*, Bose's regiment in houses in Bloomingdale and the English Guards on North River Hill. The 44th regiment was stationed at Paul's Hook for good, without the relief commands.

22 Dec. Wed. At 9 o'clock this morning, having undertaken to superintend the transport of the baggage (but only for love's sake¹) I bade my hospitable friends a cordial farewell (and left all my things and money there in a box), but secretly I took the most affectionate parting kiss from the girl, went away deeply moved, with two privates armed with muskets. I impressed a wagon on the road to transport the bakery and when I had arrived at the ferry I gave everything to the guard and crossed over alone in a boat to New York. (Here lay the baggage of many English and Hessian regiments, but could not be taken across on account of the stormy weather). I reported duly to the officers and the Colonel ordered me to assist the regimental Quarter Master again in providing forage, rations, wood, coal and beer and straw for the regiment, so I now had more to do than before.

23 Dec. Thurs. I was busy all day, till late in the night, with the above mentioned affairs for the regiment. All the Hessian Grenadiers and divers Eng-

lish regiments, also the Hessian Chasseurs, left in the meantime with the fleet, without being able to ascertain their actual destination. It was the general belief that they were bound for West Florida, because Trimbach's recruits, whose regiment was said to be in crowded quarters with Wiesenbach's at Charlestown, was also sent away. The English General *Cornwallis* left also.

25 Dec. Sat. The Commander in Chief General *Klinton* sailed to-day with a large number of officers and directly afterwards all of the fleet, that had been ordered to sail, left. A few of the ships had been wrecked near New York and the soldiers on board had been transferred to other ships and sent after the others Only a few days later there were many good and bad rumors current regarding the fleet, but they were unfounded. In the meantime Lieutenant General von Knipphaussen was Commander in Chief, and the English Major General *Baterson* of the Artillery, Commandant.

27 Dec. Mon. I had flour in the provision-store for the regiment and when I sent a wagon to get some to-day, it turned out that a soldier had stolen a barrel of it. They got on the scent and the English Commissary made a great row (for these kind of tricks were occurring daily). I took the fellow's part when the Commissary went away, although I knew nothing about it, yet I had the responsibility. The Colonel thought highly of me, so I had nothing to fear from the Commissary. But I had to decide to take up my old duties again and I therefore lost many handsome perquisites.

29 Dec. Wed. The new equipments were distributed to be worn on New Year's day. Many of them had been injured by the rats. Mine was all right.

Regiment's day and Company's day.

Pay in December 26/- ½d.

(End of the year 1779.)

1780.

Sergeant in Lt. Col. Hinte's Company in Donop Regt. of Hesse Cassel Musketeers.

January. The cold was so intense this winter that the inhabitants could not remember the like for twenty years back The North River was wholly frozen over and the East River had an astonishing quantity of floating ice. As, in spite of this, many people ventured out in boats, sad accidents happened almost daily. The wood magazines were emptied and as we could not get our wood from Long Island on account of the ice, old ships were assigned to all the English and Hessian regiments for firewood. Even then we had only half allowance and the other half was to be paid to us. The Rebels had now the best opportunity to attack us from all sides to the best advantage We expected it hourly and therefore the best measures were taken. The sailors on the ships received guns and had to serve on land and with the pickets at night. All the citizens and country people between 16 and 60 years of age received guns. The Rebels often made light attacks, but they were in most cases badly defeated.

2 Jan. Sun. On reserve picket.
4 " Tues. On *men-guarde* in Wall Street.
5 " Wed. Company's day.
7 ." Frid. On guard at the Coffee House.
10 " Mond. Company's day. I had my left arm bled, fearing to get the eruption, since nearly everybody had it. But that did not help me much. I broke out all over, especially on my neck. I hope for the best from God's mercy.

11 Jan. Tues I was on the Ferry-Watch. Two English sergeants were there who acted disrespectfully towards me, so I gave them both a thrashing, but did not arrest them, because at their request I

agreed to cross swords with them the following day. I waited for them in vain, they did not appear.

12 Jan. Wed. On reserve picket.

14 " Frid. In the evening there was a great alarm to the effect that the Rebels were approaching. Firing was heard on Staten Island (of our troops were there: the Hessian Guard Regiment Bienau, the 57th English Regt., the 54th *Rooens Corps*, and the R. P. Corps). Immediately a detachment of Hesse-Anspachers and English numbering several hundred men, was ordered over there. But no ship could cross on account of the ice, neither was it strong enough to march across.

15 Jan. Sat. They again attempted to get the detachment across, but it was impossible. In the evening a spy had, to our wonderment, succeeded in stealing over from the State of Jersey and from him we learned that the Rebels had arrived in force, that they had set fire to a Jersey magazine and driven away many cattle; but as our men had held out well in the redoubts, the enemy had not been able to gain any advantage, but instead had to leave nearly 100 prisoners behind.

16 Jan. Sund. On watch at Coffee House

17 " Mond. I risked crossing over to *Long Islandt* with an orderly, without fear on account of the thick ice. Owing to the danger I found it difficult to get a furlough Love left me no time to consider. I was kindly and affectionately received, called on several other acquaintances and felt very contented

18 Jan. Tues. After I had secretly received many farewell kisses and had paid my regards to her parents, my orderly took my box and I, although urged to stay longer, went back to the *fery* where, with greater danger than the day before on account of more ice, but still safely, I got over to New York.

19 Jan. Wed. Our equipment money, a small amount, was paid to us and I received 4 Hessian thalers, 8 English shillings, 7 pence ha'penny.

20 Jan. Thurs. On watch at *Sik Rebls Prisin*.

21 Jan. Frid. Company's day. On reserve picket.
22 " Sat. With working party on shipboard to gather firewood.
23 Jan. Sun. This evening, while on the *West Worft* watch, I had a man arrested for creating a disturbance, but persuaded by the entreaties of his female companion I let him go. At night, as we again had apprehensions of [an attack by] the Rebels, extra patrols were sent out. All the posts had to be relieved every half hour and that was to continue until further orders.
25 Jan Tues. Company's day. In the night a patrol of English, Hessians and Anspachers, numbering three or four hundred, under command of an English Major, went about 16 English miles beyond Paulus Hook and captured a Rebel picket of 30 men without giving any alarm.
26 Jan. Wed. With working detachment on shipboard to gather firewood.
27 Jan. Thurs. On the watch at West Wharf.
30 " Sund. On guard at the Coffee House.
31 " Mond. Company's day.
Pay received in January : 26 / – ½d.
2 Feb. Sund. On reserve picket.
3 " Mond. With working detachment on shipboard after firewood.
4 Feb. Tues. On provost guard.
6 " Thurs. On the rampart Bunker Hill.
7 " Frid. It was now quite cold, so I could not apply any remedy to my eruption, now entirely broken out.
10 Feb. Mon Company's day.
11 " Tues. On guard West Wharf.
14 " Frid. Regiment's day.
15 " Sat. On reserve picket.
16 " Wed. On account of my increasing eruption I took a purgative.
17 Feb. Thurs. Watch Bunker's Hill.
18 Feb. Frid. Company's day.
20 Feb. Sun. | To-day a *Baquet* boat arrived here

bringing over some promotions in the Hessian army. In our regiment Free Corporal *Schoenwolf* was made ensign in Landgraf's regiment. I wished to demand my discharge.

21 Feb. Mon. After the watch parade Colonel v. Gosen himself sent for me to see him at 1.30 P.M. He then showed me a letter from Gen'l. Jungheim in which he wrote that the Landgrave would, in consequence of my good behaviour, qualify me even as officer in Donop's regiment, as soon as a vacancy occurred; in the meantime, however, I was to have the position of Free Corporal. Colonel von Gosen promised moreover to do everything for me. In the meantime I was to be transferred to the Body Company as Free Corporal. This I finally consented to, though I was to get less pay.

23 Feb. Wed. On general watch.
26 " Sat. Company's day.
28 " Mon. Reserve picket
29 " Tues. On guard West Wharf.
Pay in February 26/- 5½d

1 March. From this day I was Ensign [Fahnen-Junker] in Lieut. Col. Hinte's Company, but with the pay of Sergeant. I was put on the monthly lists as *Free Corporal.*

2 Mar. Frid. In the morning we were mustered by an Englishman in the old *Eingiessen* Church,[1] in which horses or other animals were sometimes kept, on the square of Crown Street.[2]

4 Mar. Sat. I again took a purgative as my eruption was growing worse.

5 Mar. Sun. Company's day,
6 " Mond. The 80th, 82nd and 76th English and Scotch Regiments went from New York to Long Island. On Long Island there were now the following regiments besides the previous (English) ones

---

[1] Dutch Church, late Post Office, recently demolished for the erection of the new building of the Mutual Life Ins. Co
[2] Liberty Street.

whose names or numbers have slipped my memory: The Hessian Fusilier regt., regt. von *Dittfort* and *Hiene*, 1 Garrison battalion.

8 Mar. Wed. On watch as guard at *Sik Rebls Prison.*

10 Mar. Frid. Company's day
14 " Tues. On watch at West Wharf.
16 " Thurs. Company's day. On reserve picket.

18 " Sat On reserve picket. I wrote again as a remembrance to Gen. von Jungheim in Cassel and sent also the last two letters that had been written to Follert and Weinstock, by packet ship.

20 Mar. Mon. On watch at *Sik Rebls Prison*.

22 " Wed. Company's day. In the evening a patrol of English, Hessians and Anspachers, numbering about three hundred went out again past *Powles Hook* to *Hekinsak*, 16 English miles into Jersey. They lost a few men thereby, but brought back to New York the next evening 64 Rebel prisoners and much booty. .

23 Mar. Thur. Order was given for the whole army to be ready to march on shortest notice.

25 Mar. Sat. Sick in the barracks until the 9th of April.

26 " Sund. I was bled on the left arm and the regimental Surgeon Stieglitz prescribed something for me. I felt better. At times I had bad attacks of fever on account of the inflammation and pustules, I could only hope for the best.

29 Mar. Wed. In the regiments an account of the small equipment pieces, dating from the 1st. of January of this year, was made out and according to it I received 3 English shillings and 4 pence or, in Hessian money, 1 Reichsthaler,—which afterwards always occurred in March.

30 Mar. Thurs. Some English heavy artillery and the 42nd English Regt. embarked· Regt. Prince of *Wallis* (Wales), Volunteers of Ireland and Queen's

Rangers; the Hessian Regt. von *Dittford* and all the convalescents of that regiment and of the regiments which were in South Carolina. Therefore though nothing certain was known it was evident that this fleet had been ordered there too. Their march (departure) on board the transport ships, which had been allotted to them, took place on the 2nd of April at noon, because the embarkation was always slow.

Pay received in March 26/- ½d.

April 1. Saturday. The Sub-officers and each man received 12 English shillings, 8½ stuyvers wood money and money paid for the work on the old ships, although much was deducted on account of the working cloth injured during the work.

To-day the 37th English regiment arrived here in New York to strengthen the garrison. We heard through the papers here the first startling news, viz: that General *Klinton* had certainly captured *Charlestown* and that the English fleet had also taken many Spanish ships.

9 April Sun. I went out again in spite of my suffering with the eruption and being under medical treatment.

10 April Mon. All the regiments had to begin drilling 3 times a week.

11 April. Tues. I was summoned to an examination of a musketeer named Herbert, a man of my Corps, who had already deserted almost all his masters. He said I was the cause of it because I had punished him several times. They did not want to examine me on that account, but I went directly afterwards to Col. von Gosen and Lieut Col. Hinte who exonerated me.

12 April. Wed. Company's day.
13 " Thurs. On provost guard watch.
14 " Frid. While on watch I got a boil on my left leg, which grew worse, causing me much pain I was troubled with it until April 28th

15 April. Sat. On reserve picket.

16 April. Sun. Company's day. I got back the 3 guineas that I had previously lent to Captain Donop, principally through the actions of the deserter Herbert, who declared me to be the chief cause of his deserting. Having perhaps, at times, noticed something, he had, contrary to my desire, insinuated that I must be on very good terms with the Captain, since the latter was in my debt. Although it was not true I could not help fearing disagreeable consequences. I consoled myself with my innocence and wrote to that effect to Col. von Gosen. But I had to wait and see what the future would bring about, hoping for the best. Now I am living again in the greatest perplexity. Hardly does my luck make a start to flourish, but it is crushed again by some execrable coincidence or other. What am I to do? Undoubtedly my fate was thus fixed at the very time of my birth! My heart, my thoughts, all have so changed that I am myself no longer contented with it and wish I could die! Oh, if death would but release me! Could I but end this life or live contentedly! Ah!—and how is my misfortune going to end? Only through God's mercy, without that I am again lost!

21 April. Frid. On watch very near the barracks with one company and 27 privates. My eruption increased so much that I had no rest, neither did I wish to be seen.

25 April. Tues. Regiment's and Company's day.
26 " Wed. On baggage watch.
28 " Frid. The two English regiments quartered in New York took away all the young men that could be spared from the inhabitants and forced them to become soldiers.

29 April. Sat. Company's day.
30 " Sun. On watch at West Wharf.
Pay received in April. 26/- 3d.

1 May. Mond. At about 12 at night a fire broke out in a bakery-shop in Maiden Lane and all the

regiments had to make ready to help, but it was quickly extinguished, though amidst great uproar.

3 May. Wed   Company's day.
6 " Sat.   On reserve picket. I was again under examination, but I noticed immediately the kindness of the Colonel, because the auditor only touched upon the worst points and I [my case] was soon finished.

7 May. Sun.   On baggage watch.
8 " Mon.   Company's day.
10 " Wed.   On baggage watch.
12 " Frid.   On picket reserve.
13 " Sat.   Company's day.
15 " Mon.   A fleet left here again with all the Braunschweig soldiers that were here and had ransomed themselves from Borgo's [Burgoyne's] former army. From all regiments and corps in which they had taken service, they were again given to General Riedesel, who was here on parole, and were sent back by him to Canada with the fleet; also Capt. von Schlageteufel, who was surrendered (and who is to be found in my journal for 1777); also the other three companies of von Losberg's Hessian regiment were sent there, where, it was said, the other two companies together with some men of Knipphaussen's regiment had, while with the former fleet, been driven by stress of weather. Consequently some recruits for the Hessian regiment and men, who had been here, were also sent there. Of the English there went away with the fleet the remaining companies of the 44th regiment and many others General Riedesel and many others from *Borg's* army and those of Saratoga were exchanged in the month of October, but only officers and such as belonged to the suite of Riedesel and the English Major General Philips. General Riedesel had insisted on taking command in the meantime of some troops on Long Island until his departure to Canada.

16 May. Tues.   On baggage watch.

18 May. Thurs. On working command with 19 men at a redoubt.
19 May. Frid. Company's day
20 " Sat. On reserve picket.
22 " Mon. On watch at West Wharf.
24 " Wed. Company's day.
26 " Frid. As a finish-up of the drill period we four Hessian regiments, in garrison in New York, had a manœuvre.
27 May. Sat. On provost guard.
29 " Mon. Company's day. We received the news that Charlestown had capitulated to General *Klinton* on the 12th inst. Whereby of the Rebels nearly 5000 had been taken prisoners and only about 100 had been killed or wounded on our side. Moreover our soldiers had taken much booty for the King of England.
30 May. Tues. To-day the regiment received per man 1 sh. 11 pence sterling arrears of wood money.
31 May. Wed. Regiment's day.
Pay received in May 26 /–½d.
1 June. On watch at Coffee House.
2 " Frid. Regiment's day.
3 " Sat. Company's day On working command with 8 men, making cartridges.
4 June. Sun. To-day was the King of England's birthday, and on that account guns were fired at 12 M, in N. York from Fort George and 1 P. M. from all the ships.
6 June. Tues. On picket reserve. From this day forth I was on the march to Staten Island and New Jersey, until the 24th inst.
At 3 A. M. an unexpected order came for all to march. I took the necessary steps, gave my money and papers in the safe-keeping of Lieutenant Col. Hinte, and at 10 A. M. we—Donop's regiment—set sail on schooners and *shluppen* (sloops). Towards evening we landed on Staten Island. Our regiment encamped around a church-yard and that night I slept on a grave-mound.

7 June Wed Company's day. Before day-break the whole army, English and Hessians, marched past us. We followed them to protect the baggage, and marched to the narrowest part of the water where we were to be ferried over to New Jersey, which was a very tedious affair, partly on account of the ground being so muddy before we reached the water's edge, partly on account of the baggage. The English and Hessians and Anspacher regiment all went straight ahead, but our regiment had to follow with the baggage, together with some English Dragoons. We marched through the pretty little town of *Liesbethtown*, which is of a long shape, and there I took part in the side patrols. We constantly heard firing ahead of us and the Rebels gave much annoyance to our army which numbered nearly 9000, as they had also done while we were crossing, having batteries and trenches near the water. We had one English General and many privates wounded. After mid-night there suddenly came an order for the baggage to go back, because the army was about to do so immediately. We did so shortly afterwards and in the greatest haste. We encamped in the form of a square in front of the little town, just before daybreak. We had an unannounced number of dead and wounded. The Rebels kept on making attacks all night.

8 June. Thurs We thought we were to return to New York. The Rebels began to attack us with unusual vigor. The 22nd English regiment was sent out to check the Rebels, but after mid-day the firing grew so intense that Bose's and our regiment had to advance. The English regiment had twice fired without hitting and many of them had been wounded, killed and taken prisoners. We saw an astonishing number of Rebels, nearly all in the bushes excepting a troop of *Leithorst*, which, however, was far off, and, according to the statement of a deserter, Washington himself was there. We remained in our positions for several hours, firing constantly with our cannons, and 3 of our men were slightly wounded by rifle shots, which was surprising

considering the distance. Thereupon we marched back to our old position.

9 June. Frid. On field-picket on the flank.

I barely escaped being shot while on picket to which I had been detached by the regiment that was there on command. We of the picket had our post close by the road behind the fences. In a short time when our sentinel had fired at some Rebel *Ld. Ross* (Light Horse), some Rebel riflemen came along and shielding themselves behind fences they opened fire and in spite of the distance hit so near us that we did not dare to let ourselves be seen standing upright. I imprudently crawled forward a short way, but when I had seen some bullets strike the ground at my feet and listening to the appeals of my comrades I had finally got up, at that very moment a rifle-ball struck quite deep into the ground just where I had been lying. Heaven had bidden me arise. We got some of our Yagers to cover our post and procured 2 cannons whereupon the Rebels retired. We slaughtered two cows and two calves here and ate them.

10 June. Sat. At an early hour we and our regiment were relieved and placed, in a line, in hut-camp. The names of the English regiments I could not accurately ascertain. The Hessians, however, consisted of: The Body regiment, Landgraf, Bose, Donop, Garrison regiment of *Pienou* and the Anspach regiment, besides their and our Yagers, the whole army estimated at 9000 men. Several ramparts were erected. The Yagers stood in front of us. There were constant short attacks. To night I took my coat off for the first time since leaving New York.

11 June. Sun. Company's day. This morning our regiment was again on *sharp commando*, where the Yagers had stood, and the latter advanced further on to the bridge.

12 June. Mon. in *Liesbethtown*, where there was firing every minute, and our entire regiment had to be prepared to cover them. Therefore no one was al-

lowed to undress and every day we had to be in arms one hour before daybreak.

13 June. Tues. Remained standing. On reserve picket. It rained so hard that we suffered much in our huts. And it was constantly unquiet, because our outposts and pickets were constantly being attacked, which did not end without dead and wounded on both sides. Our Yagers were the most frequent victims.

14 and 15 June Wed. and Thurs We remained standing, also on the 16th. Then it rained very hard again although it had been raining some every day. Ditto the 17th and in the afternoon the Beyreuth regiment arrived from New York, also some English troops. To night I was detached with 1 Lieut. and 3 more sub-officers and 56 privates on active picket on the banks of a stream, which one could wade across when the tide was low We were undisturbed till after 12 o'clock in the night, when the Rebels moved up a cannon close in front of us, which they had obtained from a deserting English ship's boat. We had a breast work of fences in front of us and derided their firing. They fired three times very rapidly, it was directed, however, towards the horses of the cavalry and a newly erected rampart. The second ball had struck the staff out of our color-bearer's (Col^{bs}) hand, as he stood in front of the regiment, but without injuring him. After the third shot all was quiet and we could hear them dragging off the cannon.

17 June Sat. On field picket, *Liesbethtown*.

18 " Sun. Still remained standing there. To-day General *Klinton* had returned from Charlestown with all the Grenadiers and several English troops. These he landed on Staten Island. In Charlestown had remained. General *Cornwallis*, with some English troops, and the Hessian regiment v. Tillford and the Garrison regiment of Hiene.

19 June. Mon. Company's day. In the afternoon General *Klington* reviewed all the regiments which were obliged to be in their camps beyond the front.

20 June, Tues On watch at General Knipphaussen's quarters. Again all was quiet, except casual firing by the outposts.

21 June. Wed. Ditto On reserve picket

22 " Thurs. At 7.30 A. M. I got a furlough from Col. v. Goosen to New York. I went on foot (across a very pretty bridge connecting Staten Island and Jersey. It consisted entirely of sloops and schooners) away to the end of Staten Island, a walk of three hours. Thence I proceeded on a provision schooner to New York where I arrived at 5 P. M. In the barracks, where things seemed to be in great confusion, I got in order the few things that I had left there. I slept in the barracks.

23 June. Fri. It was my desire to remain here longer, but hearing some loud firing in the direction of our camp and ascertaining from reports, that our army had marched further on, I immediately prepared for my departure. My ambition compelled me to go. All flat boats having gone to *Staaten Island*, I got on board a ship that had been ordered to General Knipphaussen. We sailed at 4 P. M. and arrived towards 9 P M. near the ship bridge But after passing the watch ship, it being dark, we ran aground and could not get off till morning at high tide. Here we heard that the greater part of our army had advanced as far as Springfield, but had been obliged to return again. Before day break the whole army hastened with all possible speed across the ship-bridge. This was then broken up and Donop's regiment had been obliged to stay behind in some ramparts to protect it. Soon after, he too embarked in flat-boats and, unseen by the Rebels, crossed to Staten Island. This caused much reflection and wonderment. N.B. While I was sailing from New York I saw all the Grenadiers and English regiments passing from Staten Island in large ships and sailing up the North River, where they landed at *Philipp's House* and were obliged to pitch a hut camp.

24 June. Sat. At day break, looking from our schooner, we saw our whole army on *St. Iland*, and the rising tide lifting us again we sailed back, landed and I returned to my regiment. A short time after, we marched on, but to night we were obliged to sleep in the pouring rain.

25 June. Sun. At 9 A. M. we received an order to the effect that Donop's and the 43rd regiment were to march immediately to the *Ferry* to be carried over to Long Island and thence to march to Brooklyn Ferry, a distance of about 3 hours, and thence back to New York in garrison This took place in regular order and we all arrived towards evening, & marched to our old barracks, where Lieut. Col. Graff's Grenadier Garrison Battalion was quartered and where we were to be as a *commando* of Mirbach's regiment. Thus we were obliged to spend the night lying in front of the barracks.

26 June. Mon. All was in confusion and it took several days to get things to rights again. The duty was very hard, too. The 43rd English regiment left New York again. The whole army again lay in hut camp near Philipp's House

27 June. Tues. On field picket at Col. *Beyers* house North River.

29 June. Thurs. On watch West Wharf.

30 " Frid. Company's day.

Pay in June 26/–3d.

1 July. Sat. In the afternoon we went among the cherry-trees, had plenty of them, but got soaked through by the rain.

3 July. Mon. On general watch at General Clinton's.

4 " Tues. On picket reserve.

5 " Wed. In the evening bathed in the North River. To-day on working command making cartridges

6 July. Thurs. Company's day.

7 " Frid. On foundry watch at cannon foundry.

11 " Sat. On watch East guard watch.

13 July. Thurs. Bathed in the North River.
14 " Frid. On working command making cartridges. To-day all the baggage of the army returned, because they had received the order to march.
15 July. Sat. On watch at General Knipphaussen's.
16 " Sun. Company's day.
19 " Wed. On commissariat watch.
20 " Thur. Watch at West Wharf.
21 " Frid. Several English regiments and also the Anspach, Bayreuth and Hessian regiments, Body and Landgrave, had left their camps at Philipp's House and marched into camp just above the city. The two latter went by ship to *Roth Island* as also the Bienau Garrison regiment from Staten Island, which was relieved by Bose's regiment.
23 July. Sun Finally the whole army had left Philipp's House and marched until within a short distance of Martin's Wharf. It had embarked there not far from *Hellegott*, lying quietly on the ships for a few days and then sailed for *Roth Island*, although they did not arrive there.
24 July. Mon. Company's day and regiment's day. At 7 A. M. Graff's Grenadier Battalion left New York by ship, and a few days after sailed, like the other thereto appointed regiments, for *Roth Is* Here French and Rebels were almost daily taken prisoners, large and small ships captured, which were sometimes richly laden
25 July. Tues. On watch at Foundry Redoubt.
26 " Wed. At 6 this evening Major Gen. v. *Hine* of the Garrison regiment, who had died here of fever was buried in the German Church in New York. All the English Generals that were here were present at the funeral, also Sub-officers, officers and Hessians, also the two Grenadier Companies of the Anspachers and Bayreuthers, besides Donop's regiment. Guns were ordered to be fired at his funeral.
28 July. Frid. On watch at Gen. Knipphaussen's.
29 " Sat. Reserve picket.

31 July. Mon. Commissariat watch.
Pay in July 26/-1d

3 August. Thur. On watch West Wharf. In the afternoon an order was issued to the effect that our regiment and the Anspach and Bayreuth regiments were to be ready to march at a moment's notice. All our troops that had sailed to *Roth Island* had returned again and had halted, some on Long Island, others near King's Bridge on York Island. For their previous voyage to *Roth Island* had not been completed, because the French were reported as being too strong there, both on land and water. The order to be ready to march was kept up, and many steps were taken in preparation. The militia of the city was daily increased and well divided into several regiments and equipments.

7 Aug. Mon. On provost guard watch.
8 " Tues. On reserve picket.
10 " Wed. On watch at barracks
11 " Thur. Company's day.
13 " Sat. At examination of a soldier of the Body [Leib] regiment.
14 Aug. Sun. On watch at New Hospital.
16 " Tues. On working command with 20 men in the Store-House.
18 Aug. Thur On watch at East Wharf.
19 " Fri. Company's day. At 6 A. M. the 22nd English regiment and Hessian Body regiment and Landgrave left their Long Island camp in boats and crossed over to New York. The Hessian regiments took up their old quarters, the 22nd English regiment took the camp in which the Anspach and Bayreuth regiments had been, while the latter removed to quarters in Bloomingdale. Most of the regiments, also Hessians, Grenadiers, Yagers and English Light Infantry were still on Long Island, as protection on account of the *Roth Island* scare.

24 Aug. Thur. Towards 8 o'clock a fire broke out

in the suburbs, not far from *Bonkershill*, in a rope walk and a brewery owing to the great quantity of pitch there. But it was soon put out.

28 Aug. Mon   Sick again with a boil on my foot. From this day to the 31st I was sick with a sore foot and confined to quarters. Pay in August 26/- $\frac{1}{2}$d

2 Sept. Saturday. Again Hessian promotions had arrived by a ship. Our Col. v. Goose was made Major General in *Prinz Carl's* regiment, our Col. v. Hinte commanded Donop's regiment temporarily. Curses be upon Fate! that persecutes me. I shall hope no more. But from this moment I shall endeavor to get away from the Hessians at the first opportunity. Oh! could I but manage to escape on board a pirate vessel! Could I but die, or at least have no more suffering! I am beside myself!

4 Sept. Mon.   Watch on West Wharf.
5   "   Tues.   Company's day.
6   "   Wed.   I demanded my discharge without knowing, myself, to what service I should turn. But Lieut. Col. v. Hinte and Capt. v. Donop talked me over by all manner of promises. I yielded. No one was to be preferred to me again. So the next day I wrote again to General v. Donop and v. Junker in Hesse.

10 Sept. Sun.   On watch at General *Klinton's*.
11   "   Mon.   Company's day.
13   "   Wed.   On watch Sugar house with 1 Corporal & 21 privates.

16 Sept. Sat. Admiral *Rotny* (Rodney) arrived with 10 ships of the line, without the other ships, from the West Indies. He himself came to New York on the 18th, but the fleet (the destination of which was not yet exactly known) lay in proper order off Sandy Hook. Much was also spoken about a French fleet, as to where it was likely to go. Also about several captured English transport ships of the fleet that had left here a short time ago for England, with which the English Generals *Tryon*, *Pattison* and *Mattheow* had gone, on being ordered to England.

17 Sept. Sun   Regiment's day.
18 "   Mon.   On watch at Sugar House.
19 "   Tues. On reserve picket.
20 "   Wed   Company's day.
21 "   Thurs. Pay parade.
22 "   Fri.   At 3 P. M. the whole garrison of New York, English, Hessians and Militia, had to turn out and form a line on the North River (in honor of the victory of Lieut. Gen. *Cornwallis* in South Carolina over the Rebels, by whom tents, flags and guns, besides many dead, wounded and prisoners were left to our side,) and fired three rounds *of joy*, at a signal of 7 rockets from the ramparts of *Bonkershill* and their guns, besides the shouts of joy. The Hessian regiments had their line in the valley below *Bonkershill*.

23 Sept. Sat. On commissariat watch. At the regimental parade a deserter from . von Knipphaussen's regiment ran the gantlet.

25 Sept. Mon. To-day I had one of the boils cut open that had troubled me for some time under my arm.

26 Sept. Tues. On watch Sick Rebels Prison.
27 "   Wed. Company's day.
28 "   Thur. To-day some distinguished inhabitants of New York were arrested for having been in correspondence with the Rebels. They were all betrayed, in a list of names, to General *Klinton* by a deserting Rebel General who had arrived here, named Arnold, a German ; for the same reason more inhabitant were daily taken to the prison (Provo). An Adjutant, Major André of the 54th English regiment of General *Klinton*, having been sent on a secret errand, was caught by the Rebels and hanged as a spy, which caused much excitement among the English.

Pay in September 26/- 3d

7 Oct. Sat. At 8 A. M., after my round, I was put on sharp command at a little place on the North

River called *Paulus Hook* whither every two weeks 1 Captain, 3 subalterns, 9 sub-officers, 2 drummers and 100 privates of the Hessian and Anspach regiments in New York, were sent, in addition to the English regiment (then the 54th) which was stationed on *Paulus Hook*. But owing to contrary winds, we had to lie on the water till 3 P. M before the boats could get us over. Every *commando* of the 3 Hessian regiments had quarters in different barracks; Donop's regiment in the so-called *Stackat* redoubt. N.B. In the day-time only 1 sub-officer and 3 privates were sent as watch to the 2 log-houses that stood there on one side; but in the evening a picket as re-enforcement In the middle log-house, however, near the crossing to New Jersey, there was, day and night, a considerable body of men, and in the ramparts behind the 3 log houses the *commandos* lay.

8 Oct. Sun. On watch in block-house on the right.
13 " Frid. Do.
14 " Sat. Field picket at block-house on the left.
15 " Sun. Early this morning the Hessian regiment of Bose, which was on Long Island, left by ship (though themselves not knowing whither), but halted for further orders at Sandy Hook till the 8th of November, Wednesday The English Guard regiment and some Light Infantry Grenadiers went with them to Charlestown, as it was asserted. Also Major General Bose as commander. Also recruits and other men belonging to the regiments in South Carolina and Georgia. In the direction of the sea we often heard reports of cannon. Some English frigates sailed out from New York, but came straight back again and soon after arrived (as we were informed later on) the English recruit fleet from England, which was a beautiful sight from *Paulus Hook*. But the long delay of the Irish provision fleet for us caused us to hope little good. We received nothing but salt beef and oat-grits meal and bad zwieback.

18 Oct. Wed. We on *Paulus Hook* heard that the

Body regiment and ours had received orders to march next day, the 19th, into the winter-quarters assigned to us, the Body regiment to Bloomingdale, Donop's to Fort Knipphaussen in their former huts. The detached commando of these regiments was to be relieved on the arrival of the other regiments in New York As soon as I heard this I obtained a furlough, gave my effects in the safe-keeping of the Lieut. Colonel's baggage and had myself immediately taken back by the *Paul's Hook* ferry I saw in New York the newly arrived recruits being distributed among the regiments, also the Chasseurs, who had also arrived, the same that last year were to have gone to Charlestown, but had been driven to England. They entered their regiments again Among the recruits that had arrived there were some unfortunate persons of high social rank, such as one Lieut. v. Makebrand who had been in Prussian service in the Free Corps and the former Prussian Councillor of War *Schmalz* who had been presented by the Landgravine of Cassel with the *port épée* of an officer, but who otherwise was only a sub-officer with the Yagers—and several others whose names I have not recorded.

19 Oct. Thur. On watch in block house on the right.

21 " Sat. We had been anxiously waiting to be relieved ever since yesterday, but there was a calm and, as we could not sail, we were taken over to New York in flat boats to be relieved. In New York there were now the following regiments. Hessian· Erb Prinz, Prinz Carl, Landgrave. English: 42nd and 22nd regiments. The 42nd Scotch and the Bayreuth and Anspach regiments. At one o'clock we arrived in New York At 4 we went out again and at 8 o'clock P. M. we arrived at our hut camp at Fort Knipphaussen. After the companies had played, (drawn lots) we, being the Lieut. Colonel's Company, got our huts on a different hill from last year, but we had enough repairing to do on the old huts The whole neighborhood

was, in comparison with last year, quite unrecognizable, the woods and bushes having been cut away. We now had our fire-wood furnished us, and a sorry affair it was.

24 Oct. Tues   Reserve picket.

NB 25 " Wed.   On watch at Fort Knipphaussen. Last year the occupation of Fort Knipphaussen was counted as sharp *commando*, but now, the line having been built across the front, it was only occupied by a Sub-officer's watch. Every regiment that was out here, gave out separate watches and *commandos*. We every four days, N° 8, as *commando*. Donop's was the only Hessian regiment out here. English the 80th, Robinson's, the 57th of Marte. Scotch: 76th and 100 Hessian and Anspach Yagers. On Long Island were the Hessian and English Grenadiers, the Hessian Yagers and Anspachers, the English Light Infantry and a few English regiments. On Staaten Island, Hessian regiments: Garrison, von Bienau. English: *Renny* Corps, *Thumer's* Hussars and a few other English. Mirbach's regiment again remained in their old hut camp at Martin's Wharf and Harlem.

31 Oct. Tues.   To-night, after thundering and raining hard, it began to grow very cold and it commenced to snow for the first time this year. N.B. We only sent out two pickets, our regiment before the front of the regiment, on the North River in the redoubt N° 8, but the latter only every 4 days.

Pay received in October 26/ – ½d.

1 November.   On field picket in front of the regiment.

2 " Frid.   On working command with 11 privates at *Morisini*. All our wood for fuel, building and fortifying was procured in *Morisina*, a piece of land back of number 8 redoubt and which once belonged to a Rebel Colonel. In his fine house not far from our camp the Generals were in the habit of

lodging, at present our Brigadier Major General von Lossberg. To cut and bring in wood from this place, until it be all used up, men are daily sent from all the regiments around here, and the royal wagons. This morning the recruits for *Knobloch's* regiment left here for New York and thence to the fleet which had been lying at anchor for some time off Sandy Hook, in order to get to their regiments

6 Nov Mon Company's day.

8 " Wed. The whole army again received bread for only 5 days (5 lbs.) and rice for 2 days. The captive Rebels in New York had now been all exchanged for Hessian prisoners of Knipphaussen and Lossberg's and other regiments, also English soldiers who were hourly expected in New York.

To-day the fleet spoken of on the 15th October had sailed from New York and Sandy Hook.

9 Nov. Thur Reserve picket

10 " Frid. At last the long wished for provision fleet from Cork arrived here, but some of the ships had been captured. There were many unfavorable though doubtful stories afloat regarding General and Lord Cornwallis in South Carolina.

12 Nov. Sun. On active command in Charles Redoubt. N.B. The officer of the 76th Scotch regiment who was in command of the Charles redoubt sent out some men beyond Philipp's House on a foraging expedition. We Hessians were below the redoubt in the watch-house besides 4 English Dragoons who had, by day, a post above the river. The latter joined the expedition and I sent three men also, who, a few hours later, brought back plenty of apples and potatoes.

13 Nov Mon. Company's day.
15 "   Wed. Watch on Fort Knipphaussen.
18 "   Frid. Company's day.
21 "   Mon. Watch at front
24 "   Frid. At 5 A. M., at day-break, a body of about 16 Rebels had left Staaten Island and crossed the water from *Liesbethtown* on a foraging expedition.

Some of them, however, were caught. Our men not knowing their number began to fire and lighted the alarm signals whereat there was great excitement.

26 Nov. Sun. Reserve picket.
27 " Mon. Watch at Fort Knipphaussen.
29 " Wed. On watch at Charles redoubt.

Our regiment, being the furthest from New York and the provisions therefore having to be carried a long distance, again received their full allowance of rations, to wit; bread, rice, pease, and oatmeal. The other regiments had received theirs on the last provision day.

30 Nov. Thur. Company's day.
Pay received in November 26/– 3d.

1 December, Frid Regiments day.
2 " Sat. This evening the Graf's Grenadiers left the *Fleschen* for *Brookly. Ferry*, and on the 3rd in the evening the 80th English regiment and the *Loyal American regiment* received orders to be ready to march at a moment's notice.

3 Dec. Sun, On working command in wood magazine at foot of Cox's hill with 3 men

5 Dec. Tues. Company's day.
6 " Wed. Letters have again arrived from Hesse by an English packet boat Lieut. Donop was appointed chamberlain (Kammerjunker) of the Duke of Mecklenburg-Schwerin. Meanwhile I was congratulated by the regiment as officer But until further information should arrive, we knew nothing definite about it. My continual suffering has changed my disposition. I leave the future willingly to a higher and kind fate.

8 Dec. Frid. · Field picket.
10 " Sun. Watch at Fort Knipphaussen.

N.B. I was detached with 15 men to the watch on Laurel Hill, to relieve the English there. But when I arrived, the 76th Scotch regiment had already relieved them It was a mistake of the Adjutant General. For me, however, it was counted a watch.

11 Dec. Mon. Reserve picket.

This afternoon the Hessian Garrison Grenadier Battalion of Graf came here in the place of the 80th English regiment which left. They encamped in their huts. Likewise the 38th regiment in place of the Loyal American regiment, and also in their huts. The former regiments marched this morning, the first to New York, the second to Long Island with orders to be ready to embark. All the women and children belonging to the regiments under the above orders had quarters given them on Long Island at *Fleschings-Fleg*. The regiments, however, remained under orders ready to march, and a few days later they and some others thereto designated, sailed for South Carolina.

Now, by degrees, the last captives of Knipphaussen's and Lossberg's regiments—and several that were to be exchanged for Rebel prisoners in New York—arrived here and had their quarters for the time being in New York.

Lieut. Col *Ganson* of the 17th regiment, who the year before had been captured with his regiment on Stony Point and had now been exchanged, asked the commanding General for an examination to prove his innocence, which was accorded him and published in the orders. At the conclusion of the examination he was submitted, as being not fully guilty, to a punishment that was not made known and thereupon set at liberty again

13 Dec. Wed. Company's day.
14 " Thur. Active service in N° 8 Redoubt.
18 " Tues. Company's day.

I gave Lieut. Colonel v. *Hinte* a perspective situation plan, which I had executed myself, of most of the redoubts of this neighborhood, which greatly pleased him.

23 Dec. Sat. Reserve picket and on work command at front with 5 men.

24 Dec. Sun. Active command on North or Cox's Hill (Sub N.B.)

N.B. The circumvallation line in front of Laurel Hill being completed, that made *Nord River* and Cox Hill an out-post and there were regularly 1 officer, 2 x (?), 1 drummer and 20 privates there, composed of a combination of Donop's and Graf's Grenadiers. Now there were only 2 iron twelve pounders there under superintendence of the English Artillery.

25 Dec. Tues. The first Christmas holiday. Up to now we had had, with the exception of a few cold days, quite warm weather with thick, stinking fog mixed with rain, so that we had to apprehend many cases of sickness.

27 Dec. Thurs. On field picket.
28 " Frid. Company's day.
Pay received in December 26 /− ½d.

The following were the Hessian regiments in America and their names, as they were called on their arrival there, and as they were subsequently changed (but the Brigades changed too often).

Yager Corps under the command of Col. v. Donop (since 1777 Lt. Col. v. Wurmb),

1st Grenadier Battalion of Linsing,
2nd   "   "   " Munchenroth [since '80 Loewenstein],
3rd   "   "   " Lengecke,
4th   "   "   , a garrison battalion, of Koehler,
(since '7– Graff, since '81 Blatte).

1st Musketeer Regt. Leib Regmt (since '83 *Erb Prinz*),
2nd   "   "   Erb Prinz Fusileers. Since '83 Prinz Field Inf'try,
3rd   "   "   Prince Carl,
4th   "   "   Landgrave, (since '79) formerly von Wuttgenau since '83 Leib regiment.

5th	Musketeer	Reg'm't	Fusileers Tittfort,
6th	"	"	von Donop,
7"	"	"	von Mirbach (since '80 von Yung Lossberg),
8th	"	"	v. Trimbach (since '79 v. Bose)
9th	"	"	v. Lossberg } fusileers
10th	"	"	v. Knipphaussen }

Garrison Regiments.

11th Grenadier Reg't. von Rall (In '76 still Woellwurth) since 80 v. Dangschinelli,
12th   von Wiesenbach (since 80 v. Knobloch),
13th   von Seitz—since '78 (formerly v. Stein),
14th   von Bienau,
15th   von Hiene (since 80 v. Benning).

(End of 1780.)

P. S. The winter of this year was hardly noticeable, and pleasanter than some autumns. And very desirable for us on account of the huts and the scarcity of wood; for nearly all the sticks around here were pulled up and even of the smallest bushes there was very little to be seen. My eye was hardly able to recognize the place again, not having seen it during one year's absence.

1781.

Free Corporal in Lieut. Col. Hinte's Company Hesse Cassel Musketeer Regiment of Donop.

January. In the hut camp near Fort Knipphaussen.
2 " In the night upwards of 100 men of the Rebels at the instigation probably of one of the traitors in New York (who are to be found there and throughout the island) were so rash as to cross over the North River from Jersey in flat boats in order

to take Gen Clinton out of his own quarters in New York. The accomplishment of the act would have been very extraordinary, if they could have succeeded in spite of the many sentries stationed about. It was enough that they certainly meant to succeed. But Heaven itself had not wished it to be so; for the row galleys [Rohgellen] which were usually there had gone away and of course it had been immediately made known to the Rebels. But they had the wind and tide so against them, that they could not land and so they had to go back All this was afterwards reported to Gen Clinton, (but how, I do not know), and he formed the intention of revenging himself in a way which was before unknown.

3 Jan. On watch at Fort Knipphaussen.
4 " On reserve picket.
5 " Company's day.
6 " At 6 o'clock in the morning Gen. Clinton went to *Staaten* Island with English Grenadiers, 2 Hessian regiments and other troops, not alone on account of the above (his attempted capture), but, among many other things, more especially on account of the rumored mutiny which some regiments of the Rebels are said to have attempted. He sent some parts of them across to Jersey, but they came back a few days afterwards without having accomplished anything of importance. So much we heard about it in our camp.

7 Jan. On active duty at N° 8.
9 " I was detailed on working command, in pretty cold weather, with 4 Grenadiers of Graf's Battalion (because we did service together) and 6 privates of our regiment to make fascines (not far from *Jonschen's* house) to repair old works.

11 Jan. Regiment's day.
12 " Company's day.
16 " On field picket. In the morning we were again mustered by the former English Inspector in front of the quarters of Gen. v. Lossberg at the so-called Morris House.

17 Jan. On the watch at Fort Knyphaussen.
18 " On reserve picket.
19 " On active service on *Cock's* or North River Hill.
21 Jan. Company's day.
22 " At four o'clock in the morning our reserve picket had to move out, because some Rebels (number not given) had stolen through the outposts of the refugee camp [revougl] on *Moresine* At first they did not fire, but cut down the first guard and burnt quite a number of houses of the refugee camp,¹ the great fire of which alarmed us. Some Rebels even stole along under N° 8 and cut off the ferry cable² there. At last, through some musket firing, assistance was sent out consisting of the reserve pickets, which pursued the Rebels a few miles, but did not accomplish anything more than to kill, wound and capture a few The Rebels gathering together in pretty large numbers, our men had to turn back, but without loss.
29 Jan. Company's day.
31 " On active service in N° 8.
Pay received in January 26/- ½d.

February In the hut-camp near Fort Knyphaussen.
1 Febr. On reserve picket.
2 " On watch, Fort Knyphaussen.
5 " On field picket
7 " Company's day.
14 " On active service in N° 8
15 " On reserve picket.
17 " On watch, Fort Knyphaussen. Many promotions arrived here again from Cassel, but for none

---

¹ There were "some huts of negroes and plantations and houses" south of the road which led up from the Harlem at the crossing-place or *Holland's Ferry* to Redoubt N° 8.—Delancey's corps used to occupy this locality protected by the guns of N° 8, and the fortifications across the Harlem on Laurel Hill The locality was called Morrisania. Doubtless the word (which seems to be) *revougl* was intended for this settlement

² Holland's Ferry across the Harlem to the foot of Laurel Hill.

but staff-officers. The Donop regiment got Col. Heymel for its commander (He had been Lieut. Col. of the Knyphaussen reg'm't.)

19 Febr. Company's day.
24 " On field picket.
25 " Regiment's day.
26 " On active service in N° 8.
27 " Company's day On reserve picket. We received the usual winter *douceur* again to-day · sub-officers and privates were paid 9d $\frac{1}{2}$ p'y each.

28 Febr. I bled myself again and for the first time in my left foot.

Pay received in February 26 /− 7$\frac{1}{2}$d.

March. In the hut camp as before.

1 March I received from the Company my annual small equipment money, 13 English shillings and 4 Stuyvers, which made 4 Hessian thalers. Gen. Clinton had announced in his orders the advantage which the Brigadier Gen. Arnold (who had deserted from the Rebels) had gained in Richmond with the English troops and others he had with him. He had burnt all the stores of provisions and ammunition there and lost but few men.

2 March. On regiment's watch
4 " The 16th Scotch regiment, which had been stationed here on Laurel Hill, marched to New York, pursuant to the order which had been given some time before, to march with the English light infantry, the Hessian Grenadiers, the 42nd English and the Hessian Crown Prince regiments. On the other hand there came out here to reenforce us in the fort, the 57th English regiment and the Knyphaussen and Lossberg men who had come out of imprisonment; also some of Bose's regiment and several recruits, which together were called the "Composition" [Componirten], amounting to 230 men.

5 March. Company's day. The above mentioned troops embarked, excepting the Hessian Grenadiers

who again remained behind. They cast anchor off Staten Island until soon after they set sail. The cause of their departure is a secret to us.

10 March. After the reading of the new articles of war, I had to carry the flag into the new quarters of the Commander Col. *Heimel.*

11 March. N. B. In the morning I went to see Col. Heimel because he had already asked for me, as my Lieut Colonel had spoken of me to him and recommended me to his attention. Of this he willingly and very kindly assured me and out of politeness I was obliged to pay him my respects as Commander of the regiment.

12 March. On field picket.
13 " On regiment's watch.
14 " On reserve picket
15 " Company's day.
18 " On active command to guard the royal wagons while getting wood 3 English miles beyond *Independence.*[1]

19 March. In my hut.
21 " Company's day
22 " On the watch, Fort Knipphaussen.
23 " On reserve picket.
25 " Sunday, Church parade in a stable near Morris' House.
30 March. On active duty in N° 8.
31 " Company's day.
Pay received in March . 26/- ½d.

April. In hut camp as before.
1 April. On the watch, Fort Knyphaussen, Church parade in a stable near Morris' House.
2 April. The Hessians had been ordered by Lieut Gen. von Knyphaussen to re-commence drilling to-day; but as it rained it was not done until the 4th.

[1] Fort Independence, called by the British after its capture by them, No 4 The residence of Wm Ogden Giles now occupies its site. Gen Richard Montgomery owned the farm on which the fort was erected in 1775

3 April. On field picket. I, as well as the privates, received 1 English shilling for the superintendence of the wood cutters in the magazine for one day.

4 April. On reserve picket. Company's day

6 " Our captain of arms in the Company being sick, and it being my turn to make the grand rounds, I had to go with two other sub-officers and 30 privates of the regiment to Long Island and near Newtown (beyond two churches which stood near together). There I had them dig clay for coloring, a little one side on the right. From Fort Knyphaussen over *Hell Gotts* ferry to Mistor's Wharf is 11 miles. For the double passage each person had to pay 7 stuyvers, which Lieut. Col. Hinte re-imbursed to him.

8 April. Regiment's day.
9 " On watch, Fort Knyphaussen.
12 " Company's day.
14 " On reserve picket.
18 " On field picket.
19 " On watch, Fort Knyphaussen.
20 " Frid. In the night a loud noise was heard on our lines, also some firing. In front of the line, from a French deserter who had come in, we learned that the enemy had approached very near to our lines. How far this was well founded will be better and more certainly determined in the future. Several men had raised a false alarm which happened very often here.

21 April. Sat. Another packet boat had arrived here from Germany, but it brought no special news. Lieut. von Donop now demanded his dismission, which he had applied for last year. As for myself, I still entertain hopes founded on the promises made me, but I am so uncertain in regard to many things that I do not know myself how I shall manage. I shall await the development of circumstances here to see whether I have been deceived or not.

23 April Mon. Company's day
26 " Thurs. On active command, N°. 8.
27 " Frid. On command in N°. 8. A corporal

of Knipphaussen's regiment *Fuchter* in the combined battalion of Major von Stein (where I was in command as Sub-officer) compromised himself by falling asleep. He believed that I was to blame and therefore sent me a card, in the afternoon, by an orderly of the Old Lossberg regiment, requesting me to meet him at a certain place where he wished to speak to me. I went there and after I had waited a long time (a good place it was and I had no one with me) he finally came. At first he only wanted to "preach," and then he did not want to fight there, but to go to another place I tried to force him to fight here and threatened him with a drawn sword. Just then 3 other Sub-officers appeared whom he had evidently appointed. Thereupon I sheathed my sword and held it defensively towards them, having no one on my side. But they assured me that they did not intend to join in the dispute, but only desired to dissuade me in a friendly way. I refused to listen to them. So he went with me to his other place. But there we found a number of Sub-officers and privates of his battalion approaching the place, from which I inferred that he had already been bragging a great deal about the affair. So he requested me to postpone it until another time which I agreed to, should I not be detained by my duties But nothing came of it, and soon after they marched away from this neighborhood Some transport ships with Hanau and Zerbst recruits had arrived in New York, but they were to proceed further to their regiments in Canada

28 April. Sat On regiment's watch.

This evening the whole garrison of New York fired salutes to "Victory" on account of the victory gained by Lord *Cornwallis* over the Rebels under Gen. Green in North Carolina, in the month of March of this year, during which engagement however the Hessian regiment von Bose had done almost all the fighting under the command of Lieut. Col. *Dubby* but had lost many in dead and wounded.

29 April. Sun. On reserve picket.
30 " Mon. This noon the combined battalion of Major von Stein which had been on Laurel Hill marched to New York, (they had not received the order until the night before), but when the Anspach and Bayreuth regiment (without the English) sailed on the 1st. of May, (their port of destination was unknown to us), they went to Long Island and the two Hessian Grenadier Battalions went to New York in garrison.

Pay received in April 26/– 3d.

1 May. Tues. Company's day.
5 " Sat. I took an emetic having had a bowel complaint for some days past.
6 May. Sun. Field picket.
7 " Mon. Provost watch.
7 and 8 May. Mon. and Tues. There was such astonishing wind and rain here that I do not remember to have experienced the like as long as we have been here. It incommoded me all the more as I was on watch.
9 May. Wed Reserve picket.
11 " Frid. In command of Cox's Hill. While in command on Cox's hill I irritated a Rebel officer exceedingly by asking him, when he passed under a flag of truce from North River towards New York, whether he was a Rebel officer? He answered with ruffled dignity, "No! But of the Independent States!" Whereupon I replied, "But against their legitimate King and subjects that had defected for a time." I spoke warmly and he kept silent. N. B. This conversation was carried on in the English language. Likewise in the evening another boat came past at 9 o'clock from New York. Hearing of it through the sentinel and Lieut. Waldeck of Graf's Grenádier Battalion placing confidence in me, I hastened down the hill to the water's edge ordering four men to follow me with their muskets. I called to them. At first they

pretended not to hear, especially when they perceived that we were Hessians. But when I assured them that I would have them fired upon, if they did not immediately send a boat to shore to me and as they did not know but what my threatened firing meant that from the guns in the redoubt, the Captain himself came to me & proved to me by his pass that he had been ordered to convey some men to a certain place. Thereupon I permitted him to proceed enjoining him, however, to keep further off from the shore, telling him that it was not customary in times of war, under any pretext whatever, to pass a sentinel at night without high permission.

13 May. Sun   Company's day.

14 May. Mon   This noon when our regiment returned from the drill, about 12 small ships came sailing up the river from New York with our refugees on board, who, for a purpose unknown to us, landed just across the river below what used to be Fort Lee, near a house. They showed their joy by firing three rounds with their small guns, with the usual English *Hura!* and after a short pause they ascended the acclivity up to Fort Lee The ships remained lying at anchor a short distance from the shore. Before it grew dark the Refugees engaged in much shooting with the Rebels in the woods, until night closed in. Then they went out to the ships in boats and the next morning down again.

Likewise a few hundred of the Refugees marched from *Morrisini* to the neighborhood of Philipp's House (in front of the line) at the same time as the first mentioned on the Jersey, and that very evening they sent in some of their wounded and Rebel prisoners. By the way, the ships of the transported Refugees remained in the North River and a three-masted armed ship came up from New York. After that thirty men of the English and the same number of Hessians took turns during six days in reconnoitering below North River or Cox Hill.

16 May. Wed   Watch, Fort Knipphaussen.

17 May. Thurs. In the afternoon there were terrific thunderstorms, which were the cause of a soldier of the 57th regiment, on sentinel duty, on the east side of Laurel Hill being struck dead by lightning, and another while fishing.

Our Refugees on Jersey were now rather quiet. They had fortified themselves considerably on the site of the former Fort Lee and they kept in there every evening, as also in one of their ships, under *Retiret Schuss* [within range of their guns]. The Rebels did not care to attack them any more. Our Refugees made some brave sallies.

18 May. Frid. Regiment's day.

This morning, at daybreak, when our Refugees landed, as usual, from their ships and went on Jersey, some of the Rebels had already placed themselves in ambush, so that a sharp exchange of fire began, with small guns. Finally our Refugees began to thunder with the 2 small amuzettes which they had with them. A couple of flat boats came over here from them to get more Refugees from *Morrisini* to go to their assistance. By those who had come over we were informed (for the firing had stopped) that on our side only one man had been slightly wounded, but two taken prisoners. About the losses of the Rebels they could tell us nothing definite, as our men were still in pursuit of them.

19 May. Sat.   Reserve picket
21   "   Mon.   Company's day.
22   "   Tues. We stopped drilling. Now and then we received good tidings from a part of our army in North and South Carolina to the effect that they had gained several important advantages over the Rebels. On the part of the English Lord Raden had especially distinguished himself; among the Hessians, Bose's regiment. Also from the sea there came many uncertain reports in regard to the French and Spanish as is usual in war times. But I shall never note down any-

thing that I do not positively know and only such things as concern our army. There are thousands of things that we hear nothing about, tho' sometimes they take place very near us. The foreign newspapers know sooner and better than we, especially when our side has been unfortunate. I myself have read European papers which contained accounts concerning occurrences in our army covering the past two years, in which I myself had been engaged, and they reported more correctly than many of us had been able to inform ourselves here.

23 May. Wed. On active command Cox's Hill.

Towards morning our Refugees had set fire to their fortifications on Jersey and some huts erected there and that very night at 12 o'clock they had again boarded their ships and after proceeding a few English miles towards New York they dropped anchor and lay in correct naval battle array, till towards evening when they all started for New York. This took place entirely contrary to our expectation, because they had previously and up to the last seriously endeavored to accomplish something important. But on the other hand they were in all cases superior, but too weak in themselves in resistance. All the prospects for this year are not of the best for us as against the enemy, and on account of our weakness we will not be able to undertake anything this year. Since therefore we shall probably remain here until winter, there are few places in our camp which have not been made into gardens. I too had two pretty spots near my hut for my garden in which I raised almost all the necessary vegetables, the seeds for which I procured in New York.

25 May Frid. Regiment's watch.
26 " Sat. Reserve picket.
27 " Sun Field picket outside.
29 " Tues. It being left to the discretion of every commander of the Hessian regiments to continue the drilling exercises a few times beyond the

regular drilling time, if they thought it advantageous to the regiments under them, our Col. Heymel, being dissatisfied, wished to continue the exercises. Therefore we were obliged to drill this morning at half past six with the flags which I as Real Free Corporal had to carry, and the articles of war were read to the regiment.

30 May. Wed. Company's day.
31 " Thur. Reserve picket.
Pay received in May 26/- ½d

2 June. Sat I was again detailed on work command to *Laurell Hill* with 18 men of Donop's regiment and Graff's Grenadier Battalion (without the English) to make repairs here and there on the fortifications.

3 June. Sun. Watch, Fort Knipphaussen. We had to house ourselves near the Fort and began to wear linen trousers while on duty

4 June. Mon. The second Pentecost holiday. That night Lieut. Col. Emmerich who really only belonged to the "Suite" of Gen. *Klington* without being himself in command of any troops, crossed over the North River (below our picket hut and opposite Fort Lee) with a few other officers and several privates of our regiment and they caught a Rebel spy there in a house, returning without being discovered by the Rebels.

N. B. An amusing incident, which seemed, however, to us Germans to be a repulsive occurrence must be related here. I met a soldier of the 38th English regiment who asked me to tell him where our clergyman lived. He said they had none in their regiment and the one in Donop's regiment had refused, when he had desired to be married to a woman whose acquaintance he had made in the street a few hours before. He said he had received permission from the commander of his regiment to marry. I gave him a short answer, but could not help laughing and proceeded on my way. Such things and a thousand others of like or worse character were not rare here. A certain Sergeant of the above named English regiment, a handsome young fellow, had been married sixteen times to loose women of the town by different English and German chaplains, through shrewd contrivances, without the consent of his officers and told me too that he hoped to do so often again, before making up his mind to take the last one in real earnest.

 7 June. Thurs. Reserve picket
 8 " Frid. On commando in N° 8
 10 " Sun. Company's day.
 11 " Mon. Watch, Fort Knipphaussen.
 14 " Thurs. Field picket. At daybreak the Graf (Hessian) Grenadiers that had been here marched off and into camp with the other three Hessian Grenadier Battalions before New York. Into their old huts came the Young Lossberg's regiment, and in the huts deserted by him at Martin's Wharf, there stood only one watch of *Pr Ch*. At New York were still in camp, of the English, the 22nd and 43rd regiments and the 76th Scotch. The Hessian Body regiment was in camp at *Johnschen* House; the *Prz. Charl* regiment by the 7th mile-stone, east side.

 17 June. Sun. Church parade in stable near Morris' house.
 19 June. Tues. Regiment watch.
 20 " Wed. Reserve picket.
 22 " Frid. On command in Charles Redoubt.
 23 " Sat. Company's day.
 24 " Sun. Being Saint John's day (Johannis Tag) most of the men in our camp made merry and had music I went walking during the day, and did not retire till late, after having laughed at many a soldier during the dances or sighed over them, but chiefly despising them for their imprudence, when I saw what promiscuous exchanges were made with their wives. And any modest observer who wanted to could see through it all, but their husbands could

not. I could not help deploring such a state of things and became acquainted with many very strange occurrences.

27 June. Wed. Regiment's day Towards evening letters arrived for our regiment by a packet-boat bringing news from Hesse. We did not get them, however, until the following day I was placed on watch after which Lieut Col von Hinte sent for me and showed me a letter from General von Jungken-Münzer of Cassel in which he regretted that, Lieut v. Donop and Ensign von Knoblauch having obtained their desired dismission from our regiment, their places had been filled by v Haussen and Henckel as Ensigns in consequence of many applications by them to the Landgrave. But he (Gen. von Jungcken) assured me through the Landgrave that I should certainly be placed in the next occurring vacancy. Lieut. Col. v. Hinte seemed to be very sorry for me I thanked him, but asked for my immediate dismission, stating my resolve (which was fixed) to apply to Gen. *Klinton* for a free passage to Europe. But he dissuaded me very seriously with all possible further promises. But I would not be deterred. Finally he advised me to be patient, he would speak seriously with Lieut. Col von Hinte, with which I had to content myself. But I wanted to call on von Lossberg who had just become Lieut. General. But he had ridden in to New York There was an old sergeant major in our regiment who had been made an Ensign in the Garrison regiment of Benning. I was beside myself and so full of grief as I had hardly ever been before, which my scarcely-to-be-dried tears proved.

28 June. Thur. Watch, Fort Knipphaussen. The Hessian Yagers arrived here today from Long Island and went into camp below Cox Hill at the place where the huts of the former 17th English regiment had been and they received tents from the Landgrave regiment and ours, because they could get no bushes or wood around there to build huts with.

29 June. Fri.   Reserve picket.
30 "   Sat.   Company's day.
Pay, June, 26/- 3d.

July. From the 7th. on, in the tent camp, near the hut camp, and from the 14th on, in Fort Knipphaussen itself, first the Body regiment for a few days and then the Lieut Col. Company.

In the beginning of this month several hundred men of the Waldeck regiment arrived here, who together with the 60th and 16th English Regiments had [started] for West Florida [and had been] taken prisoners by Spanish ships from there [mit accord] and brought here. Their lot had been unfortunate; but we here heard almost nothing except what the prisoners themselves told us That shows how little or at least how contrarily we heard the dark sides of our affairs.

2 July. Mon. Lieut. Col v. Hinte sent Capt. Donop himself to me to persuade me to stay and my grief having somewhat subsided and it being moreover dangerous to wander around here with no one to depend upon but yourself, I went to the Colonel and Lieut. Colonel and promised to be patient, whereupon I received much encouragement. Almost every day now we had much vexatious trouble about going on patrol, since the arrival of our Yagers; and the Rebels gave us much annoyance too On both sides there was loss. The Rebels were at times extraordinarily bold. One of the Mounted Yagers, the Yager Cavalry Captain von Rau, who had already received permission from the Landgrave to return home for two years, had requested leave to join one of the patrols, and he received two shots one in the breast, the second in the leg.

3 July. Tues. On field picket When, the night before, a patrol of ours had gone out, the Rebels had been waiting in ambush in the ditches below Independence and had suddenly opened [Pelotons] fire on our men and thereby wounded many; for they had not

expected it. Some Rebels had also crossed over the North River in boats, from Jersey, and they marched within full view of us, in whole regiments, flags flying and bands playing, down around the lower Courtland House. Many of them, however, were wounded and killed by our Yagers, also some brought in prisoners. On our side also about 40 Yagers were wounded and only one mounted Yager killed One man deserted from the detachment of our regiment. Our regiments held themselves in readiness for further orders. The firing by the Yagers continued till the afternoon. The Rebels, as we were informed by two deserters, had gone into camp at Philipp's House with the French numbering 16,000. What further will happen must transpire without any more conjecturing

4 July. Wed. We Sub-officers and privates got some wood money that was due to us, each man 3 English shillings 3 *and* $^3/_3$ pence

5 July. Thurs. Regimental watch.

6 " Frid I stayed till break of day with an English Corporal who "treated" me.

8 July. Sun. Company's day.

10 " Tues. All the bed clothes of our regiment had to be given up, and since the 7th we had to put up out tents along the front.

11 July. Wed. Reserve picket.

14 " Sat. At 4 this afternoon our Company together with the Body Company had to move unexpectedly into tents in Fort Knipphaussen, on the right side, because the Rebels were constantly expected, according to what was heard of the measures they were taking. Gen. *Klington* was here this afternoon too, inspecting everything. But it was an execrable life there in the Fort, and we hope for a speedy better issue.

13 July. Frid. Field watch.

16 " Mon. On command in N° 8.

17 " Tues. Field picket.

18 " Wed. Company's day. We had a muster-

ing again by the same inspector of the English troops, at 7 A M. taking turns. The whole regiment has quarters in front of Fort *Knyph*.

19 July. Thur This afternoon two frigates and several transport ships arrived here with guns, also sloops that a few days ago had sailed up the North River on what kind of an expedition we did not know. They now returned and brought back one captured Rebel sloop. As long as these ships were *forwards* and out of our sight, except those watch ships that lay alongside of us, guns were fired every day on the ships towards the land. Looking over towards the Heights of Jersey we could see many Rebels there.

20 July. Frid Working command. N. B At work with one Corporal and 30 privates of the regiment, to demolish the lines that had been built by the Rebels and by us, as has been related, on the north side near Fort *Knypph*.

21 July. Sat. Watch, Fort Knipphaussen.

22 " Sun. At 9 A. M. the combined forces of the Rebels and French, in whole columns, came marching over, where Independence had been, and up towards us, in different divisions and 2 of them, below what used to be King's Redoubt, had guns with which they shot at our fleeing Refugees, and also at the camp of our Yagers, which latter had retreated within our line after taking down their tents. From Laurel Hill a few shots were fired from the Fort with 24 pounders at the Rebels, whereupon they immediately retired behind the height. Afterwards we saw that several columns of the Rebels marched off behind N° 8 to the end of *Morrisinie;* but being terribly bombarded from Harlem, from *Shnek-hill,* they were seen retreating into the thickets and returning again. A French regiment lay not far from N° 8 to protect the others. Altogether one could see by their camps, which were on the plain above Independence, that they must be very strong. To night, though we had certainly expected it (an attack), they were very quiet.

23 July. Mon This morning, at the request of Lieut. Col. von Hinte, I repaired, with 12 men, the parapet on the two front bulwarks (bastions) in Fort *Knypph*. which in consequence of the concussion by the morning and evening cannonading had caved in a little. This morning our Lieut Gen. *Klinton* rode up the front of the line with a small following and some Light Horse to reconnoiter and he was saluted by guns, "loaded blind", from our 3 exterior redoubts. The whole afternoon the Rebels attacked our outposts, but mostly in *Morrisinie*, in Harlem whence however they always had soon to recede before our fire. Towards evening the whole Rebel army began to move away again, in a very changeable manner, that is, not knowing exactly where to go. Our Yager Corps pursued them a short distance, but on account of their good order could not get at them. On their return our Yagers went into their old camp and now everything was quiet again. We heard that the Rebel army had encamped 14 English miles forwards from our line. Very fluctuating reports kept their intentions very dark to us.

— July — The Anspach and Bayreuth Regiment, as also that of v. Bose (but, as has been said, still lying at Sandy Hook) had arrived and were to disturb Rhode Island which was supposed to be the cause of the departure of the Rebel army from our line here. Many pontoons were floated up here from New York and were placed in the "Line-barrier" and had to be watched for a reason unknown to us. The truth must soon appear.

26 July Thur. Company's day.

27 " Frid. On watch in Stone Redoubt with 7 privates.

28 July. Sat In the night an alarm was raised among us (probably by a spy) giving out that the Rebels and French were again marching up against our line. N° 8 was reenforced and our Yagers, as before, again left their camp and came, with bag and

baggage, in with us. We all were obliged to remain awake, but nothing happened. We heard nothing of the enemy, nor saw anything the next morning. It rained very hard.

30 July. Mon. Reserve picket.
Pay received in July 26/- ½d.

3 August. Frid. Provost watch.
5 " Sun. Field picket in N° 8.
7 " Tues. Company's day.
8 " Wed. In the tents in the Fort we, the two named Companies, had much to put up with. We were almost burnt up by the sun and almost swimming in the rain. Meanwhile our gardens, which the Companies below had to take charge of, were very useful. If we had wished to sell them we would have been able to make a handsome sum of Thalers. But as it was we used them for our own enjoyment.

9 Aug. Thur. Active command in N° 8.
11 " Sat. Watch, Fort *Knypph*.
The recruit fleet arrived in New York with Hessians, Zerbst Free Corps and Hanauers (the Zerbst Corps was sent to Paul's Hook under command of Col. Emmerich), but they were not allotted to their different positions until the fore-noon of the following day. This was in the city. In the evening they came to our regiment to the number of 34 men and also the before mentioned two Ensigns. Also one Sub-officer. But they were not allotted to their places in the Companies until the following morning. An insubordinate fellow ran the gantlet to day 6 times between 200 men.

13 Aug. Mon. On working command on *Forsed Hill* making banquettes on the palisades.
16 Aug. Thur. Watch, Fort Knipphaussen.
18 " Sat. This morning the two Hessian, i. e. Body and Charles, regiments marched from their camp at Jones House and occupied the Hessian Grenadier camp in New York, the latter taking their

former camp. In the afternoon the 54th English regiment came here from Paul's Hook and pitched their camp in front of the 38th regiment (near New York).

19 Aug. Sun. In the afternoon the *Pienau* Hessian Garrison regiment arrived here from Staten Island and had their camp between the 4 Hessian Grenadier Battalions and the 54th English regiment Likewise the English Grenadiers and Light Infantry from Long Island encamped at *Hell Gowns Pass*. The pontoons which for some time past had lain at the principal barrier were now taken for a bridge in *Harlem's Creek* near the Pioneer Huts. All these changes led us to anticipate, a few days hence, some as yet unknown expedition by Gen. *Klinton*.

20 Aug. Mon. Field picket in front of regiment.

21 " Tues. I went walking with Sergeant Heynemann, of my Company, to the Lengeck Grenadier Battalion which was now, like the rest, in camp at Jones House and saw again, after a year's separation, my old friend Mrs. Breitsprach, who was very glad to see me—but I was not. She had changed very much.

23 Aug Thur. Company's day. The *Pienau* Garrison regiment again left its camp and marched to New York, where the Grenadiers had stood. That put an end to our expecting an expedition. Likewise the Refugees left their camp near *Hol Ferry* and returned to their dwellings in *Morisini*. With the exception of one *commando* which they left behind (and a long distance from us) the French and Rebels had all retired to Jersey. Whether they will undertake anything from there or not, we must wait and see

24 Aug Frid. This morning all the Grenadiers left their camps again and marched to Long Island and from there to New York.

25 Aug. Sat. Watch, Fort Knipphaussen.

In the night the 57th regiment marched from Laurel Hill to N°—, thence to Staten Island. During the day the 54th regiment took possession of the camp at

Jone's House where the Grenadiers had been. And until further orders two Companies of Young Lossberg's regiment took the place of the 57th regiment.

28 Aug. Tues. In the evening our regiment (Lossberg) and the 38th English regiment had to give a watch as far as the 4th mile stone towards New York, because the 54th regiment had marched away again. But during the march to New York they had received the order to march back and they relieved our squads.

30 Aug. Thur. In the Royal Wood Magazine on the East River with 12 privates to unload wood.

31 Aug. Frid. Watch Stone Redoubt.

Pay received in August 26/- ½d.

1 Sept Sat. The 37th English regiment had encamped on the East side of *Mac Gowns Pass* where Prince Karl's regiment had been. The 37th regiment had been encamped on Long Island. To night the 38th English regiment unexpectedly received the order to march immediately. Also the 54th and 100 Yagers. They were to march to Long Island, but the 38th left their tents standing and all the women and children and disabled remained behind as hut and camp watch.

2 Sept. Sun. Field picket, front, on left.

3 " Mon. Active command N° 8.

4 " Tues. In the afternoon an English artilleryman deserted from Fort Knipphaussen. He quickly took off his clothes, jumped into the North River and got safely over, before our very eyes, to the Jersey side. Several shots were fired at him from the Stone Redoubt, but without injuring him, as he could dive well.

On the same day orders were given for us to be ready to embark. And the 37th and 43rd English and 42nd Scotch and 17th Drag.r regiment, English Light Infantry, Grenadiers, the Hessian Grenadiers and 400 Yagers, the Body regiment, Prinz Carl and the Garrison regiment of Bienau were all embarked by the 6th of this month, Thursday, and, as was said, were sent by

Gen. *Klinton* himself to the South to the aid of Gen. *Cornwall* where he was reported to be sadly penned in (especially by the French).

5 Sept. Wed. Company's day.

The pontoons below N̊ 8 were again removed and replaced in the line at the barrier, their old place. But the next evening they were again taken back to New York. Meanwhile we had very severe duty. The above named regiments were still at New York on the ships and several *dis-ordres* (countermands,) could not make us understand why they did not start, except that they said a strong French fleet, superior to ours, prevented General *Klinton* from permitting them to leave New York until a decisive naval battle had been fought. This same afternoon the watch ships lying in the North River sailed to New York.

6 Sept. Thur. On main barrier watch.

9 " Sun. This morning the remaining mounted Yagers with the horses of those who had been taken for the last fleet (and had been obliged to leave their horses behind) took possession of the tent-camp at Morris House, but the remaining Hessian Yagers remained in camp below Cox's Hill. A few days ago the —th English regiment had arrived in New York from England by ship. At first there were said to be many regiments, but the number gradually decreased and this is now certain. To-day I took an emetic having had, for some time, a bad taste in my mouth that resulted from a stomach complaint. After that I felt very well.

The above regiments—of the 1st inst.—namely the 37th 54th— and 100 Yagers and some others led by General *Arnhold* had come back from the South and gone to New England, where he had set fire to many of the Rebel stores in the town of New London and plundered them, besides several other places. Afterwards, however, he had to retreat with heavy losses and the wounded were now arriving here.

11 Sept. Tues. Watch, Fort Knyphausen.

. 12 Sept. Wed. But he took the remainder and crossing over from Long Island went on the ships which were still lying off New York, to join the expedition. Our duty here changed from day to day and was very severe, and fevers commenced.

13 Sept. Thur. Field picket N° 8

14 " Frid. The 38th regiment had their tents taken down and their baggage sent after them—off New York

15 Sept. Sat. The above mentioned fleet sailed from New York but remained at anchor off Sandy Hook for what reason we didn't know.

The Loyal American Regiment had encamped at Jones House.

16 Sept. Sun. Watch, Fort Knyphaussen.

17 " Mon. The 37th English regiment took possession of the hut camp at Martin's Wharf.

18 Sept. Tues. Active command, Charles Redoubt.

NB 20 Sept. Thur. I was on the active picket, (a short distance in front of Jones House), called Landing Place, with 6 privates

A morning and evening gun being fired every day from Fort Knypphaussen, in a circuit around the fort, and the negligent aiming of the gunners causing most of the embrasures to be destroyed, Lieut. Col. von Hinte asked me to take as many soldiers as were necessary to do the work and repair the damage. At which I was occupied for several days.

21 Sept. Frid. This morning it was made known in our order that all the above named regiments and corps which had been off Sandy Hook were to leave the ships again and encamp on Staten Island until further orders.

22 Sept. Sat Regiment's day.

23 " Sun. Watch, Fort Knypphaussen.

All the officers and privates that belonged to the regiments in Virginia and had gone on board the ships the evening before were disembarked and placed in huts and barns at the Flag staff on Staten Island.

Received rations for 4 days

25 Sept. Tues. Company's day.

26 " Wed. Reserve picket. In New York the Royal English Prince Henry William had arrived from England.

27 Sept. Thur. Several desertions having occurred among the Hessians, a gallows was built in front of Fort Knyhaussen in order to excite fear

28 Sept Frid. Watch, Fort Knypphaussen.

29 " Sat. Field picket, N° 8.

Pay received in September 26/– 3d.

1 October. Mon. In *Shnak Hill* block house

This morning the portraits of the 3 Hessian officers who had deserted, von Masco, Fuhrer and Kleinschmid, and who had been away a long time, were fastened to the gallows In the afternoon our regiment had orders to prepare to march at short notice, and

2 Oct. Tues at 4 P. M. the regiment received orders to march immediately and to encamp until further orders at *Macc Gown's Pass* where Prince *Charl's* regiment had been. That same night all the watches and the detachment of our men in N° 8 were relieved, but not *Snak Hill*. As soon as our regiment had gone the *Hanau* Free Corps immediately took its place

4 Oct. Thur. Reserve picket.

6 " Sat. Field watch. N. B. On field watch. My tent was so pitched that my head and feet were just against graves and I consequently right in between them. But I slept without fear.

8 Oct. Mon. This morning I went on a "small tour" to Morris House, where our Lieut. Colonel still dwelt, to report a soldier to him for an offence. At 10 o'clock the English prince passed our regiment to view the line, where he was saluted from the fort with several guns. As soon as I arrived at the camp, I was obliged to go on fatigue command to take 4 deserting sailors to New York to head-quarters. Gen.

Klinton met me on the way there and I had to give them to the Landgrave regiment, which was encamped just outside the city, and I hardly got back to our camp by evening.

10 Oct. Wed. Company's day.
11 " Thur. Active command at Harlem
12 " Frid. The above mentioned troops on Staten Island went on board the men of war and transport ships, even the Prince and General *Klinton* accompanying them. But they did not start till the 18th and afterward returned without having accomplished anything

16 Oct. Tues. Watch at Gen. von Lossberg's.
19 " Frid Company's day.
20 " Sat. Field picket, landing place.
22 " Mon. Active command at Harlem.
24 " Wed. All day and night we heard loud and continuous gun and musket firing of the Rebels, the origin of which we at first did not know. But shortly afterwards we heard with sorrow, that the otherwise so celebrated Gen. Lord *Cornwallis* had been taken prisoner by the French and Rebels in the South, where, besides the English, also the Hessian Bose and *Erb Prinz* regiments were captured, and it was not wrong to conjecture that *Savanna* would soon follow in this pitiful run of ill-fate. It afterwards was deserted by our troops. Lord *Cornwallis* soon after came on parole to New York and from there to England.

26 Oct Frid. v. Lossberg's watch.
26 " Mon. That part of Knypphaussen's regiment that had been in Quebec, Canada, arrived in New York, having been ordered back
31 Oct. Wed. On a "small tour", again at the Lieut. Colonel's where I had to get the Company's pay.

Pay received in October 26/- ½d.

November. In camp near *McGown's* Pass until the 24th..

1 Nov. Thur. On active service in *Shnak Hill* block house.
2 Nov. Frid. On reserve picket.
3 " Sat. Company's day.
5 " Mon. On field watch N. B.
On the field watch there was such a cruelly cold wind that being in the open air and finally in the rain I had much to bear. The above named ships arrived back here again and the men were disembarked on Staten Island and Long Island.
9 Nov. Fri. Company's day.
11 " Sun. In the night we had the first snow, but it melted quickly.
12 Nov. Mon. Active command Shnak Hill block house.
—Nov. — The arrangements for the winter quarters of all the troops that were still here, were named in the order to-day (they are described in the supplement hereto) Shortly after almost all the regiments and corps went to the winter quarters allotted to them. But we had to continue in camp and had much to bear on account of rain, wind and cold Two barracks were begun here and we were not to march until they were completed. The work progressed very slowly.
14 Nov. Wed. On Gen. Lossberg's watch.
15 " Thur. I took another walk to the Hessian Yager camp, because they too were to march next morning to their winter quarters.
16 Nov. Fri. The Loyal American Regiment marched also from the other side of *Mc'gons Pass* and as we had to perform their services, we had a very hard time of it. I took a walk today.
17 Nov. Sat. Company's day On reserve picket.
20 " Tues. N. B. I was detailed from the field watch with 9 men to *McGon's Pass*.
22 Nov. Thur. Field picket at the landing place.
23 " Frid. On active command, Harlem. Through the endeavors of our Maj v. Wurmb we

finally received orders in the afternoon to march next morning into the winter quarters allotted to us.

24 Nov. Sat. So at 9 A. M. we marched out of our camp which had become almost intolerable and I got my quarters at the 5th mile stone, below a tavern named *The Dove*, with six privates. My host's name was ——— and he still had a pretty daughter at home. This was not agreeable to me, having regard for my sensitive heart and tranquillity To day we went into winter quarters below Martin's Wharf.

25 Nov Sun. Company's day.

27 " Tues. Regiment's day. N. B. I had to stay home from the Regiment's *jour*, because I had to fix my shoes which I had got only the day before and had chafed my right heel. [I was kept at home] until the 6th of Dec. when I went out and took a walk to New York.

Pay received in November 26/– 6d.

2 December. Sun. I wrote and sent a letter to Col. Heymel and requested him therein to write by first mail to Hesse and ask for my dismission as officer.

6 December. Thur. Got over my sickness.

7 " Frid. Watch at Artillery Forage Storehouse.

8 December. Sat. This morning Col. Heymel unexpectedly had me called from the watch and only he who has been in like circumstances, as myself, can feel as I did when, with a frank, cheerful face, he handed me a commission as Ensign, from Cassel, in Bose's regiment, with monthly pay from October 1st. In the afternoon I went to dine with Lieut. Col Hinte. He expressed his joy at my good fortune and I was chiefly indebted to him for it.

9 Dec. Sun. I dined with Col. Heymel.

10 " Mon. In the morning I went to New York. First, to his Excy. Lieut. Gen. Knypphaussen, where I reported myself and asked him for permission to serve a while longer in Donop's regiment, which he

willingly granted. Thereupon I went to the Quarter Master, Lieut. Col. *Duppy* and Lieut. Col. von Munchhaussen, the latter the oldest and both of Bose's regiment, to pay them my compliments. For seven guineas I got the necessary equipments at the merchant Hatzky's, of the Hessian Commissariat, for which Lieut. Col. Duppy gave me an order on Hatzky, (as Munchhaussen had refused me one, telling me to keep the *douceur* in the future). When I had received this I returned to my old quarters.

Lord Cornwallis left here for England, also some ships with inhabitants of New York who probably expected nothing good here in America, and also the Hessian invalids. Also officers who had resigned and been discharged, among whom was Lieut v. Donop.

11 Dec. Tues. This morning I wrote to Col. Heymel and Lieut Col. Hinte and both accorded me everything I asked, especially Lt. Col Hinte who did everything for me.

12 Dec. Wed. At noon today, while dining, my nose began to bleed freely of its own accord and not being able to recollect that this had happened ever before in my life, I believed I ought to consider it a premonition of some change in my friendship, although that is not one of my firm convictions.

13 Dec. Thur. In the afternoon I had myself bled again on the left arm. I again perceived indications of scurvy, God help me! Furthermore I was greatly vexed by the two fellows who were in quarters with me, one of whom I soundly thrashed and then sent to the watch, at which Col. Heymel was very angry. The other fellow was removed from my quarters. I am painfully waiting for my things to be made, so that I can go out.

15 Dec. Frid. This morning the detachment which had been stationed at *Mᶜ Gouns Bass* and had been detailed from the Body and Prinz Carl regiments, returned to their regiments. In the afternoon some others came to relieve them. Meanwhile I had some

trouble with Capt. Donop in regard to my money and when I pressed him for it, he gave me much vexation on account of the above mentioned fellow.

17 Dec. Mon. In the evening I received my uniform furnished by the tailor, and had to pay him $6 Spanish for his work.

20 Dec. Thur. All the soldiers and officers which belonged to the regiments in South Carolina, Georgia and East Florida, went on the ships to which they were assigned.

Pay received in December 26/– ½d.

(End of 1781.)

1782

Ensign ("the second from above") of the Worshipful Hesse Cassel Musketeer Regiment of Lieutenant General von Bose.

1 January. From the 1st of January on, I was detached [zugefuhrt] with the Grenadier Company of Major v. Orelly in the Grenadier Battalion of Lieut. Col. von Lengecke, in the rank of the 2nd Battalion.

In *New York town.*

4 January. The 4th of January was my first service in the field picket, towards evening, near Gen. Clinton's quarters, where I went again the next morning with 1 x and 17 Grenadiers, but the watch remained stationed there. I had to lead it off to the chief parade ground, but only part of the way and for the first time I saluted before the Generals who were there.

5. Jan On reserve picket, and at the same time, barrack inspection. The inspection of barracks was to visit the barracks and to hold the watch there under rapport. Attended at a Court Martial on account of a Grenadier who had been stealing while on watch. [He was sentenced to] run the gantlet 12 times on one day through 200 men.

7 January. On provision-store watch with one x and 21 privates. The officers' watch room was far off in King's Street, and as my quarters were just opposite the privates' watch across the street, I stayed at home and had it very easy on that account.

11 January. On barrack inspection and reserve picket.

16 January. On reserve picket.
18 " On barrack inspection and reserve picket.
21 " On field picket.
24 " On guard at Naval Store: changed from the head watch.

26 January. On barrack inspection and reserve picket.

Pay: of my Ensign's pay of £3. 8/-4d St'g I received from the regimental Qr. Master Flachshaar £3. 8/-4d. st'g. I also sold this month $3 St'g. worth of wood.

February. In *New York town*.

1 February. Barrack inspection and also reserve picket.

3 February. On field picket. N. B. In the evening I was on field picket in the so-called Red House on the North River, behind St. Paul's church, with 1 drummer and 2 x and 30 privates.

8 February. On Naval store guard watch, and I exchanged with Lieut. Giessen to my following ones.

10 February. Reserve picket and barrack inspection.

17 " Reserve picket and barrack inspection.

18 " Attended on Court Martial of a rascal who was sentenced to run the gantlet 12 times in one day through 200 men.

19 February. On field picket.
20 " At a gantlet 12 times run.
24 " Reserve picket and barrack inspection.
27 " In the morning at 10 o'clock the Grenadier

Battalions of the Hessians were mustered in the *Common Platz*, but as I was only standing there detailed, I was not mustered and only paraded with them.

Pay· I received 3 guineas and a half thaler St'g. less ha'penny, after deduction of 3 Hessian thalers equipment money, and received double rations This month I sold wood again for $3 St'g.

March. In New York town until the 5th, thence forth until the 12th on ship board, and then again in New York town.

1 March. On working command [which was made up of the Hessians and the 40th English regiment which was in New York and consisted of 1 Staff officer, 4 Captains, 10 Sub-officers and 500 privates] to dig a canal behind the Brew House on the North River and make the necessary ramparts. This made us apprehend that the General-in-Chief expected nothing good. Yet this very day the news had come by an express-ship from Charleston (if it was true) that our fleet in that region had defeated the French and that on land also the French had been defeated.

2 March. In the morning a review was held of the Composite battalion which consisted of the recruits of Crown Prince and von Bose; also those of the Garrison Regiment von Zeis, not 200 men altogether. Because I, as Ensign, only did interim service with the Grenadiers, I was mustered here too.

3 March. At the Magazine watch.

5 " At 11 A. M. I went with a detachment of 2 x 1 drummer and 28 privates of the Grenadiers on the ship Jersey, on which were 400 sea-prisoners. This command was relieved once a week. The prisoners increased and decreased daily. The officers of the command were in the habit of eating with the commander of the ship, Lieut. Gremen, and they all paid, as I did, one guinea for 7 days. This old and now unseaworthy ship was about 50 or 60 years old and had been a 64 gun ship of the English Line.

14 March. On field picket in the Red House.
16 " On the chief watch.
18 " On working command.
20 " On Court Martial of 1 rascal, sentenced to run the gantlet 18 times on 2 days through 200 men.

24 March. On chief watch. I exchanged my watches with the youngest Lieutenant Kosbott of the Landgrave Regiment Grenadier Company; but as I was made Assistant to the Engineers a short time afterwards I had to have done it without pay (sic).

25 March On field picket.
26 " On working command.

From the 26th on I was ordered to duty as Assistant Engineer at the new line and I was Ass't Engineer until the last of May.

Pay I received, after former reduction, 3 guineas 1 shilling 5½d—[received already on 23 Febr.] Sold wood again for [blotted].

April. In New York. Assistant to the Engineers on the new Line.

Pay received for April. 3 guineas, 1 shill. 10½d, after above deduction, but I got it already on the 26th of March. Again sold wood for $6 St'g.

2 April. Tues. I drew from Hessian commissariat fine white linen and 3 pairs of white linen stockings, two cotton night caps and some coarse linen on account in advance for my engineer's pay, receipting for its payment within three months.

9 April. Tues. This noon I had a decayed tooth in my left under jaw extracted, because it caused me much pain.

22 April Mon. This morning I had £1½ paid to me from the Royal Pay Office, as Assistant, for 6 days of the month of March, because from the 1st of April it is a new quarter.

1 May. Wed. Orders had been given that no expedition was to be undertaken, without the order of

the commanding General in Chief, against the enemy which was understood to apply to the Refugees because they among other things had committed a cruel outrage upon a Rebel and the Rebels wished to have revenge for it.

6 May. Mon. Lt. Gen. Carleton (who formerly had commanded at Quebec in Canada) arrived here from England to take the command from Lt. Gen. *Klinton* (which for a few days past has been held by Lt. Gen *Robison*) and likewise another Chief Engineer, Capt. *Maas*.

7 May. Tues. At noon, after work, I went out with Ensign *Biskamm*, with whom I had disagreed a few days before, and wounded him slightly on the right hand.

10 May. Frid. It was publicly announced that the English fleet in the West Indies had gained a glorious victory over the French, taking the French Admiral, M. de Grasse, prisoner

13 May. Mon. At noon Gen's *Klinton* and Knypphaussen went on board the frigate Pearl to return to Europe. English and Hessian soldiers to the number of about 700 were ordered to place themselves in two rows, reaching from Gen. *Klinton's* quarters down to the water, in order to pay the last honors to them

14 May. Tues. My madchen's father died and was buried on the 16th

15 May. Wed. Lieut. Gen. Carleton, with the new Chief Engineer Capt. Maas, came at noon to view the line and I spoke with the latter. In the evening after work. I went to my madchen's and after 11 P. M. I got back to my quarters pretty wet from the heavy rain.

16 May. Thur. In the evening Lt. Gen. Carleton issued the order that all work already begun in front of the city and on Long Island should be suspended until further orders.

20 May. Mon. Returned to service in the battalion. At noon the whole garrison of the New York and Donop's, Prince *Carl's* and the Body Regiment at

Macc Gouns Pass had to pass in review before the new Commanding Gen. in Chief, Gen. Carleton, in front of the new line on the East side; the other regiments around New York were reviewed the next day. They talk so much of enemies, of marching and of the resumption of the works begun that on account of the different and contradictory rumors nothing is certain.

22 May. Wed. This morning from 6 to 8 we drilled by order of his Excellency Lt Gen. von Lossberg and so thereafter as long as the work was suspended.

23 May. Thur. On Naval Store guard.

25 " Sat. On field picket at West Wharf.

26 " Sun. At 2 o'clock this morning I was detached with a certain number of men on fatigue to get paint for whitening, on Long Island across *Hollgotts* Ferry to Newtown, where I obtained a horse through the kindness of *Lengerke* (now Colonel) from the battalion and at 4 o'clock in the afternoon I was back in New York.

May 27. Mon. This noon I dined with Col v. Lengerke. To-day on barrack inspection and reserve picket.

31 May. Frid. Field picket *Bunkershill*.

Pay this month · £1, 1Sh. 11 h.d, st'g was deducted from my commission, so I got only $9, Spanish 2 Sh 11d st'g and had sold wood for $9 Spanish.

June. In New York. From the 16th on, in camp on North side in front of New York, near Greenwich.

1 June—Sat. At a gantlet.

2 " Sun. Barrack inspection and reserve picket At examination of a man for insubordination.

3 June. Mon. On Court Martial of a deserter

4 " Tues. At a gantlet. It being the King's birthday all the Royal troops had to fire after sundown in the evening. We in New York town fired in front of the newly established line, from the East to the North River.

5 June—Wed. After the watch parade I got into

a dispute with Ensign von *Kleist* of the Landgrave regiment, on behalf of another officer. We fought outside the city and I received a little cut across the middle finger of my right hand, but I wounded v. Kleist quite severely on the right arm. At a gantlet to-day.

6 June—Thur. I received a letter (which I still have) sent to me from the Chief Engineer, in which he makes known to all Assistant Engineers that we are no longer needed as Assistant Engineers, and this to date from the last of the previous month; at which our provision, forage and wood allowance ceased.

7 June—Frid. I received my pay from the Engineer Pay Office for two months, 5 shillings a day, which made $65 st'g and 3 York shillings. I paid the debt of April 2nd to the Hessian Commandant consisting of £5, 1, 9.

8 June—Sat. At the Magazine watch. All the regiments, battalions and corps received orders to be prepared to go into camp at the first notice.

10 June—Mon. Field picket, Gen. Carleton.

11 " Tues. Barrack inspection and reserve picket.

14 June—Fri. Ditto. Had some things taken to Cornelia's brother's house, to be kept for me.

15 June—Sat. We received orders and on the 16th Sunday at 3 P. M. we marched into camp, the four Hessian Grenadier Battalions together in an irregular [hacken-] line on the plain below Klinton's summer house, in front of the new line.

17 June—Mon. Field picket. I was assigned to field watch which I had exchanged with Lieut. *Zanthier* and he being sick I had to ask some one else to take the field watch for the night, so that I could do my picket service along the North River.

20 June—Thur. This evening we got orders that in a few days all the troops on York Island were to be cantoned on the North River and the officers were to camp near them. But this order was revoked on

the 21st, Friday, and all were to remain as they were.

21 June—Fri. Called on Cornelia with Lt. Zanthier.

25 June—Tues. Field picket.

26 " Wed. Field watch, now as inspection only. Reserve p'k't.

27 June—Thur. Had a good time for a few hours, hunting.

29 June—Sat. Today I received my Hessian forage money for the past half year amounting to £4, st'g. One quarter of a year I, like all other Hessian officers, had due to me in cash. With the said £4, I paid for my sword which I had until then borrowed, and besides for a blade, together $7, Spanish.

Pay: I paid £.1 st'g of my Sergeant's pay in Von Donop's regiment, which was £.4½, 10, 10. Thus I cleared $10 Span· 1 sh. 11d. St'g (having already sold wood, May 26, for $5 Span.) by the battalion and Engineer's service.

1 July—Mon. Lieut. Hartmann came out, with whom I slept in his tent, and who had been sick until now.

In camp on North side before New York near Greenwich.

3 July—Wed. Field picket and working command at the Line. Lieut. Hartmann having kindly invited me to live in his tent, I acted kindly towards him and took the field picket for him on the 3rd.

4 July—Thur. Field picket and field watch inspection.

5 July—Frid. Field watch inspection.

6 " Sat. At tattoo the whole Hessian Grenadier Brigade had to turn out in front of the camp, without muskets, before the Prince and Gen. Carleton. The former had been away on a ship for sometime, but had soon returned.

12 July—Frid. Watch at Gen. Carleton's.

I dined at 3 o'clock at Gen. Carleton's, as before at 8 o'clock I had taken tea there. The watch was relieved at 6 o'clock.

14 July—Sun. Field watch inspection. I did not leave the camp on account of field watch inspection.

16 July Tues. It was made known that our troops had left Savannah All the troops here received orders from Gen. Carleton to practice target shooting for a time, for which cartridges were furnished, and we found it quite irksome.

18 July. Thurs. In the morning after the watch parade I had to take the usual oath over a deserter (who subsequently was condemned to run the gantlet 30 times) in the Court Martial, which was my first.

19 July. Frid. On Thursday our Cork provision ship arrived here in New York

20 July. Sat. I was at work at Fort George in New York, when the batteries along the water were changed and repaired We worked from early daybreak till 8 A M., but not at all in the afternoon.

21 July. Sun. Field picket. At 7 A. M. the English Prince and *Sea Admiral* (as had been announced the day before) came to our field church to attend divine service.

24 July Wed. Early after watch parade I went up the *Bloomendal* road with my gun, shot 6 birds, but so completely lost my way in the thickets that I was badly scratched. Attended at execution of a deserter.

26 July Frid. N. B. The field watch inspection was again counted a watch because an officer was under arrest and the officer having the watch had to stay there day and night.

Pay· I again paid £1 St'g for my Sergeant's pay in von Donop's regiment and received, after all deductions $9 Span . 1 Eng. Shill. 5 coppers, and had sold wood for 9 shill. currency [*correnssi*] only.

2 and 3 August—Frid. and Sat. I changed my

Friday watch to Saturday through the picket, with Lieut. von Kosbott.

3 Aug. Sat. Field watch. To-day proclamations of peace were published everywhere in the papers. Although it is not, generally speaking, reasonable of me to so consider them, they are nevertheless thunderbolts to me.

5 Aug. Mon. This evening all the citizen watches in New York were discontinued on account of the peace, by the English and Hessians. How desponpent I now am owing to my circumstances and how much rather would I die than survive the completion of peace!

6 Aug. Tues. To-day the 42nd Scotch regiment marched into quarters in N. Y. to do duty there

7 Aug. Wed. Field picket.

8 " Thur. Field watch. N. B. I again exchanged, on field watch, the picket for Lieut. *Lui Kosbott*. I again had hopes of a longer war, because many things seemed to tend that way.

9 Aug. Frid On work command.

10 " Sat. N. B. I exchanged with Lieut. *Lui Kosbott* for my future work command and therefore did his to-day.

11 Aug. Sun. This morning the Hessian Garrison Regiment of *Knobloch* arrived from Savannah, where it had been left together with the 7th English regiment, and some of the King's Americans arrived here with a fleet consisting of 9 ships. The Hessians and English had lost a fearful lot of men by disease. They disembarked at *Broklyn* Ferry and were distributed in quarters on Long Island, but transferred, a few days after, to New York with the Yagers

12 Aug. Mon. Chief watch

15 " Thur. At a gantlet. 2 thieves, 3 times.

17 " Sat. This morning after watch parade I went to see my madchen. I took my gun along and shot 7 birds, whereby I had a curious adventure. The cries of different birds attracted me towards a high

bush to see what was the cause. I shot an old bird and the young one which ran crying around the dead one I had to strike dead, but not without emotion because it was very touching. Meanwhile I perceived a black snake over two yards long (which the cries of the birds had awakened) up on the bush. I shot it in two and found a young bird swallowed whole falling out of its body. It was a frightfully hot day and as I drank so much butter-milk in the heat I got sick and had to vomit; but afterwards I was better. N. B. This evening I went on picket for Lieut. *Lui Kosbott* and on the next day he took my city watch. From to-day one officer was again detailed to the reserve picket.

19 Aug. Mon. Work command.

20 " Tues. In the morning after the watch parade I shot a dozen different birds.

22 Aug. Thur. Field picket. At noon I walked out above the 3rd milestone and shot 10 big birds of different kinds

23 Aug. Fri On Court Martial of a deserter [sentenced to] 24 times through 200 men

24. Aug. Sat Reserve picket.

25 " Sun. Field watch

26 " Mon. Held examination over a deserter. At a gantlet

27 Aug Tues At a gantlet At present there is every indication of peace. Our recruits have arrived at *Hallefax*. Our troops which are said to have embarked at *Charlestown* are expected here Much more, but everything indefinite. But it must be explained on the arrival of the first packet ship from England. To-day I shot 4 *picasinen* 1 young hen in the bushes and 8 other different birds. The young hen and 3 *picasinen* I gave to Cornelia and the rest I ate with my good friends.

29 Aug. Thur. I had to go to Capt. Donop at Fort Knypphaussen to ask for the balance of the debt due to me, when I received a receipt for the regi-

mental Qr. Master *Zinn* who said he would pay me the next Tuesday. This debt was $3 Spanish for my white hat plume which he pretended to have lost. On Field picket.

30 Aug. Frid. This morning after watch parade we heard that the order referring to *Charlestown*, namely, that it was to be evacuated by our troops —was revoked until further orders.

Pay: I again paid £1 St'g Sergeant's pay. Received, already on 25 July, $10 Spanish, 3 coppers. Sold wood for $2. Spanish

2 September—Mon. Field watch. This noon the order came that all should be ready to march to *McGow: Pass* and that the foragers and sharp-shooters were to be sent there next morning at 9 o'clock. In the evening another order was given by which the Grenadier Brigade was to be stationed in Bloomingdale. Our baggage was to be arranged, as if the army of Hesse had come here. I was embarrassed what to do with my things. There are rumors about expeditions, blind alarms and much else, but everything uncertain.

3 Sept. Tues. Field picket. This afternoon our foragers and sharp-shooters returned. They had measured at the camp, but could find no water on account of the great heat of this year which had dried up everything.

4 Sept. Wed. Work command. Men were sent out to dig wells. They came back in the afternoon and could not find anything but the faintest and poorest springs, even at a depth of 30 and 40 feet and besides very little. And all the wells and ditches round about were dried up.

5 Sept. Thur. Field watch. I exchanged with Lt. *Trottijour*. By a packet ship which arrived last night we received the news that Princess Charlotte of Hesse Cassel was dead. To day the fleet consisting of 22 ships of the line arrived here from the West

Indies under Admiral *Picott*. All measures for the continuation of the war are again seriously undertaken. Our Brigade, Grenadiers, Hessians, Landgrave, Bienau and Knipphaussen regiment are daily expecting orders to march to our camp as laid out (which on account of the dearth of water has been postponed) at *Mͨ Gow's* Pass near North River. We now have in our Grenadier Battalion on account of fever sickness only 4 officers on duty and consequently I can hardly undress.

9 ' Sept. Mon. Reserve picket. This evening we again received orders to send some men into the camp assigned to us again (because all the other regiments of Long Island and in other places had already gone into camp, but were suffering greatly for want of water) and to have them dig for water. They found some, but not much.

10 Sept. Tues. Chief watch.

11 " Wed Finished city watch (at rear of Artil Barrack G'd).

12 Sept. Thur. Chief watch.

13 " Frid. Field picket. I shot a large seabird which was good to eat.

14 Sept Sat Work command.

15 " Sun. Reserve picket. This morning at day break Gen. Carleton himself with 2 Hessian regiments, also English and cavalry, went over King's Bridge on a foraging expedition with many wagons. In the afternoon he returned.

16 Sept. Mon. Field watch.

17 " Tues Reserve picket.

18 " Wed. Field watch. This morning a few transport ships under cover of some frigates sailed—so it was said—to Charleston, to get our troops and stores there.

19 Sept. Thur. Toward evening another order came, that next morning the regimental Qr Masters of the troops stationed outside of New York were again to go to the new camp for water. From this day on, sick in camp.

20 Sept. Frid. In the afternoon I had fever twice and grew deathly sick.

21 Sept. Sat. This afternoon order came that we were to march the next Monday at 7 o'clock.

22 Sept. Sun. This evening I received my quarter ticket in the *Bowery* at a German's named *Kayser*, N° 30.

23 Sept. Mon. At 7 o'clock we all marched and at 10 A. M. I had our things (and as Lieut. Hartmann had been forgotten with the Qr. Master for a few days) sent on a wheel-barrow to the quarters and we went on foot. Here in the city the citizens and Regiment *Waldeck* and 2 Battalions of Skinners did service From this day on I was sick in the city in the Bowery.

24 Sept. Tues. This morning the Hessian Chief Surgeon Bauer, for whom I had sent, paid me a visit, which he promised me to do every day. He prescribed for me the next day *Laxon* from the Apothecary. I did not feel well all day, having to vomit naturally. Then I slept through the night very well in a heavy sweat. (Until 29th inst. under treatment which is detailed).

27 Sept. Frid. There was a general complaint that all the men would die soon for want of water. Pay: I paid again 1£. St'g Sergeant's pay and had cleared, already on 26 August $10 Spanish, 13 Coppers. Sold wood for $2 Spanish.

1 October—Tues. I felt pretty well, but when I stood up for a few moments I felt quite faint about my heart and I had to sit or lie down. The Chief Surgeon said my weakness was due to my having lain so long and he consequently prescribed strengthening medicine.

4 October—Frid. To day the Prince, the Admiral and all the Generals reviewed the whole army which was in camp drawn up in three lines of battle, in the neighborhood of Harlem. We had until now received

no wood. It had been entirely forgotten. In camp ⅓ fuel is given. From the 1st of October on ½ — which we received to-day.

9 Oct. Wed Only now and then I have slight attacks of fever, otherwise feel quite well and began to use *Gena*.

11 Oct. Frid. Feel nauseated and feverish symptoms almost continually.

14 Oct Mon It being tolerably warm the surgeon advised me to take a walk. I did so for a few hours and felt tolerably well after it.

17 Oct Thur. I go walking almost every evening. Owing to slight attacks of fever I still use *Gina* powders, and have to be careful of my diet.

20 Oct. Sun. Lieut. Hartmann, my room-mate, was taken sick and the Surgeon advised me not to stay in the room any longer. So I moved, temporarily, to Arnold's house, N° 82, where I went towards evening (in the *Pump* Street).

21 Oct. Mon. In the afternoon Lieut. Hartmann began to die and he was in agony until 8 o'clock when he died very hard. In spite of all urging he did not want to have any clergyman or in regard to his own arrangements. I took the sick *auditeur* Weissenborn, who was lying opposite me and had been ordered to Knypphaussen and Bose's regiment, quickly with me and had everything fastened up as well as possible and taken to my quarters This same night I sent a report of all this to Col. *Lengerke*. The next morning at 10 oclock, it being the

22 Oct. Tues. The Regimental Qr. Master Spangenberg and Capt. *Leliva*, sent by Col. Lengerke, came to me, took off the old seals and put on new ones of the battalion. All the effects of the deceased I had to keep until they were sent for to be taken to the battalion. This day at 1 o'clock I crossed swords with the Skinner Ensign Henndorf (who had formerly been an Ensign in Old Lossberg's Hessian regiment). I was so weak I could not hold my sword tightly and

I received a wound in my right middle finger, just the same wound I had received before from *Kleist*, but not so deep.

23 Oct. Wed. At 3 P M Lieut. Hartmann was very nicely buried by the Waldeck's, 2 officers and 50 privates. I attended also, but the cold air disagreed with me extremely. I was again taken very sick and had a fever during the night.

24 Oct. Thur. This morning I went to see the sick Chief Surgeon Bauer who again prescribed *Gina*.

25 Oct. At noon to-day, after dinner, I found on reaching my quarters that all the effects of the deceased Lieutenant had been inventoried by Spangenberg, the regimental Qr. Master, and again sealed. I and Lieut. von *Kuntz*, both of us sick, having been present, had to sign To-day two guns were fired in honor of the King of England's Coronation Day.

26 Oct. Sat. It rained hard. I only went to the city to the regimental Qr. Master Flachshaar to get my pay and then returned home.

27 Oct. Sun. I stayed at home and felt pretty well. I wrote a letter to *Charlestown* to Lieut. Gen. v. Bose, proposing myself as 2nd Lieut. in the Landgrave [regiment], now that I was the oldest Ensign. I wrote another letter to his Adjutant, Lieut. Henel, for acquaintance sake and I had the letters taken to a packet-boat

28 Oct. Mon. At 8 o'clock this morning the English Dragoons all the Hessian Yagers and the Hanau Free Corps had left their camp and marched as far as *Morritz House*, when they again encamped until further orders.

30 Oct. Wed. I made up my mind to return to my old quarters at Kayser's in the upper room. To-day it rained most astonishingly.

31 Oct. Thur. I could not go out on account of the rain. Pay: I paid the final sum on my Sergeant's pay—10 sh. 10 d. sterling: but I received back provision money for 12 days of the previous month, in

view of future reduction. Hence I cleared $14 Span. and had sold wood for $1. Spanish, 2½ York shillings.

1 November—Fri. My orderly removed my things.

2 " Sat. Towards noon when I was going home, the quarters for our battalion were made in the whole district where a year ago Donop's regiment was stationed. When I got home to my new quarters I refrained from putting things in order, because it was my intention, if God would only preserve my health (as I was now feeling quite well) to go to the battalion in a few days.

3 November Sun. At noon the 42nd Scotch regiment marched into York to their winter quarters. I stayed at home all day, not feeling well.

4 November. Mon. The English regiment arrived here in winter quarters. Also the Hessian Grenadier Battalion of Loewenstein and of Linsing. Of the latter and Young Lossberg's Company, Lieut. Kersting came into my quarters, because the sick officers were to go to their battalions, or, if very sick, they were to get other quarters. But the Lieut. managed to get with me. I had my things all taken back, so as to have them altogether.

5 November. Tues Again with the battalion on the East River before New York. At noon Lieut. Kersting lent me his horse (as the day before when I reported myself to Col. Lengecke and inspected my quarters) and my landlord Kayser, a cart, and so, through heavy rain, I drove to my quarters at Martin's Wharf in Leffert's house, where Gen. Carleton had lodged this summer and where now 6 officers occupied the large number of rooms. On the way I met all the English and Hessian regiments which were on their way to the garrison in New York. The Company to which I belonged lay near the city and most of the officers, through the kind arrangement of the Colonel, were at some distance from the Companies.

6 Nov Wed. Reserve picket and barrack inspection—to visit all the watches. My orderly had to go almost 4 English miles to get provisions; but in future I received them from the Donop Grenadier Company of *Giesold* which was stationed in barns around here. We officers had no duty except inspection of the watches and the *Tortle Bey* watch.

14 Nov. Thurs. I and Lieut. v. Trott—of General v. *Prinz Carl*—had to take other quarters at the order of Col Lengecke at the 5th milestone at *Shmid's* house.

15 Nov. Frid Inspection. Visited all the watches.

16 " Sat In the afternoon I stood as godfather for Cornelia's sister who was married to a man named *Roll.* It was a girl and the Lutheran Staff chaplain Becker baptised it.

20 Nov. Wed. This morning Col Lengecke ordered me on fatigue command to New York, although it was not my turn for that duty, to order the bedding and wood repairs for the quarters of the battalion, because I was well acquainted in the English barrack office and Engineer Dep't.

21 Nov. Thur. In the night it was cold and stormy and the first snow of the year was falling. It was 3 o'clock in the morning.

22 Nov. Frid. *Tortle Bey* watch

26 " Tues. I went to New York to get my pay Did not stop long. Asked for the Staff chaplain Becker, to come the next day to christen a little baby girl. I bought a few things and then went home again.

28 Nov. Thurs. Turtle Bay watch for Lieut. von *Kospott* Junior.

2 December—Mon Watch for Lieut. v. *Kospott,* Jr.

When I was on watch at *Tortle Bey* there was an alarm to the effect that the powder magazine there and the ships lying near were to be set on fire by the

Rebels. Gen. Carleton sent me his Adjutant with orders to use every precaution during the night and I was re-enforced during the night by a picket of 1 Sub-officer and 12 men. Everything, however, remained quiet. One frigate came from New York the same afternoon and anchored off there to protect us.

4 Dec. Wed. Barrack inspection. This morning I was called by request of our regimental Qr. Master Spangenberg to go on horseback to New York for provisions, wood and *état*.

5 Dec. Thurs. Work command. This morning I went with 2 *F.* and 60 privates to Master's Wharf to have some old fascines put on boats, and the latter to New York. To-day I wrote to Major *Scheer* who was a prisoner in Virginia, and gave it to our Regm't'l Qr Ms't'r. Flachshaar to deliver, who had been ordered there to take money and clothing to our prisoners Also sent my regards to the other officers of the regiment, who were there. Again many papers [Zeitungen, news?] from *Giebraltar* were circulated on *Long* by way of *Roth Island* with the uncertain news that all was in our hands, but they were soon contradicted. A large number of empty transport ships have arrived here from England and *Hallefax*, but for what purpose, is yet unknown. To-night I slept for the first time in my quarters.

7 Dec. Sat. I again went to *Tortle Bey* watch for Lieut. *Kosbott*, Jr. for a silver *tabatge* (as the first time for a green and gold purse).

15 Dec. Sun. To night there was such a heavy snow-fall that I did not go to my quarters for 3 days.

27 Dec. Frid. To-day I went to New York to get my pay from the Reg't'l. Qr. Mstr. Ludwig of the *Erb Prinz* Regiment (because Flachshaar had been sent to the prisoners), but I had to wait until the

28 Dec. Sat. When I received my whole pay, and what the provisions amounted to I paid to Captain *Seliva*. This morning I bought some blue uniform

cloth again with my pay, for $7 Spanish, from Lt. von Trott, Senior, because I had sold mine the previous spring.

Tractement Liste as follows: Provisions [rations] in 1782: I received, already on the 29th of December 1781 double provision in the "Composite" Battalion from the 23rd of January 1782,—one in the Grenadier Battalion and the other in the "Composite" Battalion, because it would not have sufficed for one person; and it had been so arranged by the Reg'm't'l. Qr. Mstr. The latter I gave up for some time, as I received double free provision from the Engineer Department; but I took it again a month later.

From the 1st of June I received no more provision from the Engineer Department. The portion from the "Composite" Battalion I gave away.

From the 18th of September I received no more provision from the "Composite" Battalion; but I gave away the commutation money instead.

Tractement List. For the month of November, but already paid 26 October to me only the balance of the $3. German for arms and 1 portion of provision deducted—$15 Span. 6 York shill. less 1 copper and had sold wood this mo. for 10/- York.

Month of December (received already on 26 Nov) $15 Span. 3/- English, 2 coppers.

(End of 1782.)

1783.

Ensign (2nd in rank) in Regiment von Bose, Grenadier Company of Capt. Eigenbrod, transferred on 1st of January to Battalion A. von Lengecke.

January. In winter quarters in front of New York near the 5th mile stone, on the East River.

3 Jan. Frid. I had to go to New York to report

a Grenadier of the Eigenbrod Comp. to Col. v Lengecke, who had been missing for 2 days. Our fleet had arrived here from Charlestown and had debarked the 5th but not all on this day. There were the following regiments· Hessian: v. Dittford, de Dangely, v. Benning, English, 1st Battalion Delancey N Y. Volunteers, a detachment of the King's American regiment, 2 Battalions Skinners, Prince of Wales Volunteers, Detachments of 22nd and 23rd regiments, 17th Infantry Regt, 3rd and 4th Battl. 60th Regt., Detachment of Bose, the Yagers and English Artillery join their regiments and Corps. All these were assigned quarters on Long Island.

5 Jan. Sun. Went to New York to recommend myself in person to Gen. v. Bose. He was somewhat sick from his journey, but I interviewed him. He was very kind and said he would propose me as 2nd Lieut. at Gen'r'l.

7 Jan This morning at daybreak I drove to York in a Cariole which I had borrowed. On my way back to my quarters I paid my compliments to my new Capt. Eigenbrod which he very politely returned. This evening I had the fever again badly which I may have got from severe cold or some old trouble, but it left me with God's help soon.

12 Jan. Sun. This morning we officers went to Capt Eigenbrod's Comp. to the Captain to draw for a scarf and I got one for 30—. It weighed $31^{5}/_{8}$ halfounces. All the scarfs for Bose's regiment had arrived last year with recruit transports at Halifax and had now been sent here with many small equipment pieces Inspection.

10 Jan. Frid. Watch at *Tortlebey*. N. B I came to the watch at *Tortlebey* and only make note of it here, because I never in my whole life saw such deep snow lying on the ground inside of 36 hours, as there. I had almost 2 English miles to walk and through blasts of wind I had to relieve two men continually so that they could help each other; and I had to have swept

out of my wooden watch room the snow which the cruel wind drove in.

13 Jan. Mon. I sent the orderly attending me—Spohr—back to duty in the Company and took an old Grenadier, Klein, in his stead.

14 Jan. Tues. At 10 this morning the whole Company, with upper and lower arms, had to turn out before the quarters of Capt. Eigenbrod—for Capt *Leliva* to take command of the Company in the presence of 2 Commissaries (Capts.) appointed for that purpose. I dined to day with Capt. v. Leliva and Eigenbrod

16 Jan Thurs. There was a mustering at the 3rd English milestone at 11 A M. with our Battalion, and I, now with the Grenadiers, was mustered with them. As usual I hired for this purpose a servant for half a Spanish dollar.

19 Jan. Sun. Watch Turtle Bay.

17 " Frid. The whole army (except officers who had received candles before) after Gen. Carleton had arranged the economical management, received pewter lamps and fish oil to burn.

20 Jan. Mon. For a few days past there has been such a persistently cold wind that many of the men have had ears, hands and feet frozen. I had taken cold so badly in the whole left side of my face that I had scarcely any rest day and night for a week.

21 Jan. Tues. Inspection.

22 " Wed. Execution, 3 men for fighting.

23 " Thurs. In the afternoon I went to New York to learn about the *douceur;* but it being a day of repentance I found no one at home, so I came directly back.

27 Jan. Mon. This morning went to New York and received my English douceur of £4, 2, 6 st'g for 165 days in 1782, from the Regmt Qr. Master Ludwig. Dined with Lieut. Haussmann of Donop's regiment, who afterwards when Capt. resigned and removed to America.

30 Jan. Thurs.   Watch at *Turtlebey*

31 " Frid.   Inspection. I dined with Capt. Eigenbrod

Pay in January. I received after deductions for equipments and provisions $16 St'r'g, 3 York shillings and 3 coppers; and for the mountain wood I sold this month $5. St'l'g, 2 York sh

February. In winter quarters, [same as above.]

1   "   Sat.   In the forenoon I went over to New York and paid $7. St'g and 7 York shill. which I had borrowed the year before from Hatsky, and got a receipt for it, after which I at once returned home Through the close management of Gen Carleton we officers were to lose the £2, st'g, (goods or money), which we usually received in winter, but afterwards we received our pay in July.

2 February. Sun.   Such a cold, stormy wind again that I did not go out, partly on that account and also on account of the deep snow.

12 February. Wed   By this time there was a general circulation of rumors about peace and a packet-boat which had been seen by a faster sailing ship that had arrived here, was daily expected.

18 February. Tues.   The surest signs of peace were corroborated by the proprietors of deserted lands being called back to their possessions by the English. Meantime the above mentioned English packet boat had been, it was rumored, captured and taken to Philadelphia.

25 February Tues.   This morning took a walk to New York, dined with the Grenadier Lieut. Gersting of the regiment of Young Lossberg and the Gren. Battl'n of Linsing.

26 February. Wed.   Dined at noon with Capt. Eigenbrod and had a pleasant time till evening.

Pay : after previous deduction $15 St'g, 5 York sh. 7 Coppers. Febr. 5th received again double rations from Capt Eigenbrod. Sold wood for $5. 2 Yk. shill. 7 Coppers

March. In winter quarters, [as before.]
1 " Sat Watch.
2 " Sun. Inspection.
3 " Mon. I went to New York, intending to pay my respects to Gen. von Bose, but did not find him at home and therefore returned at once.

4 March. Tues. Went again to Gen. von Bose and dined with him Afterwards from the baggage-house of our Battalion I took for my own use 20 German yards of Hessian furnishing linen [lieferungslinin] to be paid for to the Regimental Qr. Master Spangenberg, but I did not pay for it until the 28th of August, giving Capt. Eigenbrod $2 St'g and 15 Coppers.

11 March. Tues Regarding peace there was still such a confusion of rumors that we could not gather the least particle of actual truth therefrom. The packet-boat already mentioned was hourly expected. All the royal Refugees and well affected received liberty to go to New Scotland or Old England this month.

13 March. Thurs. Inspection.

19 " Wed. The long expected packet boat arrived in New York by which we learned that the English had granted the Americans independence; but not to leave the country entirely until the negotiations for peace with France and Spain had been completed, all of which another packet-boat from England must soon explain. Lieut Gen Carleton's recall to England has been granted and in his stead Gen *Gree* is soon expected here, but the latter was subsequently left behind in England.

21 March—Frid. This morning I went to New York and wanted to draw something from the Hessian Commissariat. but I heard that the day before almost everything had been sold at public auction, because they did not know how matters stood with regard to peace. (I was directed by General Order to put all the tents of the army in order quickly.)

23 March—Sun. Watch.

24 March—Mon. Inspection.

25 " Tues. To day in the newspapers general peace was made known, but a packet from England must give further information.

29 March—Sat. This morning I was in New York and bought a trunk on account of the rumors about marching away. But notwithstanding the rumors about peace the Rebels at *Paulus Hook* made prisoners of several men in a night raid and accordingly order was given us to be on our guard in all our watches and to pay no attention to the rumors of peace yet

31 March—Mon Today the 54th Regiment went from York Island to Staten Island, crossing the East River in boats, and from there the 40th Regiment came over here in the same boats. A few days ago the Grenadier Companies which were here, but belonged to regiments in the West Indies, marched to quarters in N. Y in order, as was said, to leave for their regiments the first opportunity. A few days later, however, all but a few returned.

Pay In March I received from Capt. Eigenbrod my pay on the 1st. $14 St'g. 2 York Shillings, 7 Coppers and I sold wood for $3. St'g and 4 York Shillings.

April. Still in quarters at the 5th mile stone. Youngest Second Lieutenant.

1 April. Tues. At an early hour all the Companies of the Battalion were inspected by Col. von Lengecke as to equipments.

2 April. Wed As usual the drill-time began, by order, four times a week.

3 April. Thurs. In the night, being on watch on *Tortle Bay* I heard, towards 11 o'clock, a terrific noise, shooting, crying and horn-blowing and just across the water on Long Island; whereupon the next morning I found out that 900 Spanish dollars had been stolen from an inhabitant there by a boat full of robbers from N. Y. one of whom they had captured. At noon to-day I dined with Capt. Eigenbrod, and Lt.

v. *Trott.* Sr , with whom I lay together in quarters, remained on watch for me a few hours.

4 April—Sun. Inspection.

5 " Mon After the drill I went to New York and bought some things. There I heard that a packet boat had arrived from England the day before and had brought confirming news of the peace, and concerning other things among the Hessians, my Commission as 2nd Lieut.

8 April—Thurs. Ensign Biskamp and I received our Lieut. Commissions. N.B. I received from Col. v. Munchhausen, as Commander of Regiment von Bose, my commission as 2nd Lieut. (which had been signed on the 15th of Sept. 1782) and the same day I reported to Col. v. Lengecke and the next morning early

9—April Frid. I and Lieut. Biskamp were in New York at the quarters of Gen. v. Bose, Maj. Gen. v. Kospott and Lieut. Col Du Berry [Buy] to report as 2^{d} Lieutenants

12 April—Mon. Watch.

13 " Tues. Inspection.

16 " Frid. This morning I was In New York again buying a ham and other necessaries for my departure, for, according to appearances, our departure cannot be very far distant. This evening the Governor here, *Robertson*, went on board ship for England. Also most of the Refugees embarked to go to Nova Scotia—also the Brunswickers.

20 April—Tues. Watch.

21 " Wed. Inspection.

23 " Frid. On Court Martial. 1 deserter sentenced to receive 24 lashes

24 April—Sat. At punishment of 1 deserter.

21 " — Ditto.

27 " Tues. Watch. Early before leaving watch I had a man who had deserted sworn into the Company again. The wood furnished to us officers ceased every year on the last Saturday in April: thenceforth

only a half-burning was made good—as ¾ feet of wood a week, but no candles.

29 April Thurs. Directly after drill I went to New York and bought some things. Clothing had become dearer, because the country-people (since peace was known) came in in crowds and bought thereof.

28 April — Inspection.

Pay In April I again received $14. St'g. 3 Yrk. shill. 1 Copper; but this on the 28th of March—and sold wood to the amount of $2. St'g, 5 York shill

May. In winter quarters, [*id. ut sup:*]

2 " Frid. Watch. N.B. I changed with the Garde Lieut. v. Zanthier of the Landgrave regiment to my future watch.

5 May Mon. Inspection All the prisoners of the Hessians, Hanauers Brunswickers, English and of both armies, to wit · *Borgonne's* and *Cornwallis'*, were daily expected here. Gen. Carleton sailed up the North River on the 4th accompanied by a large suite and as we heard he had dined with Gen *Wassinton* at *Tapan*, and he stayed away from New York until the 7th

6 May—Tues. We drilled for the first time in Battalion at *Marston's* Wharf.

12 May—Mon. Watch.
13 " Tues. Inspection.
14 " Wed. I dined with Capt. Eigenbrod. We were informed in the order of Gen. Carleton that all English deserters, who should come back, were to be received; but not in service again on account of their perjury, but with leave to be taken back to England.

16 May—Frid. To-day I again had my left arm bled on account of frequent nose-bleeding. I commenced again to notice a scrofulous breaking-out on my body.

18 May—Sun. Watch.
19 " Mon. Inspection.

20 May—Tues. This morning I went to N. Y. to the regimental Qr. Master Flachshaar, who had returned from visiting our prisoners (who were soon to arrive) and I received a polite answer through him from Major Scheer.

22 May—Thurs. Examination. I had to examine a negro drummer for theft and, because he denied it, had him spanked.

24 May—Sat. Watch. I was drilled by order of Gen. von Losberg for the last time this year.

25 May—Sun. Inspection.

26 " Mon. The watch drew up this morning at 8 oclock. Among other prisoners of Cornwallis' army, the v. Bose regiment arrived and went the next day in boats from Staten Island across to Long Island at Jamaica. A few days before the prisoners of *Borgonne's* army, principally the Brunswickers and Hanauers, had arrived here on ships, but they lay, without disembarking, before N. Y. in the North River, in order to go, as was said, in the next boat to Canada with the rest of the Refugees who were bound for Halifax in one fleet.

29 May—Thurs. This morning I went to New York and bought another ham for my voyage.

Pay in May I received (but on the 27th of April) $14. Stl'g 2 York shill. 7 Coppers and the little wood that was furnished, I gave away.

1 June—Sun. Watch. A packet boat has arrived in New York from England and brought many orders concerning our departure, and has assured us of the early arrival of the necessary transports to take us away from here. Among others changes made in the Hessian troops, the Body Regiment called the *Erb Prinz* Landgrave, has been changed to Body Regiment; and what had been *Erb-Prinz* to *Vacant Erb Prinz* Regiment.

2 June—Mon. Inspection.

3 " Tues. This morning I went to New York

and bought 2 linen undershirts and went directly back. From the 2nd of June on we received a different allowance of wood, the subaltern officers only ½ allowance every 7 days.

4 June. Wed. After sunset this evening our Battalion had to go, along with the others, in front of the city-line, as it was the King of England's birthday. At a given signal of rockets and then three rounds of 21 guns from Bunker's Hill, three rounds of musket fire was given by us also, with loud cheering by all the troops. From this day on we were drilled with powder, so as to be able to exercise better with powder at the next review.

9 June. Mon. Went to New York and spent a short time with Reg. Qr. Master Flachshaar.

10 June. Tues. Watch. At execution of sentence on 3 Yagers and one negro who ran the gantlet N.B. until the 23rd my watches were at Gen. Carleton's. Our Hessian forage-money was paid for ½ year, but was retained in the regimental cash-box until further notice.

11 June. Wed. Inspection.

13 " Frid. I settled my accounts with Regiment v. Bose through the Reg^t Qr. Master up to the end of 1782 and thereupon also with the Grenadiers Battalion v. Lengecke through the Reg^t Qr. Master Spangenberg and, after squaring up, got my receipts.

14 June Sat. At last by order of Lieut. Gen v. Losberg the Hessian forage-money above mentioned was distributed to those officers who owed nothing; but I voluntarily left mine in the Equipment Cashbox. This afternoon I was in N. Y. because aware of the serious measures taken for our speedy departure. Seventy transport ships having already been inspected by our Genrl. Qr. Master *Duppy* and other Commissaries. From time to time several other transports arrived here.

17 June. Tues This morning after the firing I went directly to N. Y. to say good-bye to Gen. von

Bose, who went on board ship this afternoon to sail to Europe with the first favorable wind.

19 June. Thurs. N.B. I changed my watch until the 23rd with Lieut. von *Trott* Sr. for mine, but at Gen. Carleton's in Beckmann's house. This afternoon Gen. Carleton came out here from N. Y. to the 4th mile stone on the East River, to Beckmann's house, generally used therefor, to spend the summer. And the officers of our Battalion who were quartered there in the adjacent houses among which were my quarters also, had to change to other quarters for the General's Adjutants. I got permission from Col. v. Lengecke to lodge (at a private house near the 5th mile-stone).

20 June. Frid. Inspection.

23 " Mon. Being on watch at Gen. Carleton's I had to breakfast and dine there.

25 June. Wed. Watch.

26 " Thurs. Inspection.

30 " Mon. This morning I went to New York again and bought a few supplies.

Pay in June. As my pay as 2nd Lieut. Battalion (B!.) was cut down one half I did not clear more than $11 St'g. 2 York shill. 8 Coppers, received on the 28th. of May. Capt. Eigenbrod reduced the above twice. From the 28th of May on, we English and Hessian troops received no more provisions daily than 1 lb. of bread or flour, 12 ounces of pork or 21 ounces of beef and rum as before.

1 July—Tues. On watch at Gen. Carleton's. I again breakfasted and dined there. They had supper.

2 July—Wed. Inspection. This afternoon I went walking to *Macgown's* pass in great melancholy, which has been following me for a long time now. Our merciful Father protect me from all evil!

3 July—Thur. This afternoon I wrote 2 letters to L. I. one to Major Scheer, the other to Capt. v. *Leliva* in order to report myself as Lieutenant and through the second to bid good-bye to all the officers.

4 July—Frid. In the morning I went to the city and delivered the letters and received a visit from our Ensign, Wagehals, of Bose's Regiment, who dined with me and towards evening I took him back as far as the city.

6 July—Sun. Watch at *Tortle bey.*

8 " Tues. Inspection.

9 " Wed. This morning 3 Companies of Hanauers Free Corps sailed down the East River on flatboats to embark at N. Y. and afterwards the other two Companies on the 15th of this month in order to go to Germany. Also the Waldeckers embarked and the Zerbsters followed the former. Shortly after they sailed from New York.

11 July—Frid. Watch at Gen Carleton's. I exchanged the General Watch with Lieut. v. Trott Sr., he to take mine at *Tortle Bey.* I had my meals as before at General Carleton's.

14 July—Mon. We were again mustered—our battalion at 9 A. M. at the *Dove,* by the old Commissary and I had my servant for 1 Spanish dollar. Directly afterwards I sat on a Court Martial, in which Col v. Lengecke was President, over one deserter and accomplices of Donop's Grenadier Company and he was condemned to death, but afterwards his punishment was mitigated by Gen. v. Losberg to running the gantlet 30 times through 200 men on 3 days.

15 July—Tues. Watch at Gen. Carleton's. This morning the Company called the Vogt Grenadier Company by the Body Reg'm't. marched to York to Linsing's Battalion for which they had been appointed and in exchange we received from their Battalion Capt. v Malet's Grenadier Company of Young Losberg's Regiment. I dined again to-day at Gen. Carleton's

17 July—Thurs. Inspection.

19 " Sat. I took the General Carleton watch for Lieut. v. Trott. Sr. (because on account of his dirtiness he was forbidden by Col. v. Lengecke to take

it himself) for a gold shirt pin. Dined again at Gen. Carleton's.

21 July—Mon. This morning I went to New York again principally for the reason that the Refugees, also officers, who had served under the King of England and desired to go to Nova Scotia, received, privates as well as other subjects, 300 acres of land, subaltern officers 2000 ac. Captains 3000 and so on. But there were so many doubtful considerations involved that I quite gave up all the ideas about it that I had at first entertained.

23 July—Wed. We received, after all, the so-called furniture-money mentioned in the Spring, but believed to be lost, and amounting to £2 Sterling.

24 July—Thurs. Watch at *Tortlebey*. This evening while on watch I took a purgative and owing to the mosquitoes and the great heat, the like of which I have never yet experienced, since the first Dog-day of this year, I had much to bear.

25 July—Frid. In spite of the heat to-day I went, after the watch, to New York to buy some things.

27 July—Sun Inspection.

Pay July. After deduction of the other half of my pay (patents) I received (on the 29th of June) $11 St'g and 2 York shill

30 July. Wed. Today the Anspach Yagers and 3 days later the 2 regiments belonging to them marched to N.Y. where like all the preceding troops, they embarked in men of war and on the 9th day after they entered the sea for Europe.

2 August—Sat. Watch at Gen. Carleton's. Dined there.

1st 2nd and 3rd all the English and Hessian regiments, which were on Long Island, near New Town Creek, went into camp there, excepting Bose's regiment and the *vacant Erb Prinz* and one or two other English regiments came there into settled quarters (cantonment).

4 Aug. Mon. Watch at Gen Carleton's. At punishment of two Yagers deserters, who were made to run the gantlet. Dined at Gen. Carleton's. I had my watch at *Tortlebay;* the same day I had been changed with Lt. v. Trott, and in future I regularly took his General watch and he mine in *Tortlebay*, for which he made me a present of a gold shirt pin and a somewhat broken ivory box inlaid with gold and silver.

5 Aug. Tues. This afternoon I went to New York and remained there over night with Lieut. v. Trott, but got a furlough beforehand from Col. v Lengecke.

6 Aug. Wed. Inspection. This morning I crossed over to Brooklyn on the Ferry boat, dined at Maj. Scheer's and afterwards went to *Buschwik* with an officer of Bose's regiment and called on my old host and hostess Skillmaenn, especially Sally. She was very affectionate to me, when we were alone, and as it had grown very late, I was urged to stay there over night. But on account of the other officer I declined with thanks, took tea there, and after many kisses and promises to come again very soon, I returned to Brooklyn. It had grown very dark. At first I was inclined to stay there, but I took leave of the other officers. (Meanwhile the following Hessian regiments have since 2 days received orders soon to embark for Europe, to wit Regiment v. Tittfort, v. Knipphaussen, Vacant Erb Prinz and v. Bose. Garrison regiments v. Bienau, Benning, D'argschinelli and Knoblauch.) In the evening I crossed over to New York again on the ferry-boat and spent the night with Trott.

7 Aug. Thurs. In the morning I returned home and in the afternoon reported to Col. v. Lengecke.

9 Aug. Sat. This morning as our Company had not been paid by the Reg^t Qr. Master Spangenberg for a long time and since I had to report it to Col. v. Lengecke and the latter found several other things out of order, he ordered me to arrest him, but as

privately as possible. But I did not find him at home, near the City and went back to the Col's and then back to Spangenberg's and finding that he had been away for two days I left a sub-officer and a private with necessary instructions as watch.

10 Aug. Sun. This morning I was ordered on fatigue *commando*, as also Capt v. Eigenbrod and Auditor Bauer of the Garrison Grenadier Battalion *Plate* and as it had not yet been reported to the General, for the time being (until more definite news) to seal Spangenberg's papers and to continue above-named watch in his quarters. I dined this noon with Capt. v. Eigenbrod.

11 Aug. Mon. This morning I went to York again and from there to Brooklyn in L. I. and took leave of all the officers of v. Bose's regiment. Thereupon I returned to New York and slept at Trott's

12 Aug. Tues. This morning after having some things bought in the market I returned home. To-day the following regiments embarked v. Tittfort, v Knipphaussen, Garrison regiment, v. Bienau, v. Knobloch, and D'angschinelli at Brooklyn and then

13 Aug. Wed. the *Vacant Erb Prinz*, v Bose and Garrison regiment v. Benning embarked, all under the command of Major Gen. v. Kosbott and later v. Bischhaussen and v. Knobloch. They waited for water to be placed on board the ships, then for good wind which came on the third day afterwards, when they sailed. These regiments were all embarked in transport ships.

On watch to-day at *Tortle* bay.

14 Aug. Thur. Inspection. After returning from the watch I went to N. Y. but did not stay there long. A packet-boat had come from England, but had been unfortunate on the way and had been wrecked on a sand bank. The passengers and some goods were saved. By this vessel we learned from letters from Hesse that the Vacant Erb Prinz Regiment was to be given to his oldest son Prince Frederick and Col. von

Borbeck of Knobloch's regiment received the Vacant Garrison Regiment of v Seiz.

15 Aug. Frid. We heard in the orders that the English *douceur* for the remaining part of the army which had not yet received it, was to cease immediately. Likewise the cannons in the outworks and other things were to be brought in and a return of provisions made and more such things—A sign that our embarkation is not far distant.

18 Aug. Mon. Maj. Gen. v Kosbott now being absent, Major Gen. Hachenberg received the command of the Hessian Grenadier Brigade consisting of four battalions.

19 Aug. Tues. Watch. To the whole army, that was here, was made known by Gen. Carleton the order of the King of England to the effect that the 17th Dragoon Regiment, the 7th, 22nd, 23rd, 38th, 40th, 43rd, 70th, 74th 76th, 80th and 82rd regiments were very soon to return to England, and on their arrival there to be reduced to a certain number—officers as well as privates, of whom, however, the reduced officers were to receive half-pay. N.B only reduced the 17th Light Dragoons Reg^t, the 70th, 74th, 76th 80th, 82nd Infantry regiments The 3rd and 4th Battalion of the 60th regiment, the 2nd Battalion of the 84th regiment and the 4 Corps of Col. *Etmond Bennin*, Lt Col. Robert *Sonkin*, Tarleton, v. *Simko* are shortly to be entirely disbanded (reduced) The regiment of Gen. Morrison, the 33^d, 37th, 54th, 57th regiments, the 1st Battalion of the 42^d regiment are to be reduced to 471 men including officers of whom some also who have already been discharged have already been deducted.) The 17th Infantry regiment and also the 33^d, 37th, 42^d, 54th and 57th regiments hold themselves ready to go to Nova Scotia at the first order. The sub-officers and privates of the above-named reduced regiments who are willing to go to Nova Scotia are to receive, each sub-officer 200, each private 100 acres of land, ten years free from all taxation and one year's free provision besides their

present equipment, arms and ammunition. All this has already been subscribed in London since June of this year.

20 Aug. Wed. This A. M. the 43rd and 76th Inf. Regiments came from Staten Island to Long Island in cantonment until further orders. From to-day I received my provision near by here from Capt. Malet's Comp. for Lieut Kersting, who belonged to this Company, and on account of the nearness he got my equal provision from the Company.

22 Aug. Frid. On watch at Gen. Carleton's. I dined there again as usual

23 Aug. Sat. Inspection.

24 " Sun. As before I again exchanged watches with Trott and dined at Gen. Carleton's. To day the now Hessian Body regiment came over from Long Isl and camped close to the East River near York till further orders

27 Aug. Wed. Had to stand my *Tortle Bay* watch myself, because Lt. v. Trott had a hearing and could not repay the watch I had stood for him.

28 Aug. Thur. This afternoon Major Gen. von Hachenberg, who died the day before was buried and in his place we received as Brigadier Major Gen. von Gosen.

29 Aug. Frid. This morning I went to New York and bought some things

30 Aug. Sat. This morning I went walking to visit my Company, because the Captain was sick, and the Company was very far distant from me (near York). I did so now very often weekly. To-day General Carleton left his summer quarters and returned to New York.

Pay in August after deduction of double provision and of the usual clothing money I cleared on the 29th of July, $14 St'g .. 2 York shill 7 Coppers.

September—In settled quarters at same place: but from the 3rd inst I had my quarters at *Kebsensbe* (Kip's Bay.).

1 September—Mon. Inspection. This morning I was in New York and bought some provisions.

2 September—Tues. This morning I was at Col. v Lengecke's and got the dismissions of 2 privates, foreigners, signed, to go to Nova Scotia.

3 September—Wed. This morning I had quarters assigned me in *Kepsens* Bay where also 30 Grenadiers of my Company were stationed. The people of the house were very grouty, for which I administered to one of them a good kick.

5 September—Frid. I sent my orderly (who had stayed hitherto in a tent near the house of a friend) to *Kepsen's* Bay to live there and occasionally, when I needed him, I had him come to me.

7 September—Sun. Watch at *Tortle-bey.*

8 " Mon. Inspection I was ordered to attend the publication of the sentence upon the Grenadier in favor of whose being hung I had voted in Court Martial. To-day some of the regiments which I mentioned above as intending to go to N. Scotia embarked. Some 30 transport ships had come up from Sandy Hook to get troops.

10 Sept. Wed This morning I took an emetic, having sensations of fever and feeling it increasing.

11 Sept. Thurs. This morning I received my English forage *douceur* from Capt Eigenbrod—£8, 15, St'g Attended at the punishment of a deserter who received 30 lashes.

12 Sept. Frid. Watch.

13 " Sat. Inspection. Being relieved from the watch I went to New York and bought some things for my journey.

15 Sept. Mon Went to New York again and bought some things. Again we had many sick with fever and on that account had to have two Vice Corporals in the Company. All the royal refugees were notified through the papers that up to the 21st of this month no more ship service of theirs would be paid for. On that account they often gathered to embark.

18 Sept. Thurs. Again in New York buying things for the voyage.

19 Sept. Fri. Watch.
20 " Sat. Inspection.
22 " Mon. This forenoon in New York. It being the Coronation Day of the King of England, cannons were fired in the fort and ships.

23 Sept Tues }
24 " Wed. } Slept at *Kepsen's Bay.*

26 " Fri Watch. Was present at the execution of sentence on a black drummer of our Company who had been sentenced by Court Martial to 24 times gantlet on 2 days through 200 men, and then to be driven out. Such an act as his had never been heard of before.

27 Sept. Sat. Inspection.
28 " Sun. We again had orders that several horses of the army were to be sold and that correct embarkment lists were to be handed in—and the same day still another *post order*, because a packet boat had arrived from England, viz. that from to-day all the troops here were to be ready to embark, so that they could start as soon as further orders were received.

29 Sept. Mon. Again in New York.
30 " Tues. Dined at Capt. Eigenbrod's

Pay. As after the last deduction I got up to 28th August $14 St'g., 3 York Shill.

October—Quarters as last mentioned up to the 27th, then at *Paulus Hook.*

2 October—Thur. This morning I went to the suburbs of New York to the house called *Keyser's*, where I had once had my quarters and bought a young pig for the voyage for $4 Spanish and had it immediately slaughtered and sausages made and salted for smoking. From the 1st of this month we had half our fuel made up to us. I therefore had ¾ barrel weekly.

3 October—Frid. Watch.
4 " Sat. Inspection. Went to N Y. and bought some things for the voyage.

8 October—Wed. This morning I was in N Y. buying something, but there was the greatest storm, wind and rain that I have seen in a long time and it continued through the day. I got terribly wet before I reached home. To-day and the following days the remaining English regiments, which were ordered to Nova Scotia and St. Augustine, embarked. Accordingly changes were made in the English quarters and camps, especially at King's Bridge.

13 October—Mon. This morning I bought a pair of silver shoe buckles for $3 Span. and 6 York shill. at an auction in New York.

16 October—Thurs. Inspection. After pay parade this morning I went to New York and bought a pair of gloves.

17 October—Frid. The Hessian Body regiment moved from their camp in quarters on the East River into a former hospital.

19 October—Sun. Watch.
22   "   Wed. I bled my left arm.
23   "   Thurs. I was at the execution of sentence on 2 Grenadiers who had deserted their watch to go marauding. Dined with Capt. Eigenbrod.

24 October—Frid. This morning in New York. Another change had been made by Parliament concerning the Refugees, viz Each officer now received only 1500 acres of land, and privates 50; and those who had lost any part of their property and could give sufficient proof thereof, were to receive apart from that royal compensation, but not exceeding £2000.

25 Oct. Sat. An order came that Lengecke's Battalion was to go to *Paulus Hook* before Monday the 27th, and *Blate's* Garrison Batt[n] to McGowns Pass in barracks with the Yagers.

26 Oct. Sun. Inspection. This morning I went to my quarters at *Kepsen's* Bay and had everything packed up.

27 Oct Mon. Commanded the fatigue with the baggage. Henceforth at *Paulus Hook*. I got up at

1 o'clock this morning and after breakfast and touching leave-taking from my friend I went to *Kepsen's* Bay and thence at 6 o'clock to Capt. Eigenbrod's Company. At 8 o'clock we arrived with the whole battalion at High Wharf, North River New York. I was ordered by Col. Lengecke to stay there until the cannons and all the baggage had been transported to *Paulus Hook*.

Thereupon I got over to *Paulus Hook* towards evening and received a little room, N° 4, as quarters in the 3rd barrack.

28 Oct. Tues On watch in the citadel of *Paulus Hook*

29 Oct Wed. After dining at Capt. Eigenbrod's I went with an officer to the little town of *Bergen*, but not further than the church, because it was getting late. Then we returned to *Paulus Hook*, about 3 English miles. We regularly did all duties 2 days in succession and the 3rd day the 43rd English regiment which was here in a very weak condition on its return from captivity. From 25th we received full amount of fuel and lights (candles) $\frac{1}{2}$ lb. every week and 1$\frac{1}{2}$ feet of wood, and 1 Subaltern as much as 6 soldiers would receive or for half a room.

30 Oct. Thur. This afternoon I sent my orderly together with a Grenadier of the Company with a boat specially ordered to New York, to fetch over my trunk from the baggage house there which was done by 10 o'cl. that evening.

Pay. In Oct. after usual deduction I got $14 stg. 2 Y'k sh. 7 Coppers.

November. At *Paulus Hook* up to the 21st (then) on board the ship "Sally" (on the North River behind the quarters of Gen. Carleton) lying at anchor; the 25th under sail and at sea for England.

1 November. Sat. At 2 o'clock this afternoon I crossed over in the regular boat to York and on account of violent wind in 12 minutes.

2 November. Sun. In the afternoon, having promised to return soon, I went over to York and in the evening after the expiration of my leave, obtained from Col. v. Lengecke, I returned by the above mentioned boat to *Paulus Hook*. To-day the Hessian Body regiment, *Erb-Prinz, Prinz Carl*, Grenadier Battalion v Linsing, v. Loewenstein and Garrison Battalion *Blatte*, likewise the Hessian Hospital and Commissariat received orders under the brigade of Major Gen. v. Wurmb, and it took place, to embark on the 8th of this month. Also the Hessian Artillery Corps. None of the English went away this time. We were also informed by the orders today that we were to receive the 165 days English douceur.

3 Nov. Mon. This morning the 2 Hessian regiments Body and *Erb Prinz* had to maneuvre at New York with firing. After dinner I went walking across the street on the right hand side past the house of the formerly well known spy who had been shot.

4 Nov. Tues. The baggage of the Body and *Prinz Carl* regiments and of the Battalion v. Loewenstein and *Blatte* was put on ship-board.

6 Nov. Thur. Inspection. N. B. Every officer who had the inspection, now had to visit the barracks and go the visitation rounds at night. To-day the whole Battalion had to go through the pay parade with arms and drill a little. To-day the baggage of the Grenadier Battalion v. Linsing and *Erb Prinz* regiment was put on board. From to-day the Grenadier Battalion v. Lengecke, the Yager Corps, regiments v. Donop and Young v. Lossberg were formed into a brigade under Major Gen v. Gosen.

7 Nov. Frid. Watch at *Paulus Hook*.

8 " Sat. At 9 o'clock this morning the above-named regiments embarked, back of the burnt down church on the North River. I dined at noon at Captain *Giesolt's* During my absence to-day orders were made known in the Battalion that 2 transport ships which were then lying in the East River for

repairs, one the "Sally" of 450 tons, the other the "Young William" of 360 tons, had been assigned to us and that the Battalion was to be informed as soon as they were repaired.

10 Nov. Mon. At 10 A.M. I was again at *Paulus Hook*.

11 Nov. Tues After dinner I took a walk to a little town comprising about 13 or 14 houses called *Communebah* at a distance of about 3 miles, situated near the water towards *Liesbethtown*, and I took back with me two polite country-men, travellers, and helped them over to New York.

12 Nov. Wed. After 6 this morning all the troops named above, and which had been waiting on board ships till now, set sail upon a signal given by firing cannons. The weather was a mixture of rain and snow.

14 Nov. Frid. Upon reporting to Col. v. Lengecke I was ordered to see to the embarkation of the baggage on the ship "Sally," which, by lot, had fallen to the Companies *Prinz Carl* and Eigenbrod. To-day I received my English forage *douceur* amounting to £4, 2, 6, stg.

15 Nov. Sat. Fatigue command. N. B. at 8 o'clock I was detached with 2 Sub-officers and 8 privates to New York to take all the things from the baggage-house there below the North Church, to the ship "Sally" for the above-named 2 Companies. I was occupied at that until 2 P.M. and after I had, myself, put everything in order on the very good ship and had sent 2 boats over to *Paulus Hook* for the baggage there I spent the rest of the day on a visit.

16 Nov. Sun. At 10 o'clock I returned to Paulus Hook. In the neighborhood of Morris House I found on the road a new black silk woman's scarf with beautiful lace. The day before Gen. v. Lossberg went on board ship with his suite and left the command with the only remaining Hessian Major General, v. Gosen, over us Hessians who were left. We were informed

by order of Gen. Carleton that Gen Lossberg, on his arrival at the Downs in England with the Hessian troops and after making report thereof, would hear from Lord North as to whether we were to depart again or stay there.

17 Nov. Mon. In the afternoon I took a short walk along the first causeway in front of *Paulus Hook* and supped at Capt. Eigenbrod's.

19 Nov. Wed. Inspection. I spent the day in York and on my return had a tiresome, tedious passage to *Paulus H'k*, there being no wind and contrary tide. We now had definite orders to be embarked by noon of Friday, but this was kept secret from the privates to avoid desertion.

20 Nov. Thur. Finished packing my things. On account of the apprehended desertion I went several times during the night through the Company. The night was dark and dismal and indescribably sad and full of apprehension for me.

21 Nov Fri Last evening a little after seven an orderly of our Company was missing. I immediately called for the keys to the outer gate and hastened after him with a Sergeant Major and another sub-officer, but I got on the wrong trail and despite all search found no trace of him. This morning I arose early, because I had slept so little and yet so anxiously with worrying dreams. As the day broke we saw our ships weigh anchor and approach *Paulus Hook*. At 9 o'clock Donop embarked; at 10 Young Lossberg; at 11 the Yagers, at 12 Lengecke, and several English; at 2 I also went on board; but I was absent-minded the whole day and night.

22 Nov. Sat I went ashore and paid some farewell visits in York and in the evening returned on board This evening the 43rd regiment came over from *Paulus Hook* quite late

23 Nov Sun. We lay quietly at anchor hourly expecting orders to set sail. The city was all full of Rebels, although all the watches in the city were

still occupied by the English, and it was said that we were to lie at anchor until their embarkation. Several orders were given relating to signals and in regard to setting sail, which latter, however, was as yet prevented by contrary winds. In the night time between 11 and 12 o'clock a terrible fire occurred in New York Then the ringing of alarm bells and the uproar made by the disgustingly drunken sailors of our ship who had been in the city until late, made it quite a restless night. The fire continued until 3 in the morning, when we could see no more. This noon we saw the American soldiers taking possession of *Paulus Hook*.

24 Nov. Mon. Inspection. During the fore and afternoon several ships of our fleet sailed, but not further than Staten Island N.B. We subaltern officers had no other duty on ship than inspection of the watch, and giving out provisions, which every other day fell to me and to-day for the first time

25 Nov. Tues. Every other day inspection on board ship fell to my duty. This morning signals were again given from the Commander's ship, whereupon at 10 A.M. our ship, with the tide and good wind, sailed as far as Staten Island near *Kohl's* ferry, 10 English miles from New York, where we anchored again at 11, at a given signal from the agent's ship. Here we saw several sloops with English troops and baggage arriving from New York at *Kohl's* ferry and debarking there, probably, as had already been rumored, to embark there as soon as the expected ships arrived. My whole heart is full of sadness when I see fading from my view the receding landmarks and house-tops, in whose midst I leave my whole happiness behind me. At 2 P.M. the anchors were again lifted and we sailed with our *beylot* [pilot] as far as the bar at Sandy Hook arriving there at 3½ o'clock in the afternoon, when the pilot left us. I entrusted a letter to him addressed to David Bergen at York. Here we met some ships coming from Halifax and some

from London   They were transports coming to get the remainder of the troops in New York. We had west wind. The night was somewhat dark.

26 Nov. Wed. This morning we saw our whole fleet consisting of 14 ships at different distances around about us. The Agent's ship which was nearest to us, had taken in most of its sails, probably in order to await the Commander whom we had not seen since leaving New York: accordingly all the other ships had to take in sail. Without knowing anything certain we followed the Agent's ship and hoisted sail about 10 o'clock A M. but with very light wind. At 8½ A M we met a ship coming from Halifax. At 12, noon, we were 60 miles from Sandy Hook, but there was a great calm and we had drifted towards the South and accordingly felt warm   Our whole fleet was together, which looked fine. After 4 we spoke three ships from England on their way to New York, which intensified the anguish of my heart nigh unto despair   We had bad weather and contrary wind which increased during the night.

27 Nov. Thur. In the morning I began to get sea-sick, because the storm constantly increased and it became so violent towards night that the Captain himself said he had never experienced a greater storm. As we were driven towards land and were not more than 40 miles off, our destruction was inevitable, if the storm continued   On deck a cow, 4 sheep and two pigs and about 30 fowls were killed owing to the cruel tossing and pitching of the ship. In our cabin everything went to pieces and was afloat which was attributable to the negligence of the ship's captain, Thomas Potter of London; but at last Heaven came to our rescue   The storm abated and we got a favorable wind.

Pay in November. After the usual deductions I had got, up to the 31 of October $15. St'g. 4 York shill. 7 Coppers. From this time on I get my provision again

December. Stormy voyage. Von Krafft resolves to resign and return to America Persuades Col v. Lengecke to aid in getting his discharge from Gen. v. Lossberg and makes written application to Lengecke for the same, while at sea.

22 December. Mon. Sighted land—the Lizard.

23 " Tues. Sighted Plymouth Light House and saw the fortifications on the heights. At night saw Portland Light.

24 December. Wed. Passed Isle of Wight. Rounded Beachy Head. Passed a transport which had sailed for N. Y. with English Artillery on Nov. 15th. The "Sally" a fast ship. At 6 P.M. saw the lights of South Foreland and Dover.

25 Dec. Thurs. Aground on sand bank and off again. Before daylight neared the Downs. Saw many ships there. Many sailed for London at about 8 A.M. Anchored in Downs awaiting pilot to Deal; arrived there at 20 minutes of 1 o'clock and anchored and spoke ship of 2nd Hessian fleet on which was the *Prinz Carl* regiment.

26 Dec. Frid. Several Jews came on board. Bought a silver watch for 2½ guineas. Lay waiting for General Lossberg and his orders, whether to stay there or go to Germany.

29 Dec. Mon. Order from London for German troops to go to Chatham and winter there. Smaller ships to land troops at Dover and to march overland, larger ships to sail to Chatham and land their troops there.

December. We were at sea for England until the 25th when we brought up at the Downs and remained this year. N.B. From the 27th to 31st I was under arrest in my own room.

I was the second 2nd Lieutenant from below (i.e. next above the last commissioned 2nd Lieut.)

Pay for December. On 8th of January 1784, after deduction of 12 sh. st'g for the ship-mess I cleared £3, 9, 2.

(End of 1783.)

1784.

1 January, 1784, to 4th. Lay at anchor in the Downs.
5 to 11 January. At anchor off Portsmouth.
11 " 25 " At Portsmouth.
25 Jan. to Febr. 4. In London on service.
5 to 17 Febr. In lodgings at London.
18 Febr. to 10 March. On board ship "Vigilant" in the Thames
11 March Sailed for New York in "Vigilant."
22 April. Arrived off Sandy Hook.
23 " 5 P.M. Anchored off *Fley-market Wharf.*

PLATE I.

Plan of the battle at Trenton, which took place on the 26th of December 1776, between a body of Americans under the command of General Washington, 6,000 men strong, and a brigade of Hessians under command of Colonel von Rall, in which 800 men of the latter were made prisoners of war

EXPLANATION.

A Trenton.
B Picket of 1 officer and 24 men.
C Captain von Altomborkum's company of the Lossberg regiment, which lay quartered in this neighborhood, and advanced so that the picket was engaged with the enemy, drawn up before the Captain's quarters.
D Picket of 1 captain, 1 officer, and 75 men.
E. 1 officer and 50 yagers, of which 6 yagers were near the command at
F, which with 1 officer and 30 men stood detached, and afterwards retreated with the Donop corps
G Place where the regiments rallied and fell in ranks, in default of a fixed rendezvous
H. Place where the regiments stood, after they had lost the town, and where Colonel von Rall, with his and the Lossberg regiment, endeavored to make an attack on the town, but being strongly driven back to
I, were there made prisoners of war. In the meantime Knyphaussen's regiment, which had to cover the left flank as much as it could, was obliged to retreat to
K, and endeavored to gain possession of the bank, but found it occupied by the enemy, and were obliged, after . . . having left the Lossberg cannon in
L, a dense swamp, also to surrender.
M. Knyphaussen's cannon
N. Rall's cannon.
O Attack of the Americans from the woods
P. The surrounding of the town and the return march of the Americans.
Q. 2 battalions of Americans which pursued Knyphaussen
R Final attack of the Americans.
S. The enemy's cannon and howitzers

Copied in the month of January 1781 in North America and on York Island

CARL VON KRAFFT.

PLATE II

Pro Arte et Marte in North America, on York Island and in winter quarters at Fort Knyphaussen. Copied 1781, in the month of January.
CARL VON KRAFFT

Battle at Monmouth the 28th of June 1778.

A Quarters of General Lieutenant Cornwallis on the 26th of June.
B Quarters of General Lieutenant von Knyphaussen on the 26th of June
C Order of march of General Cornwallis's division, and also of General Knyphaussen's, which had already moved forward.
D Position held by General Lee for the purpose of attacking our rear
E Position of the light infantry for resisting him.
F. The enemy's cavalry, which was attacked and driven back by the 16th dragoon regiment —General Lee, who retreated on the approach of the light infantry and General Cornwallis's column, which was prepared to attack him. The light infantry, which was supported by the Hessian Grenadiers, took the right, the brigade guard the centre, and the English Grenadiers the left wing, and were sustained by the 3d and 4th brigade, the 5th brigade being held in reserve
G. The right wing of the guard, which was engaged with the enemy in the woods, and sustained the first attack.
H The English grenadiers, reinforced by the Hessians, forced the enemy to quit the heights, which thereupon was occupied by our artillery.
I The heights to which the light infantry, Queen's Rangers, the light infantry of the guard and 3d brigade, were stretched out.
K Position of the enemy, and their artillery.

PLATE III.

Plan of the Red Bank fort, situated in New Jersey, on the Delaware, and above Mund [Mud] Island, built by the [Americans], (together with the adjacent situation).—On the capture of Philadelphia in 1777, by Admiral, and also General Howe, this fort was demolished, but after the abandonment of Philadelphia by the English, it was again erected by the [Americans].

PLATE III

PLAN
RED BANK

R.A.R.

DELA

PLATE IV.

Plan of the region between Philadelphia and Valley Forge, with the several different positions occupied by the royal army and the Americans, from the 23d of September to the end of December 1777.

A. The position which the royal army occupied, after it had crossed the Schuylkill at Norrington, in the night of the 22d and 23d of September

B The position of the royal army at Germantown from the 25th of September to the 19th of October, 1777.

C. The position which the royal army occupied at Philadelphia on the 19th of October.

D The position of the enemy, with their intrenchments, in the neighborhood of Whitemarsh, from November to the end of December, 1777.

As General Howe desired to surprise the enemy in position at D, he removed, on the 4th of December, from his quarters at Philadelphia, and advanced in conjunction with Generals Cornwallis and Knyphaussen, who held command under him, with the 2d battalion of light infantry, the Hessian yagers, the 2 English grenadier battalions, the 3 Hessian battalions, the 4th English brigade, which formed the advance guard, with 2 squadrons of the 16th regiment, the brigade of General Stirn, the English guard brigade, 1 squadron of the 16th regiment, the 5th, 27th, 26th and 7th regiments of infantry, the 3d English brigade, 3 squadrons of the 17th regiment, the Queen's Rangers, and the 2 battalions of the 71st regiment, and took position at

E, but, as his plans, having been discovered near Chestnut hill, were not practicable, he marched on the 7th of December to

F; the natural position there being very advantageous, and so returned on the 8th of December to Philadelphia

G The position of the enemy at the end of December, where they passed the winter.

Copied 1781 in the month of February in winter quarters at Fort Knyphaussen and York Island, North America

CARL VON KRAFFT

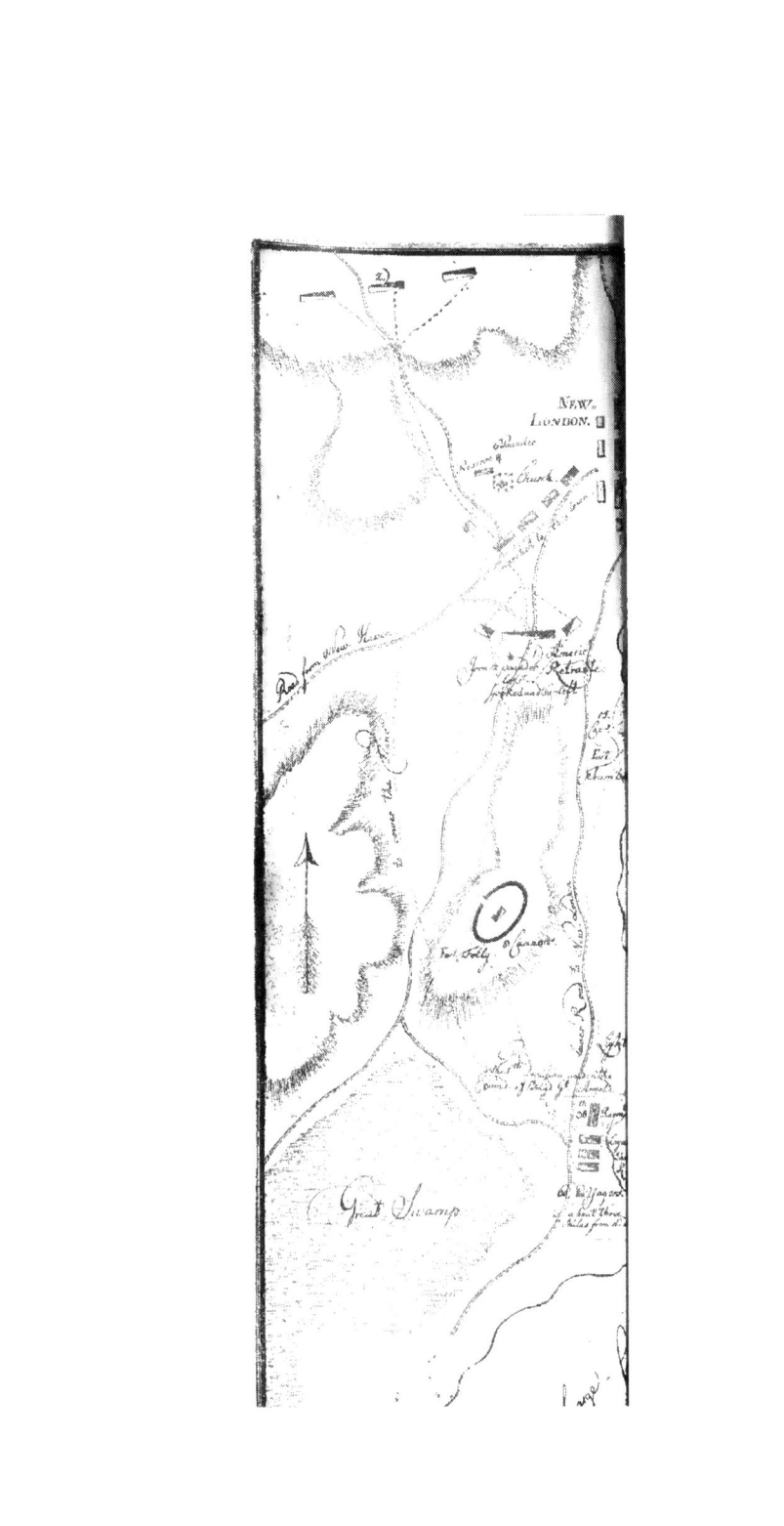

PLATE VI.

Plan of the military positions of the Island of New York in North America, but only on the east side in the neighborhood of what had been Fort Washington, but was afterwards Knyphaussen, which I sketched myself in the month of May 1779 from Laurel Hill. But this was not drawn until 1781 in the month of January, and in the hut-camp at Fort Knyphaussen.

EXPLANATIONS.

No 1, 2, 3, on "Speiten Devil."
" 4, 5, 6, 7, and Q American Redoubts
G King's Redoubt.
I. Independence.
V. Block House.

Above-named redoubts which were constructed partly by the Americans, partly by the English, were demolished in the Autumn of 1779 during the construction of the line of circumvallation, in which I was also ordered to assist the English Engineer, Lieut Sproule, of the 16th Regiment.

O Torn-down houses also hut-camps no longer existing, such as —

K Emmerichs Chasseurs' Camp
F. Hessian Yagers and Chasseurs' Camp
S Camp of the 17th English Regiment which had been taken prisoners.
E Pontoon Bridge then existing
M Queen's Bridge, destroyed.
F Storehouses, taken down
T. Former camp of the regiment of life-guards
U. Orchard cut down, for the barricades
B. The Island of New Jersey.
A North, or Cox Hill and its Redoubt
C Charles' Redoubt, and
D The Guard-House there.

The same from A on, are still in existence, as also is —

G. Upper Courtlandts, and
H. Lower Courtlandts House
N Kings Bridge
L Inhabited House.
R. Some huts of negroes, plantations and houses, called Morisina.
No 8, Redoubt
Ex. Ferry-crossing, otherwise called Holland's Ferry.
W. Laurel Hill
X. Still another place, fortified by the Americans and improved by the English.
a^{1}a The intrenchments newly constructed in the year '79.
a^{2}a. and a^{3}a called Fort Clinton
Y Huts subsequently built by the 44th English Regt before the construction of the new intrenchments

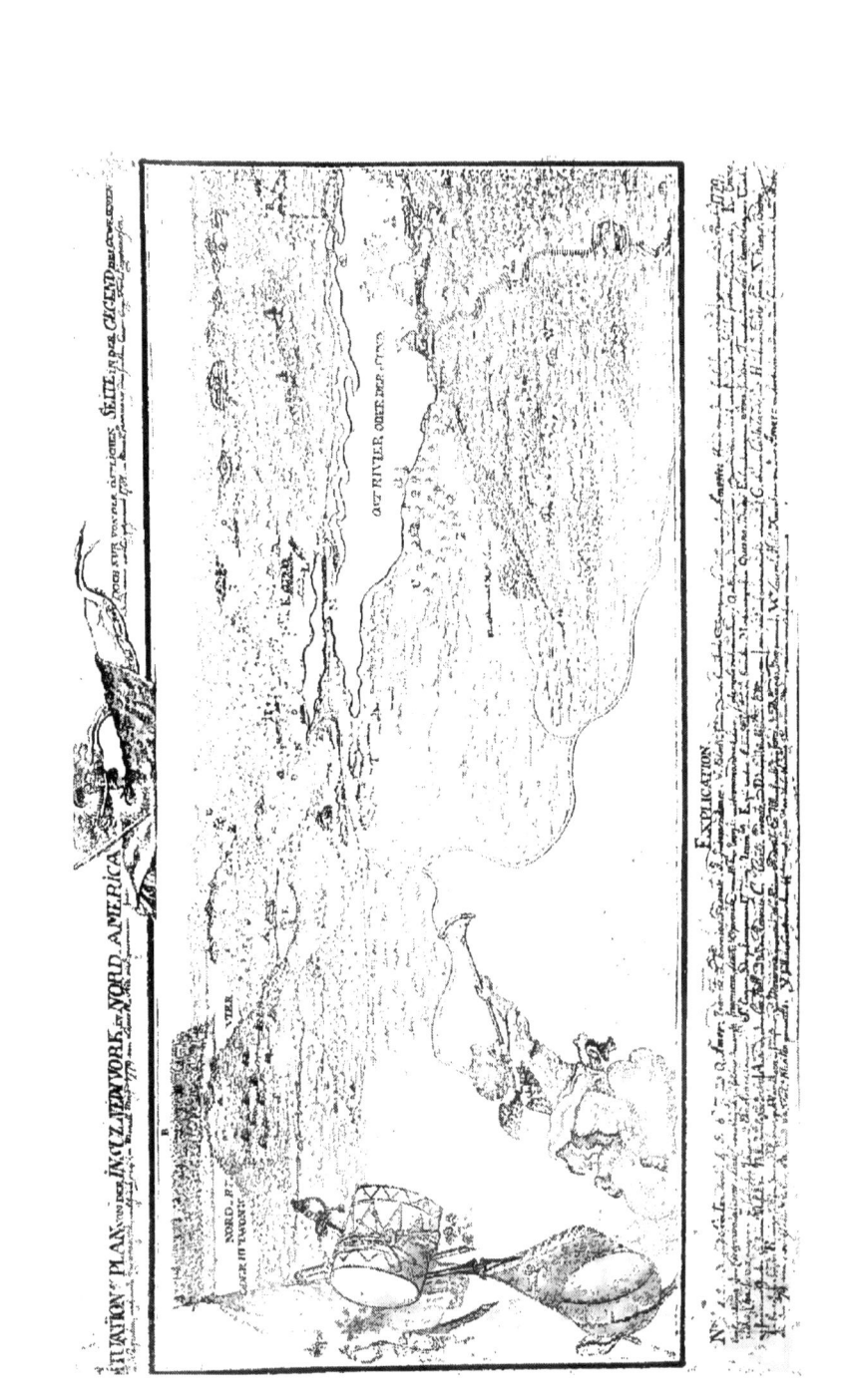

INDEX.

ALLENTOWN, 45
Amazetten (Amuzette), 57, 60, 63
American Militia, 15
American Privateer, 8
Amiott, M'lle Lisette, 7
Amsterdam, 1
Amuzette Yagers, 60
Anderson, Thomas, of New London, Pa., 14
André, Major, 120
Andresohn, Lieut. von, 63, 69
Anmerkungen, Preface, 1
Annotationes, Preface, 1
Anspach Regiment. See Troops, German
Anspach Yagers See Troops, German
Anticosti, 4
Appel, Dr , Preface, 3
Arndt, Col. Br. von, in American service at Valley Forge, 18, 20
Arnold, Gen. Benedict, deserter, 120; attacks Richmond, 131, New London, 149; plan of operations, plate 5
Arnold's House, No. 82 in the Pump Street, New York, 170
Artillery, English, 127, 201
Artillery, German See Troops, British

Backerstoss [Backenstose], Lieut., 15, 16, 17, 18
Baeren Huhel [Barren Hill] Church, Pa., 25, 26
Baggage Watch, 78, 109, 110

Baltic Sea, Preface, 2
Barlow, Capt. Godfrey Samuel, 8
Baron von Humboldt, Preface, 4
Baron von Krafft, Preface, 2
Barracks, 92, 115
Barrier, 145, 147
Bartenleben, Lieut [John von], 47
Baterson, Maj.-Gen. See Pattison
Battalions · Blatte, 127, 196; "Composite," 175 , First Delancey, New York Volunteers, 176 , First, 42d Regiment, 190 ; Fourth, 60th Regiment, 176, 190 , German (American), 18, 20 , von Graff, 85, 95, 116, 117, 126, 127, 129, 135, 139, 140 , Heine, 107 , Koehler, 70, 85, 88, 127 , von Lengecke, 85, 95, 127, 147, 175, 184, 196 , von Linsing, 85, 95, 127, 172, 178, 186, 196, von Loewenstein, 127, 172, 196 , von Münchenroth, 85, 95, 127 , Rall, 47, 55 , Second, 84th Regiment, 190 , Skinner, 176 , von Stein, 134, 135 , Third, 60th Regiment, 176, 190
Bauer, Auditor, 189
Bauer, Chief Surgeon, 169, 171
Bauermeister, Maj [Carl Leopold], 52
Bay, Kipps, 191, 192, 193 ; Turtle, 173, 174, 176, 177, 178, 180, 186, 187, 188, 191, 192

INDEX.

Bayard (*Beyer*), Col., house of, North River, 116
Bayreuth Regiment. See Troops, German
Beachy Head, 201
Becker, Lutheran Staff Chaplain, 173
Beekman's House, 185
Beer, Spruce, 3, 74, 82
Beicklandt [Pikeland], (Pa), 21
Bell, Major (American Militia), 15
Bender, Adam, 24
Bennin, Col. *Etmond*, 190
Benning Regiment See Troops, German
Bergen, N. J., 195
Bergen, David, of New York, 199
Bermann, Lieut , 54
Bettlehausen [Rittenhouse], (Pa), 35, 36
Bienau Regiment See Troops, German
Birthday, von Krafft's, 91, 111
Bischhausen, Maj -Gen [Carl E von], 189
Biskamp, Ensign, Lieut , 160, 181
Blackfort [Blackford], Md , 13
Black Horse Tavern, New Jersey, 42
Blatte's Garrison Battalion, 194, 196
Block-house, Laurel Hill, removed to Stony Point, 88, Paulus Hook, 121
Bloomingdale, 53, 101, 118, 122, Road, 164
Body Company, 106
Body Regiment. See Troops, German
Borbeck, Col. [Fred] von, 189
Bordeaux, 8
Bornholm (island), 1
Bose, Lieut -Gen. von, 80, 156, 171, 176, 179, 181
Bose, Major von, 1, 2 , in Washington's army, 19
Bose Regiment. See Troops, German

Boston, Mass , 5
Bostonier (Boston vessel), 10
Bowery, New York, 169
Brandywine, Pa., 15
Braunsberg, Preface 2 , 1, 39, 86, 87
Braunschweiger. See Troops, German
Breitsprach, Mrs , 147
Brew House, New York, 158
Bridge, King's, 90, 95, 168, 194
Brooklyn, 98, 188, 189
Brooklyn Ferry, 98, 100, 101, 104, 116, 125, 165, 188
Bunker Hill, N. Y., 105, 119, 120, 161, 184
Burgoyne, Gen , 10, 58, 110
Burgoyne's Army, 182, 183
Bureau, Equipment, 29
Buschhaussen, Col. von, 84, 189
Bushwick, L I., 97, 100, 188
Bushwick Church, 98, 99
Buy, Deu [Dupuy], Lieut.-Col., 181

Calais, 2
Canada, New, 15
Cape *Sante*, 5
Cariole, 176
Carleton, Gen , 4, 5, 6, 7, 160, 161, 162, 163, 164, 168, 172, 174, 177, 178, 179, 182, 184, 188, 190, 191, 198
Cassel, 38, 42, 107, 141, 154; Landgravine of, 122 , Princess Charlotte of Hesse, 167
Chabanell, Merchant, of Amsterdam, 1
Charles Redoubt. See Redoubts
Charles, Prince, Regiment. See Troops, German
Charleston, S C., 108, 111, 114, 122, 158, 166, 167, 168, 171
Charlotte of Hesse Cassel, Princess, 167
Chasseurs. See Troops, German
Chatham, England, 201
Cherry Street, New York, 78

Chester County, Pa , 14
Churches, 25, 26, 39, 40, 46, 59, 97, 98, 99, 106, 117, 157, 197
Churpfalz, 27
Cider, 15
Clinton, Gen. [Sir H.], 37, 40, 44, 50, 80, 81, 86, 87, 102, 108, 111–114, 120, 129, 131, 143, 145, 149, 152, 160, 162
Cocks and Hens (Mussels), 4
Coffee House, New York, 103, 104, 105, 111
Cole's ("Kohl's") Ferry, Staten Island, 199
College, English (King's), New York, 53, 71
Common Platz (Commons), N. Y., 158
Componirten, The. See Troops, German
Commissioners, English Peace, 39
Communipaw, N. J., 197
Congress, Continental, 1, 22, 39
Congress Money, 11, 12, 26
Cooper's Ferry, Pa., 40
Copenhagen, 1
Cork, Ireland, 8, 124, 164
Cornelia de la Metre, Preface, 3
Cornwallis, Gen. Lord, 88, 96, 102, 114, 120, 124, 134, 149, 152, 155, 182
Coronation Day, 171
Corps · Col. *Etmond Bennin's*, 190 , Emmerich's (see Troops, British Provincial), Hanau Free (see Troops, German), Hessian Artillery (see Troops, German), Hessian Free Yager Foot (see Troops, German), Lieut - Col Robert *Sonkin* [Simcoe] (see Troops, British Provincial), Lord Raden's (see Troops, British Provincial), of Hussars (see Troops, British Provincial), Pfenning's (see Troops, British Provincial); *Renny* (see Troops, British Provincial) ,

Robinson's (see Troops, British Provincial) , *Rooen's*, 104 , *R P.*, 104 , Simcoe's (see Troops, British Provincial); Tarleton's (see Troops, British Provincial), Yager (see Troops, German) , Zerbst Free (see Troops, German)
Courtlandt's House, 57, 58, 66
Courtlandt's Second House, 67, 68, plate 6
Cove of Cork, 8
Cox's Hill, 125, 127, 130, 135, 136, 138, 141 ; plate 6. See, also, North River Hill
Cramer, Merchant, Quebec, 4, 5, 6
Crossman, George, Barren Hill, Pa , 25, 26, 30
Cross Roads, Pa , 14
Crown Street, New York, 106

DANGELY REGIMENT, von. See Troops, German
Dangschinelli, Regiment von. See Troops, German
Danzig, 1
Danzig, Gulf of, Preface, 2
De La Metre (Delamater), Cornelia, 160, 162, 163, 166, 173
Delancey's New York Volunteers. See Troops, British Provincial
Delaware River, 39, 40
Delitzsch on-the-Hill, Preface, 2
Denstadt Company, Commissary, 31, 56
De Price, Lieut , 2, 4
Dienst Tabella, Preface, 1
Dittfort Regiment, von See Troops, German
Donop, Capt von, 30, 31, 36, 38 52, 55, 56, 62, 66, 73, 81, 83, 97, 109, 111, 119, 142, 156, 166
Donop, Col. von, 127
Donop Grenadier Company, 173 186
Donop, Lieut., Chamberlain, 125, 141

Donop, Lieut.-Gen von, 31, 38, 78, 79
Donop Regiment. See Troops, German
Douceur, English, 131, 177, 190, 192, 196, 197
Dover, England, 201
Doves [Dover] Town, Del, 13
Dove, Tavern, N. Y, 154, 186
Downings Town, Pa, 16
Downs, England, 198, 201
Dragoons, English, 112
Dragoons, Palatinate Kurpfalzer, 12
Dragoons, 17th Light, 190
Dresden, Preface, 2
Du Berry, Lieut.-Col, 181
Dubois, Saxon Ambassador, 38
Duck Creek, Del, 13
Dupuy, Brigadier Major von, 28, 29, 37
Dupuy, Gen, Quarter Master, 184
Dupuy, Lieut.-Col., 134, 155, 181, 184
Dutch Church, New York, 106, 197
Dutch Flag, 2

EASTER SUNDAY, 83
Eastern Prussia, Preface, 2
East Florida, 156
East River, 54, 61, 80, 97, 103, 148, 180, 186
Eigenbrod, Capt. [John George], 175, 176, 177, 178, 179, 180, 182, 185, 189, 192, 193, 194, 198
Eigenbrod Company, 176, 197
Eingissen (Dutch) Church, 106
Elizabeth Town, N J., 112, 113, 114, 124, 197
Emmerich's Camp, 82, plate 6
Emmerich's Corps. See Troops, British Provincial
Emmerich, Lieut.-Col. [Andreas], 64, 139, 146
Emplestown [Imlaytown], 45

Engineers, Assistant to the, 159, 162
England, King of, 39, 111, 184, 190, 193
English Artillery, 107, 148, 176
English Channel, 2
English College, 53
English Tower, 2
Equipment Bureau, 29
Erb Prinz Regiment. See Troops, German
Erskine, Gen., 61
Eudel [Eitell]. [Henry], Lieut.-Col. of Artillery, 28
Ewaldt, Capt, 62

FAHNEN JUNKER (Ensign), 106
Falmouth, Eng., 2, 55, 59, 78, 80
Fanning's Corps. See Troops, British Provincial
Ferry, Brooklyn, 98, 100, 104, 106, 188, *Cooper's*, 40; Hell Gate, 133, 161, Holland's, 130, 147, plate 6. *Kohl's* (Cole's), 199, Paulus Hook, 122, 123
Finater, Capt., 36
Fiva, Provost Capt., 83
Flachshaar, Reg. Quarter Master, 174, 183, 184
Flasche, 92, 125
Florida, West, 67, 102, 142, East, 156
Flushing Bay (*Flushings-Fleg*), 126
Fly Market Wharf, 202, Preface, 3
Follertin, Madame, 78, 87
Follert, Lohnichen (Helen), 86
Follert, Merchant, Braunsberg, 86
Foot Yagers, 95
Foreland, England, 201
Fort, at Verplanck's Point, 86, 95, *Forsed* Hill [Fort Tryon], 84, 86, 87, 88, 90, 92, 93, 146, George, 53, 111, 164, Independence, 57, 68, 90, 94, 132, 144, King's Redoubt, 73,

INDEX. 207

75, 82, 94; Knipphaussen (formerly Ft. Washington), 69, 72, 77, 80, 81, 84, 85, 90, 92, 101, 122, 123, 124, 125, 129, 130, 132, 133, 139, 141, 142, 143, 145, 148, 150, 166, Laurel Hill, 84, 85, 99, 144, Lee, 137, North River (Cox's) Hill, 72, 75, 76, 127, No. 1 (New York), 69, 73, 80, 83, 84; No 1, in the woods (near Philadelphia), 35, No. 2 (New York), 69, 82, No. 3 (New York), 69, No 4 [formerly Ft. Independence], (New York), 94; No. 5 (New York) 94, No. 6 (New York), 94, No 7 (New York), 73, 93, No. 8 (New York), 93, 94, 96, 123, 126, 130, 133, 140, 143, 144, 145, 146, 151, No 9, on the Schuylkill, 34, 35; No 10 (near Philadelphia), 38; Snake Hill, 144, 151, 153, Stone, N. Y., 145, Stony Point, 87, 94, 95, Red Bank, plan of, plate 3, Fortifications on N Y. Island, see plate 6
Foundry Redoubt, 117
Frederick, Prince, 189
Frederick the Great, Preface, 2
Free Corps, Hanau See Troops, German
Freehold, N. J, 45, 46, 48
Free Yager Foot Corps. See Troops, German
Frimel, von, Hessian yager, 30
Frische Haff, Preface, 2
Fuchter, Corporal, 134
Führer, Hessian Officer, 151

GALEE (Calais), 2
Gantlet, run, 30, 156, 157, 161, 166, 177, 184, 193
Garrison Guard Battalion of Prinz Carl. See Troops, German
Garrison Regiment Bienau. See Troops, German

Garrison Regiment, Wiesenbachs. See Troops, German
Georgetown, Preface, 4
German Battalion (American Army). See Troops, American
German Church, N Y., Preface, 3
Germantown, Pa, 21, 22, 23, 26, 33, 35, 36, 38; battle at, plate 4
Gibraltar, 174
Giesold Company, 173
Giessen, Lieut., 157
Giles, William Ogden, 132
Glenwood Springs, Preface, 4
Goldbeck, William Freeman, Preface, 2
Goosen, Col. von, 31, 38, 71, 98, 99, 106, 108, 109, 115, 119
Gosen Maj.-Gen. von, 191, 197
Graff, Lieut.-Col, 116
Grando, Sergt., 34
Grasse, Admiral [Count] de, 160
Green Dragoons, 19
Greene, Gen, 18, 134
Greenwich, New York City, 161
Grenadier Battalion, Blatte, Graff, 135, Koehler, von Lengecke, von Linsing, Loewenstein, von Münchenroth. See Troops, German
Grenadier Regiment, von Benning, Dangschinelli, von Heine, Knoblock, von Rall, von Sietz, von Stein, Woellwarth. See Troops, German
Gremen, Lieut, 158
Grenada, West Indies, 90
Grey, Gen [Charles], 179
Gross, Rev. Daniel, Preface, 3
Guard Regiment, Bienau. See Troops, German
Guards, English, 23 See, also, Troops, British
Gulf of Danzig, Preface, 2

HACHENBERG, Maj.-Gen., 190, 191
Hackensack, N J., 107

INDEX.

Haddonfield, N J., 41
Hague, The, 1, 38
Halifax, Nova Scotia, 166, 174, 199, 200
Hallmann, Adam, 21
Hanau Free Corps, 151, 171, 182, 183
Hanger, George von, 56, 57, 68, 69, 71
Harlem, 53, 84, 95, 123, 144
Harlem River, 80, 130, 147
Hartmann, Lieut., 162, 169, 170, 171
Hartong, *Fourier*, 63
Hatsky, Merchant, of New York, 155, 178
Haussen, Ensign von, 141
Haussmann, Lieut , 177
Heiligenbeil, Preface, 3
Heine Regiment. See Troops, German
Heine, Major-Gen., 117
Hell Gate, 97, 117
Hell Gate Ferry, 133, 147, 161
Helsingor, 1
Henckle, Ensign von, 141
Henel, Lieut. and Adjt., 171
Henndorf, Skinner, Ensign, 170
Henry, Prince William, 151, 164, 169
Herbert, Musketeer, 108, 109
Hesse-Anspachers, 104
Heyden, Sergeant von, a nobleman, 58
Heymel, Col. [Charles], 131, 132, 139, 155
Heijnemann, Sergt , 43
High Wharf, New York, 195
Hildburghauser, 48
Hill, Bunker, 105, 119, 120, 161 , *Forsed*, 84, 90, 92, 146 , Laurel, 84, 87, 94, 96, 99, 125, 127, 135, 139, 144 ; North River, or Cox's, 72, 75, 83, 95, 101, 127, 130, 135, 138, 149, Snake, 144, 151, Spuyten Duyvil, 57, 72, 80, 83, 93
Hindle, Lieut -Col. [Erasmus Er-nest], 29, 30, 66, 83, 103, 106, 108, 111, 119, 126, 128, 133, 141, 142, 150, 155
Hohenlohe, Princes of, Preface, 2
Holland's Ferry, 130, 147
Holly Mount, N. J , 41
Homburg, Hesse, 79
Hook, Paulus, 101, 121, 147, 193, 194, 195, 196, 197, 198, 199
Hook, Sandy, 51, 121, 124, 145, 192, 199, 200, 202
Horse, Light. 23, 25, 26, 38, 39, 40, 62, 63, 82, 85, 112, 113
Hospital, College, 53, 71 , Hessian, 196 , New, 118
House, Brew, 158 , Coffee, 104, 105 ; Col. Bayard's,116 ; Courtlandt's, 66, 68, 143 ; Jones's, 54, 140 146, 148, 150 ; Morris, 129, 132, 140, 149, 151, 171, 197 , Phillipse, 60, 66, 67, 68, 81, 86, 88, 115, 116, 124, 143 ; Sugar, 120 ; Red, 159
Howe, Admiral, 52, 164, 169 ; Gen Sir William, 27, 36, 37
Humboldt, Baron von, Preface, 4

IMLAYTOWN, N J., 45
Independence, Fort, 57, 68, 90, 94, 132, 144 , see plate 6
Indian Tea, 4
Infantry, English Light, 85, 118, 123, 147, 148 ; Prinz Field, 127 ; Queen's Rangers, 95
Inn, The Black Horse, 42 , The Dove, 154 , The General Montgomery, 14, The Rising Sun, 38, The White Horse, 16, 20, 23
In Thebe, The (ship), 9
Irish Volunteers, 107
Island, Long, 104, 110, 126, 133, 147, 160, 161 , Rhode, 117, 118 ; Staten, 104, 111, 114, 115, 116, 124, 129, 180

JACOB WOLFFRAM, The, 1
Jersey, The (Prison Ship), 158
Jews, 201

INDEX. 209

Johannis Tag, 140
Johnson, Col., 17th Regt., 87, 126
Johnson's House, 129, 140
Jones's House, New York, 53, 54, 129, 140, 146, 147, 148, 150
Junckheim, Gen. von, 31, 38, 106, 119, 141
Juncken, Maj.-Gen. von, 31, 119
Jungken-Munzer, Gen. von, 141
Junker, Fahnen, 106
Junker, Kammer, 125
Junker, Port Épée, 58

KARL REGIMENT, Prinz. See Troops, German
Kayser (resident No 30 Bowery, New York), 169, 171, 172, 193
Kersting, Lieut., 172, 191
Killmann, Sally, 100
Killmann, Thomas, 97
King of England, 39, 161, 184, 190, 193
King's American Regiment, The, 165, 176
King's Bridge, New York, 54, 58, 70, 73, 82, 90, 95, 118, 168, 194; Road, Preface, 3
King's Redoubt, 75, 82, see plate 6
King's Street, New York, 157
Kip's Bay, 191, 192, 193, 194, 195
Klein, a grenadier, 177
Kleinschmitt, Ensign, 59, 151
Kleist, Ensign von, 162, 171
Klington, Gen See Clinton
Knipphaussen, Fort, 54, 69, 72, 77, 80, 81, 90, 101, 122, 123, 128, 130, 132, 137, 139, 143, 144, 145, 147, 148, 150, 151, 166
Knipphaussen, Lieut.-Gen. von, 28, 29, 30, 37, 38, 40, 50, 56, 60, 73, 102, 115, 132, 154, 160
Knipphaussen Regiment. See Troops, German

Knoblanch, Ensign von, 141
Knoblock Regiment. See Troops, German
Koehler Grenadier Battalion. See Troops, German
Kohl's (Cole's) Ferry, 199
Konigsberg, Preface, 2
Kosbotr, Lieut. Lui von, 159, 165, 166, 173, 174; Maj.-Gen. von, 181, 189, 190
Krafft, Lieut. John Charles Philip von, family of, birth in Dresden, Saxony, officer in Prussian Army under Frederick the Great, Preface, 1; resigns, visits St Petersburg, declines cornetcy in Russian Army, sails for Holland, English confiscate his journal, 1; sails from Vaarlingen, taken a prisoner to Falmouth, loses his papers and letters, sails for Quebec to join the 53d, 2; arrives and stays five months at Port au Basques, 3; arrives at Quebec, 4; at Trois Rivieres, refused enlistment, returns to Quebec, 5; in prison, 6, in want, sent back to England, 7; falls in love with French maiden, 7, arrives Ireland, sails for France, at Bordeaux, joins American privateer, 8; near New York, 9, on coast of Maryland, 10, lands at Sinepuxint, 11; starts to join Washington's army, 12; refuses second lieutenancy in Pennsylvania regiment at Valley Forge, 16; quarrels with two captains, 19, refuses first lieutenancy under Washington, 20, escapes to Philadelphia, 20–27, becomes sergeant in Donop's Hessian Regiment, 29, puts English sergeant to flight, fights duel with Hessian quartermaster, 31; wounds

210   INDEX.

Hessian corporal in duel, 33 ; acts as second for same, 34 ; thrashes a soldier, 34 , in engagement near Germantown, 36 , arrested for quarrel with army surgeon, 36 , marches against the rebels in New Jersey, 37–44 , at Freehold, 45 , at Monmouth, 45–47 , in engagement with rebels near Freehold, 47 ; quarrel with a free corporal, 50 ; at Sandy Hook, 51 , in New York, 52 , in camp between Harlem and Bloomingdale, 53 , joins von Hanger's chasseurs, 55 , in camp at Spuyten Duyvil Hill, 57 , in skirmish, 57 ; sick, 59 ; camps [in St. John's Church, Yonkers] near Philipse House, 60 ; in fights with rebels, 62, 64 ; in White Plains, 64 , in camp near Courtlandt's [upper] house, 66 , in camp eleventh milestone below [i e , under] Fort Knyphaussen, 71 , visits New York City, 71 , wounds his leg, 75 , suffers from bad provisions, 76 , on baggage watch in New York, 78 , takes a furlough to New York, disgusted with English soldiers, quarrels with, 82 ; assists engineers on Laurel Hill, 84 , accidentally shot, 85 , suffers severely from fever, 88 , birthday of, 91 , crosses with regiment to Brooklyn, 97 , acting quartermaster, 98 , punishes impudent groom, 99 , in love, 100 , with regiment in New York, 101 , thrashes two English sergeants, 103 ; visits sweetheart, Sally Skillmaen, 104 , duties of, in New York, 105, 111 , made ensign, 106 , with regiment in New Jersey, 112 , in engagement near Elizabethtown, 112, 114 , with regiment in Brooklyn, 116 ; at Fort Knyphaussen, 117 ; in New York City, 118 , fails of promotion and demands discharge, 119 ; sick, 119 , at Powle's Hook, 121 , at Fort Knyphaussen, 122 , challenged, 134 ; garden of, 138 , deplores loose conduct of soldiers, 140 , impatient at deferred promotion, 141 , on command at Harlem, 152 ; sickness of, 154, 155 ; commissioned ensign in Bose's regiment, 154 ; thrashes soldier, 155 , in New York, 156 , on duty in prison-ship Jersey, 158 ; assistant engineer, 159 , future wife's father dies, 160 , duels with ensign, 160, 162 ; attacked with fever, 169 , quartered with one Kayser in the Bowery, 169 ; duel with ensign, 170 , with company on East River, 172 , calls chaplain to christen infant, 173 , at Turtle Bay, 174 , attacked with fever, 176 , receives lieutenant's commission, 181 , attacked with scrofula, 182 , visits Skillmaen and daughter, 188 , at Kip's Bay, 191, at Powle's Hook, 193 , embarks with Hessian regiments for England, 199 , experiences stormy voyage, 200 , arrives at Deal, 201 , in London, 202 , sails for New York, 202 , arrives at Fly Market wharf, 202 , is publicly married at First Dutch Church, becomes teacher in New York, then surveyor and draughtsman to U. S Treasury Department, removes with the Department to Washington, Preface, 3 , resides in Georgetown, visited there by Humboldt, advised by him to

visit Germany and reclaim maternal estate, is about to do so, sickens, and dies, *idem*, 4 , his person and characteristics, prominence of his descendants, *idem*, 4
Kuntz, Lieut. von, 171
Kurpfalzer Dragoons, 12

LANCASTER, Pa., 15, 18
Landgraf Regiment. See Troops, German
Landgravine of Cassel, 122
Landing Place, New York, 150
Laurel Hill, 84, 85, 87, 92, 94, 96, 99, 125, 127, 130, 131, 135, 137, 139, 144, 147 , works on, plate 6
Laurens, Col. [John], 19, 20
Lechleidner, ex-drummer, 12, 13
Lee, Fort, 136, 137
Leffert's House, New York, 172
Lehrbach, Ensign von, 30, 49
Leib Regiment. See Troops, German
Leipsig, Preface, 2
Leliva, Capt. [William von], 170, 174, 177, 185
Lengecke Battalion. See Troops, German
Lengecke, Col [George E.] von, 156, 161, 170, 172, 175, 176, 180, 181, 185, 186, 188, 192, 195, 196, 197, 201
Lepel, Lieut. [William] von, 29, 96 ; Adjt Capt von, 78
Letterloh, Col., American Regimental Quartermaster, Valley Forge, 17, 19
Liberty Street, New York, 106
Light Infantry, English, 85, 95, 118, 121, 123, 147, 148
Light Dragoons, 17th English, 190
Light Horse (American), 23, 25, 62, 63, 112, 113 ; (British), 26, 36, 38, 39, 40, 85 , Green Penn Provincial, 82
Light House, Sandy Hook, 51

Linsing Battalion. See Troops, German
Lizard, The, 201
Loewenstein Battalion. See Troops, German
Lohnichen Follert, 86
London, 200, 201, 202
Long Island, 39, 51, 104, 106, 116, 118, 121, 123, 126, 133, 147, 148, 150, 161, 165, 180, 183, 187, 191
Lord *Raden's* Corps, 95
Loose, Col von, 93
Losberg, Col von, 34 , Lieut von, 30 , Maj.-Gen von, 124, 129, 152, 161, 183, 184, 186, 197, 198, 201
Losberg Regiment. See Troops, German
Lossow's Regiment. See Troops, German
Loyal American Regiment. See Troops, British Provincial
Luck, Maj.-Gen von, Preface, 2
Ludwig, Regimental Quarter Master, 174, 177
Lundcranz, American privateersman, 9
Lyle, Capt. of American privateer, 8

Maas, Capt , Chief Engineer, British, 160
McGowan's Pass, N Y , 147, 148, 151, 152, 153, 155, 161, 167, 168, 185, 194
Magazine, Royal Wood, East River, New York, 148 , Powder, Turtle's Bay, New York, 173
Maiden Lane, New York, 109
Makebrand, Lieut. von, 122
Malet, Capt von, 186, 191
Manor House (Yonkers), 81
Maria Catharina, The (ship), 8
Marshall, Lieut., Engineers, and of 60th Regiment, 85, 86, 96, 99
Martefeldt, von, 58

INDEX.

Martinique, 9, 123
Martin's Wharf, New York, 55, 97, 101, 117, 123, 140, 150, 154, 172, 182
Maryland, 10
Masco (Hessian officer), von, 151
Matthew, Gen. [Edward], 119
Mecklenburg-Schwerin, Duke of, 125
Mercel. See Marshall
Mertz, Lieut., 62
Methiadeur, The (ship), 6
Metre, Cornelia de la, Preface, 3
Meyer, Lieut. von, 6
Middletown, N. J., 48, 49
Milestones, Preface, 3, 24, 25, 53, 140, 148
Mirbach Regiment. See Troops, German
Mistor's Wharf, Long Island, 133, 174
Monmouth County, N. J., 45, 46 47, plan of battle, plate 2
Montgomery, The General, an inn, Delaware, 14
Montgomery, Gen Richard, 132
Montreal, 6
Morhardt, Capt, 78, 79
Morrisania, N. Y., 123, 130, 136, 137, 144, 145, 147
Morris, Col., 123
Morris House, N. Y. [later, Jamel Mansion], 56, 73, 80, 129, 132, 149, 151, 171, 197
Morrison, Gen., 190
Morristown [Moorestown], N. J., 41
Mount Holly, N. J., 41
Muller, a Quaker, near New Canada, Pa., 15, Free Corp., 32, 33, 34, 82
Munchenroth Battalion, 85, 95, 127
Munchhausen, Capt. von, 27, Col. von, 155, 181
Mutual Life Ins Co., 106
Muus, Free Corp. Emanuel, 30, 32, 33, 34, 48, 49, 82

NAGEL, COL. GEORGE, Pennsylvania Regiment, 16, 17, 25, 26, 1st Lieut. von, 35, 86, 90
Negro Hut Camp, Morrisania, N. Y., 130, plate 6
Newark (Pa.), 14
New Canada, Pa, 15
Newtown Creek, L. I, 187
Newfoundland, 9
New Hospital, N. Y, 118
New Jersey, British army crosses, 41–50, troops to, 111–114, 144
New London, Conn., 149, plan of Arnold's operations against, plate 5
New London, Pa., 14
Newtown, L. I., 133, 161, 187
New York Volunteers, Delancey's, 176
North, Capt., 2; Lord, 198
North Carolina, 134, 137
North Dutch Church, N. Y., 197
North River Hill, 72, 75, 76, 83, 95, 101, 127, 130, 135, 136, 141, 149, plate 6. See, also, Cox's Hill
Notchwarb [Nut Swamp], N. J., 47
"Notes by the Way," Preface, 1
Nottingham, The, 7
Nova Scotia, 179, 181, 187, 190, 192, 194

OLD LOSBERG REGIMENT, 134, 170
Oreily, Major von, 156
Oysters in Harlem River, 80

PACKET BOAT, English, 105, 179, 193
Palatinate Kurpfälzer Dragoons, 12, 27
Parlow, Gottfried Samuel, 8
Parade Place, The Great, Philadelphia, 39
Parmy, Col., 12
Passarge, Preface, 2

INDEX. 213

Pass, McGowan's, 147, 151, 153, 155, 161, 167, 168, 185, 194
Pattison, Gen James R, 102, 119
Paulus Hook, 91, 105, 107, 121, 146, 147, 180, 194, 195, 196, 197, 198, 199, Ferry, 122
Pennsylvania Regiment, 10th. See Troops, American
Pfenning's [Fanning's] Corps. See Troops, British Provincial
Philadelphia, 9, 12, 24, 26, 27, 29, 35, 39, 40, 93, plan of operations at, plate 4
Phillipse's House, Yonkers, N. Y., 60, 61, 64, 66, 67, 68, 81, 86, 88, 115, 116, 136, 143
Phillips, Maj.-Gen. [William], 110
Picasinen, 166
Pigot, Admiral [Hugh], 168
Pikeland, Pa., 21
Pioneer Huts, N. Y., 147
Plymouth Light House, 201
Port au Basques, 3
Portsmouth, England, 202
Potter, Thomas, sea-captain, 200
Price, Lieut., 2, 4
Prinz Carl Regiment. See Troops, German
Prince Charles Redoubt, 124, 125, 140
Princess Charlotte of Hesse Cassel, 167
Prince Field Infantry, 127
Prince Frederick, 189
Prince Henry William, 151, 163, 164, 169
Prince of Prussia Regiment, 58
Prince of Wales Regiment, 107, 176
Prison hospital for sick Rebels at New York, 104, 107
Privateer, American, 8, 9, 11
Pump Street, New York, 170

QUEBEC, 2, 6, 152
Queen's Bridge, plate 6

Queen's Rangers, 95, 107
Queen Street, Philadelphia, 29

Raden [Rawdon], Lord, 90, 137
Rall Battalion See Troops, German
Rangers, English Royal, 73
Rangers, Queen's, 95, 107
Raritan River, 48
Rath, Herr von, 78
Rau, Capt. von, 142
Rawdon's Corps, Lord, 88, 90, 94, 95
Recklestown [*Racklestown*], N. J., 42
Red Bank Fort, plan of, plate 3
Red House, N Y., 157
Redoubt, Charles, 88, 124, 125, 140, 150, plate 6; Foundry, 117, King's, 82, 94, 144, Laurel Hill, 84: No 1, 83, 84, No. 2, 69, No. 3, 83: No 4 [Ft. Independence], 94, No. 5, 94, No 7, 93, No 8, 94, 96, 130, 140, *Stackat* (Stockade), 121; Snake Hill, 144, Stone, 145, 148
Refugee Camp, 130
Refugees, 136, 137, 138, 160, 179, 181, 183, 187, 194
Renny Corps, 123
Rhode Island, 117, 118, 145, 174
Richmond, Va., 131
Ridge Road, Pa, 26
Riedesel, Gen. [Frederick A] von, 5, 110
Rising Sun Inn, The, near Philadelphia, 38
Rittenhouse, Pa., 35, 36
Roberdeaux [Daniel], Member of Congress, 2
Robertson, Gov. [Gen. James], 160, 181
Robinson's Corps, 87, 95, 123
Robinson Street, New York, 71
Rodney, Admiral, 119
Roemer, Sergt.-Maj, 29, 31, 32, 33, 50

214   INDEX.

Roll (Mr.), married a sister of Cornelia de la Metre, 173
Rooen's Corps, 104
Ross, Lord, 113
Rotterdam, 2
Royal Rangers, 73
Royal Wood Magazine, 148
R P Corps, The, 104

SALLY, The, 195, 197, 201
Sandy Hook, 51, 145, 150, 192, 200, 202, Preface, 3
Sante, Cape, 5
Savanna, Ga, 152, 165
Saxony, Preface, 2
Schaefer, Corporal Conrad, 32
Schawroth, Sergt. von, nobleman, 58
Scheel, The new, New York, 101
Scheer, Major, 174, 183, 185, 188
Schlagenteufel, Captain von, 5, 110
Schmalz, Councillor of War, 122
Schmid's House, near fifth Mile stone, New York, 173
Schmidt, Paymaster, 38
Schonwolf, Corporal, 50, Ensign, 106
Schuylkill, 16, 18, 21, 27, 32, 33, 34, 36, 39
Schwartz, Sergt.-Major, 54
Seitz Regiment. See Troops, German
Sick Rebels' Prison, 104, 107, 120
Simcoe, Col. [J Graves], 81, 190
Sinepuxent, Md. See *Synntebox*
Skillmaen, Sally, 188, her father, of Bushwick, L I., 188
Skinners, 170, 176
Snake Hill, Harlem, 144, 151, 153
Sonkin, Lieut -Col. Robert, 190
South Carolina, 126, 137, 156
Spangenberg, Quarter Master, 171, 174, 179, 184, 188, 189
Spohr, Orderly, 177
Spraul (Sproule), Lieut [George], 84, 94, 96, 99

Springfield, N. J., 115
Spuyten Duyvil Hill, 57, 72, 80, 83. 93, 94, see plate 6
Square, Court, Philadelphia, 35
Staff, Capt. von, 39
Stamberg (Hildburghäuser), 48
Staten Island, 51, 92, 93, 104, 111, 114, 115, 116, 124, 129, 147, 150, 153
St Augustine, 194
Stedenfeldt, Sergt von, 32
Stein, Regiment, von, 128; Major von, 134
Stern, Gen, 40
St George's Inn, Falmouth, England, 2
Stieglitz, Surgeon, 107
Stone Redoubt, 145
Stony Point, 87, 88, 94, 95, Fort, 87, 95
Store, Naval, 157
St. Patrick Inn, Newark, Pa, 14
St. Paul, 4
St. Paul's Church, New York, 157
St Peter's Island, 3
St Petersburg, 1, Preface, 3
St Vincent, West Indies, 90
Swedish Church on the Delaware, 39, 40
Synntebox [Sinepuxent], Maryland, 10, 11, 13, 20

TAPPAN, 182
Tarleton, Col., 190
Terhorst, Capt, 2
Thames, The, 202; Preface, 3
Throsby, Capt., 2
Thumer, Capt, 81
Ticonderoga, 6, 7
Tittfort [Dittfort] Regiment, von. See Troops, German
Titus, Francis, 97
Tomson, Lieut., 9
Tonnerfeldt, Capt, 4, 6, 7
Trap, The, Pa., 22
Treasury Department, Preface, 3
Trenton, 55; plan of the battle of, plate 1

INDEX.

Trimbach Regiment. See Troops, German
Trois Rivieres, Canada, 5, 6
Troops, *American* German Battalion, 18, 20, Green Penn. Provincial Light Horse, 82; Light Horse, 23, 25, 62, 63, 112, 113, Militia, 25; 10th Pennsylvania Musketeer Regiment, 15, 16
Troops, *British* Artillery, 127, 176, 201, Guards, The, 86, 121; Grenadiers, The, 121, 123, 129, 147, 148, 180, Light Horse, 26, 36, 38, 39, 40, 85; Light Infantry, 118, 123, 131, 147, 148, 7th Regiment, 93, 95, 165, 190, 15th Musketeer Regiment, 41, 16th Regiment, 142, 16th Regiment (Scotch), 131; 17th Regiment, 85, 87, 126, 140, 141, 176, 190, Camp, plate 6, 17th Dragoon Regiment, 148, 190, 22d Regiment, 112, 118, 122, 140, 176, 190, 23d Regiment, Guards, 86, 93, 95, 101, 176, 190, 27th Regiment, 194; 33d Regiment, 95, 190, 37th Regiment, 95, 108, 148, 149, 150, 190, 38th Regiment, 126, 139, 147, 148, 150, 190; 40th Regiment, 158, 180, 190, 40th Regiment (Scotch), 101, 42d Regiment, 95, 107, 122, 131, 190, 42d Scotch Regiment, 101, 122, 148, 165, 172, 43d Regiment, 101, 116, 140, 148, 190, 191, 195, 198, 44th Regiment, 89, 92, 93, 101, 110; Camp, plate 6; 46th Regiment, 101; 52d Musketeer Regiment, 58, 54th Regiment, 95, 104, 120, 121, 147, 148, 149, 180, 190, 57th Regiment, 85, 89, 92, 95, 104, 123, 131, 148, 190, 60th Regiment, 86, 142, 176, 190; 63d Regiment, 95, 64th Regiment, 95, 70th Regiment, 190, 71st Regiment, 95, 74th Regiment, 190, 76th Regiment (Scotch), 101, 106, 123, 124, 125, 126, 140, 190, 191, 80th Regiment, 101, 106, 123, 125, 126, 190; 81st Regiment, 95; 82d Regiment, 106, 190; 84th Regiment, 190
Troops, *British Provincial* Delancey's Battalion, 130, 176, Emmerich's Corps, 60, 61, 64, 68, 82, 92; Fanning's Corps, 86, 95, Irish Volunteers, 95, 107, King's American Regiment, 176, Loyal American Regiment, The, 125, 126, 153, Prince of Wales Volunteers, 107, 176, Rawdon's Corps, 88, 90, 94, 95, Renny's Corps, 123, Queen's Rangers, 95, 107, Robinson's Corps, 85, 87, 95, 123, Royal Rangers, 73, Simcoe's Corps, 81, 190, *Thumer's* Hussars, 123
Troops, *German* [Battalions]: Artillery, 28, 196, Blatte. 127, 189, 194, 196, Graff, 85, 95, 116, 117, 125, 126, 127, 129, 135, 139, 140, Koehler, 70, 85, 86, 127, Lengecke, 85, 95, 127, 147, 175, 184, 196, 198; Linsing, 85, 95, 127, 178, 186, 196, Loewenstein, 127, 172, 196, Munchenroth, 85, 95, 127, Prinz Carl, 85
Troops, *German* [Regiments] Anspach, 63, 101, 117, 118, 121, 122, 123, 135; Bayreuth, 101, 114, 117, 118, 122, 145, Benning, 128, 141, 188, 189, 190, Bienau, 101, 113, 117, 123, 128, 148, 188, 189, Body, 53, 81, 82, 85, 99, 101, 113, 117, 118, 142, 183, 191, 196, Bose, 81, 84, 85, 89, 93, 95, 96, 113, 145, 152, 156, 175, 183, 184, 186, 187, 188, 189, Braunschweiger's, 5, 58, 181,

182, 183, Componirten, 131, 158, 175; *Dangschinelli*, 128, 186, 188, 189, Dittfort, 107, 108, 128, 176, 188, 189, Donop, 29, 34, 36, 56, 61, 65, 70, 85, 87, 89, 111, 113, 115, 116, 122, 123, 128, 131, 139, 160, 172, 177, 196, 198 Erb Prinz, 54, 56, 61, 69, 91, 101, 127, 152, 183, 196, Erb Prinz, *vacant*, 183, 187. 188, 189, Heine, 107, 114, 128, Knobloch's, 124, 128, 165, 188, 189, 109, Knyphaussen, 55, 56, 70, 80, 91, 93, 120, 124, 126, 128, 131, 152, 168, 170, 188, 189; Landgraf, 86. 88, 89, 94, 101, 113, 117, 118, 122, 127, 141, 159, 162, 168, 182, 183; Leib, 32, 56, 61, 88, 89, 127, Losberg, 34, 55, 56, 80, 93, 96, 110, 124, 126, 128, 131, 148, Lossow's, 58, Mirbach, 56, 73, 84, 86, 101, 116, 123, 128, Prinz Carl, 56, 85, 89, 92, 101, 119, 122, 127, 148, 160, 173, 196, 201; Rall, 47, 55, 128, Sietz, 56, 128, 190, Stein, 128, Trimbach, 56, 69, 70, 72, 81, 96, 102, 128, Wiessenbach, 54, 56, 61, 67, 102, 128, Woellwoerth, 41, 56, 59, 65, 67, 70, 128, Wottgenau, 88, 127, Zeis, 158, Brunswickers, 182, 183; Chasseurs, 55, 56, 57, 59, 60, 63. 79, 99, 122, Free Yager Foot Corps, 30, 38, 57, 127; Hanau Free Corps, 151, 171, Hanau recruits, 134, 146, Hessian Artillery Corps, 196, Waldeckers, 142, 171, 186, Yagers, Anspach, 123, 187, Yagers, Mounted, 142, Zerbst Free Corps, 134, 146, 186
Trottijour, Lieut., 167
Trott, Sr. Lieut von, 181, 185, 186, 188, 189, 191 : Lieut. von, 167, 173

Tryon, Gen., 81, 83, 86, 119
Turtle Bay, 54, 173, 174, 176, 177, 178, 180, 186, 187, 188, 189, 191, 192
Two Brothers, The, 2

URFF, Capt. [Frederick] von, 33

VAARLINGEN, 2
Vacant Erb Prinz Regiment. See Troops. German
Vacant Sietz Regiment, 190
Valley Forge, 16 ; operations at, plate 4
Verplanck's Point, 86, 95
Vigilant, The, 202, Preface, 3
Virginia, 150
Vogt Grenadier Co., 186
Volunteers, Irish, 95, 107

WAGEHALS, Ensign, 186
Wahls Mill, N. J, 45
Waldeck, Lieut., 135
Waldeck Regiment See Troops, German
Wales Regiment, Prince of. See Troops, British
Wall Street, New York, 103
Wallenfels, Capt von, 63
Washington, Fort See Fort Knyphaussen
Washington, Gen George, 12, 16, 17, 18, 19, 20, 27, 112, 182
Wayne, Gen., 18
Weinstockin, Miss, 87
Weissenborn, Auditor, 170
Werkhooven, The, 1
Werner, Ensign, 47
West Florida, 142
West Indies, 119, 160
Westphal, Capt, Preface, 2
Wharf, East, 118, Fly Market, 202 ; High, 195 ; Martin's, 97, 101, 117, 118, 140, 150, 154, 172, 182, *Mistor's*, 133, 174, West, 105, 106, 109, 111, 116, 117, 119, 161
Whigs, 25

White Horse Inn, Pennsylvania, 16, 20, 23
White Marsh, Pa., plate 4
White Plains, 64
Wiessenbach's Regiment. See Troops, German
Wilwart Brigade, 35, 41
Woellwarth Regiment. See Troops, German
Wolffram, Jacob, The, 1
Wood Magazine, Royal, 147
Wottgenau Regiment. See Troops, German
Wurmb, Lieut.-Col [Philip] von, 57, 66, 127; Maj. [Charles] von, 30, 32, 153; Maj.-Gen. von, 196

YAGER FOOT CORPS See Troops, German
Yagers, Anspach, 123, 187; Hessian, 123; camp, plate 6
Yonkers, 81

ZANTHIER, Lieut., 162, 163, 182
Zeis Regiment, von, 158
Zimmermann, Ensign, 69
Zinn, Regimental Quarter Master, 167

Lightning Source UK Ltd.
Milton Keynes UK
UKHW022030200722
406152UK00003B/114